# TALES FROM
# DEVELOPMENT
# HELL

## FILM-MAKING THE HARD WAY

## DAVID HUGHES

## TITAN BOOKS

# DEDICATION

**To Zahida, mi vida**

# ACKNOWLEDGEMENTS

My sincere thanks are due to several key players who rescued this book from Development Hell:

**Adam Newell**, the producer who shepherded it into production and pulled double duty as editor and continuity person;

**Rod Edgar**, the script researcher and production assistant whose diligence makes up for my negligence;

**Chelsey Fox**, the agent who negotiated the deal and made sure the writer didn't get screwed;

**Steven de Souza**, who gave me several terrific characters, and whose vast contribution seems almost sufficient to warrant shared story credit under Writers Guild regulations;

**James V. Hart**, whose tireless efforts gave me a whole subplot I would not otherwise have conceived of;

**Gary Goldman**, another great screenwriter much too gracious to take credit where it's due;

**Ryan Poenisch** at the Writers Guild of America, for opening doors;

Finally, **Darren Aronofsky** and **Rupert Wainwright**, whose great un-produced films I would far rather see on the screen than in my book.

Also deserving of a place on the credit list, in order of appearance, are the following key collaborators, all of whom I interviewed during production:

Ted Henning, Lee and Janet Scott Batchler, Adam Rifkin, Don Murphy, Forrest J Ackerman, Ralph Bakshi, David Cronenberg, Ron Shusett, Paul Verhoeven, Gary Goldman, Matthew Cirulnick, Steven de Souza, Jim Uhls, H. R. Giger, Jere Cunningham, David Koepp, Terry Moore, Neil Gaiman, William Farmer, David J. Schow, Richard Friedenberg, James V. Hart, Tom Topor, Darren Aronofsky and Wesley Strick.

Special thanks are also due to David, Dane, Angus, Gordon, James and Anette at Picture Production Co; Rudolf and Hans; Jo Boylett and David Barraclough at Titan; Marcus Hearn and the other interviewees who didn't make the final cut; Alex and Bruce for coffee and sympathy; Tamara, Ramses, Omar and Marti Blumenthal, Michael and Danny at Bigel/Mailer; everyone at *Empire*; the Beautiful Southmartins and Coldplayers; Soba, Starbucks, Soho House, Il Sogno, Terry's and Sky Bar at Mondrian; my family and friends.

This is absolutely positively definitely maybe the last book ever.

# CONTENTS

# INTRODUCTION

"Trying to make a movie in Hollywood is like trying to grill a
steak by having a succession of people coming into the
room and breathing on it."
— Douglas Adams

This is not the book I set out to write. Originally, I planned a
kind of mainstream version of my earlier book, *The Greatest
Sci-Fi Movies Never Made*, covering some of the best
unproduced scripts in recent Hollywood history. However, like so many
movie-related projects before it, a degree of 'Development Hell' crept
in, which turned this book into something else entirely. I already knew
that the stories behind many unmade movies were more interesting
than the movies themselves would ever have been. What I also
discovered was that some of the films which suffered most in
development *did* eventually get made — albeit with varying results —
and the stories behind those projects are just as fascinating. Thus, as
far as this is book is concerned, the development process was a positive
experience — which is more than can be said for the twelve cases
documented here.

Why do so many Hollywood films go into development, only to
wind up in Hell? What is this place to which so many promising-
sounding projects and perfectly serviceable scripts seem to be
banished, many of them never to be heard from again?

To understand the concept of Development Hell, one must first
understand what *development* is. Producer Jane Hamsher, whose
credits include *Natural Born Killers* and *From Hell*, has described
development as follows: "The writer turns in a script. The producers
and studio executives read it, give the writer their 'development'
notes, and he goes back and rewrites as best he can, trying to make
everyone happy. If it comes back and it's great, the studio and the
producers will try and attach a director and stars (if they haven't
already), and hopefully the picture will get made."

That's development, in theory. In practice, it's more like this:

1.   The writer turns in a script so unutterably perfect they would stick pens in their eyes sooner than change a single syllable of it.

2.   The producer or studio executive, too busy/bored/illiterate to read the script for themselves, sends out for 'script coverage' — advice on the potential of the script from a professional script reader. If this doesn't instantly lead to the script being junked and the writer being fired and replaced — either by a younger, hotter, cheaper model (a 'tyro'), or an older, more experienced and more expensive one (a 'veteran') — the writer will be given 'notes'. "Everybody gives writers notes," says screenwriter Richard Friedenberg (*Dying Young*, *A River Runs Through It*), "[even] the garbage man. And the notes always conflict."

3.   If sufficiently encouraged to do so, the producer/executive might then actually *read* the script. "This is perfect," he (or, one time in a thousand, she) might say. "Who can we get to rewrite it?" Then, in order to justify their own on-screen credits/exorbitant salaries/parking spaces, they will throw their own ideas into the mix or, more commonly, take ideas out. "In Hollywood, ideas are anathema," says screenwriter-producer Gary Goldman (*Basic Instinct*, *Total Recall*, *Minority Report*), "and the bigger the budget, the more forbidden they are."

4.   The writer then scurries away to rewrite their *magnum opus*, doing their best to incorporate all the different, conflicting notes, and resubmits the script for approval.

     *Steps 1 through 4 are now repeated continuously*, with the script continually evolving — but not necessarily improving — until finally someone decides it's good enough (though probably not quite as good as the first draft) to make into a film...

5.   This latest draft of the script is sent out to actors and directors, in the hope that it will attract one with sufficient clout to actually *get it made*. Interested *directors* — who may be attached to up to a dozen projects at a time, in the hopes that a

studio will eventually give one of them a 'green light' — will almost certainly want a rewrite, to incorporate twenty-minute tracking shots, elaborate set-pieces, thousands of extras, impossible locations, etc, any of which can add a couple of noughts to the budget the producer has in mind. Interested *actors* will almost certainly want a rewrite, to make their scenes larger, or their character more heroic, or their journey more arduous, or their dialogue more, well, you know, *gooder* — even (or *especially*) if it means stealing the best lines from other characters. In other words, as one veteran screenwriter puts it, "tweaking a draft to better suit a star who's expressed interest, only to have said star drop out of the project." Since the desires of the studio, producers, director and actors are usually mutually exclusive, all of them will blame the writer, who will be fired and replaced by a new writer... taking the whole process back to stage 1.

That's Development Hell.

The twelve cases outlined in this book could hardly be more varied. There's detailed coverage of such famously unproduced films as *Crusade*, *ISOBAR*, *Smoke & Mirrors* and *The Hot Zone*... An exploration of early, ill-fated attempts to bring *The Lord of the Rings* to the screen... An examination of how promising scripts for *Planet of the Apes* and *Tomb Raider* devolved through development into the, ah, disappointments they became... The bizarre true story of *Total Recall*'s fifteen-year development, an epic gestation almost matched by its still-unproduced sequel... Rejected scripts and storylines for the fourth Indiana Jones film and the fifth Batman film... The various Howard Hughes projects which were probably lost forever as soon as *The Aviator* took off... And more. Not wanting to repeat any of the films covered in *The Greatest Sci-Fi Movies Never Made*, I have left out the tortuous development of, for instance, *Superman*, *Silver Surfer* and *The Fantastic Four* — but that book is still available, and besides, the sorry tale of *The Sandman* more than makes up for it.

In covering these stories, I have tried not to editorialise, to pass judgment on the content of the scripts themselves. If I naturally favour the writer in most instances, that is only to be expected, since I am one myself. Indeed, I believe that my commitment to the project is illustrated by the fact that several of my own screenplays are currently rotting in Development Hell.

At least this book made it out alive.

**David Hughes**
**September 2003**

**How *Smoke and Mirrors* started life as a "weekend read", became the hottest script in Hollywood — and then magically disappeared**

"They wanted Indiana Jones meets *Lawrence of Arabia*. Most of the scripts were the latter with none of the former — though one was so confusing I couldn't figure out which line it fell on."

— *Ted Henning, screenwriter*

On a Friday in February 1993, Hollywood was buzzing with more than just the usual combination of traffic, cell phones and celebrity gossip. At two separate studios in Burbank and several high-profile agencies, the word-of-mouth concerning a 128-page script by two unknown writers was increasing from 'buzz' to cacophony, as executives at Warner Bros and The Walt Disney Company engaged in a bidding war to secure the rights to what had become, almost overnight, the most sought-after script in Hollywood.

The script at the centre of all this excitement and activity was *Smoke and Mirrors*, a historical epic inspired by actual events. The story concerned a trip which Jean-Eugene Robert-Houdin (1805-1871), the father of modern stage magic — and, incidentally, the magician who inspired Ehric Weiss to become 'Houdini' — made to Algeria in the 1850s. Robert-Houdin's task was to debunk a local tribal leader or *marabout*, Zoras Al-Khatim, who was said to be using divine magic to incite an uprising against the French occupiers. Part *Lawrence of Arabia*, part *Raiders of the Lost Ark*, the script was written 'on spec' — in other words, without a specific commission by a producer or studio — by the husband and wife screenwriting team of Lee and Janet Scott Batchler. Their only previous credits were "a small amount of TV and some kids' videos (which were produced), plus a handful of spec scripts (unproduced), all of which really amounted to 'practice' scripts preparing us to write *Smoke and Mirrors*." Deciding that they wanted to write a "weekend read" (ie a script a studio executive could read over the course of a weekend), the Batchlers recalled an encyclopaedia entry for Robert-Houdin which Lee had come across while researching something else. "As we researched and thought through various ideas, we returned to that story and pitched it, among many others, to our writers group," they recall. "The kernel of the story that would become *Smoke and Mirrors* was the one everyone responded to with extreme enthusiasm, and we knew we had found a story worth working on."

As the story begins, Jean-Pierre Robert-Houdin (they had decided 'Jean-Eugene' would be too difficult for English-speaking audiences) has turned his back on his prestidigitatorial past — "Manipulating the laws of physics on one hand, twisting people's minds on the other: it's not a fit way to make a living," he says in the script's first draft — in order to devote himself to scientific study. This decision leaves Colette, his beautiful wife (and, in the magician tradition, former assistant), only too eager to escape the gilded cage of their estate in the Parisian suburbs by venturing into *terra incognita* on behalf of the French government, in order to help quell a rebellion being fomented there by Berber sorcerers. "These non-Arab anti-colonial rebels were committing deadly atrocities against all French in North Africa, including innocent women and children, and were trying to woo the peace-loving Arab population to their cause," the Batchlers note, taking pains to head off accusations of anti-Arab sentiment at the pass. "As their credential of divine backing for their acts of terrorism, they performed very persuasive 'miracles' of black magic. A bloody civil war was about to happen if something wasn't done."

Just as all movie heroes initially resist the call to arms, Houdin is at first reluctant to accept the assignment. "Whatever days I have left," he explains, "I'm not going to waste doing card tricks for Barbarian primitives in the God-forsaken desert, just to prove that my brand of lying is superior to their brand of lying!" Yet, as is also customary, he ultimately capitulates. (In early drafts, his motivation for his change of heart is unclear: he is resolutely apolitical, and seems unmoved by the idea of oppressed Arabs rising up against their French conquerors; yet his sudden change of mind is typical of his mercurial, idiosyncratic personality.) Upon arriving in Algiers, Robert-Houdin's forthrightness and contempt for authority land him in life-threatening danger, from which he is rescued by Darcy, a fearless French Foreign Legionnaire with a wooden hand, who quickly becomes enamoured of Colette. Although Colette seems equally entranced by Darcy, her flirtatiousness is perhaps designed more to regain her husband's attention than to encourage Darcy's, and the *frisson* this creates does not stop Darcy and Houdin becoming firm friends — not least when Houdin finds a way to repay Darcy for saving his life.

The second act sees Robert-Houdin, Colette and Darcy set off for the desert palace of Bou-Allem, the most influential Arab sheik in the country. "Bou-Allem, a devout seeker of truth, is still flirting with the rebels, waiting to be convinced as to whose side to take — Berber or French," the Batchlers explain. "So he summons Robert-Houdin to a one-on-one command performance — basically a showdown against the rebellion's chief sorcerer." Though the odds are stacked against him, Robert-Houdin beats the sorcerer Zoras at his own game, totally disgracing him even in the eyes of his own men — and reminding the magician of his former glory. "We then weave elements from other historical research to create the climax for our story," the Batchlers add, "which involves the trek from the desert wilderness back to Algiers via the treacherous Kabyle Mountains, where Robert-Houdin and his party are ambushed by a loyal remnant of the disgraced sorcerer's army. Our heroes take refuge and fight it out inside an ancient abandoned tenth century citadel, which we patterned after real fortresses that once existed in those mountains. Outgunned and outmanned, Robert-Houdin must marshal all his magician's cunning in order to defeat his foes inside that fortress." Thus, the stage is set for an exciting third act in which Zoras seeks vengeance for his humiliation at Robert-Houdin's hands.

On 5 January 1993, after nine drafts, the Batchlers were finally ready to type 'FIRST DRAFT' on the title page of the script, after which they showed it to a few friends. Among them was a development executive at a small production company specialising in TV movies. "Her bosses loved the script, wanted a short-term option on it, and offered to introduce us to various agents at top agencies," they recall. One of them was Alan Gasmer from the William Morris Agency, with whom they instantly clicked, and who has represented them ever since. "Alan did a great job of talking it up without letting anyone see it, and more and more people began to ask for it. At Sundance, as well as in LA, he let it be known that this project was about to come up for auction." Gasmer had sent the script out to various studios and producers, as is customary, hoping for a call-back from at least one of the few with the power and resources to option or purchase outright a script whose historical setting, special effects, star-driven subject matter and epic scale demanded a budget which might touch $100 million: Universal Pictures, Steven Spielberg's Amblin Entertainment, Columbia-controlled TriStar, Warner Bros and The Walt Disney Company.

Among those to whom Gasmer had pitched the project was Jay Stern, a development executive at Disney-owned Hollywood Pictures, over lunch at The Grill in Beverly Hills. Stern's response was immediate, and enthusiastic. "Sounds great," he told Gasmer. "Please, I want this. That's one I would really, really like to get my hands on." Stern got his hands on the script the following Tuesday, and took it home with him, planning to read the first forty pages (typically, the first act of a 128-page script) before bed. Instead, he finished it. Stern called Gasmer first thing the following morning, and left messages with Interscope and Cinergi, two production companies with which Disney might share the costs of the mega-budget project. Arriving at his company's regular Wednesday morning story meeting, Stern pitched the story to his superiors, including Hollywood Pictures president Ricardo Mestres and Disney chief Jeffrey Katzenberg, telling them that it was big, original, well executed, distinctive — and definitely going to be snapped up fast by a rival studio if they did not make a move on it. Mestres read the script that morning and agreed that Disney should bid, and immediately sent the script to Andrew G. Vajna, the Hungarian-born founder of Cinergi and producer of such big-budget films as *Judge Dredd* and *Super Mario Bros.* Unfortunately, at nearby Warner Bros, executive Tom Lassally had made the same assessment, and called Gasmer to ask what kind of deal his clients were looking for. "I'm looking for a million," Gasmer told both interested parties, and by Friday he had Disney, Warner Bros and TriStar readying their cheque books.

TriStar had already sent the script to Wolfgang Petersen, the German-born director of *Das Boot* who would later direct Clint

Eastwood in *In the Line of Fire* and George Clooney in *The Perfect Storm*. "I don't know if they got an answer from Wolfgang," Stern told Thom Taylor, author of *The Big Deal: Hollywood's Million-Dollar Spec Script Market*, "but it was Friday afternoon and I knew that [Warner Bros executive] Bruce Berman was unreachable. I actually heard that he was stuck on the tarmac." Indeed, Berman was snowed in at New York's John F. Kennedy Airport, already sitting on United Airlines Flight 7 to Los Angeles, and therefore unable either to leave the plane, or even use his cell phone to give his colleagues the green light to write a million dollar cheque for a screenplay he had not yet read. Naturally, this being Hollywood, Stern used Berman's predicament to his advantage: "I was concerned that as soon as Lassally reached Berman and had the conversation, that they would just put a million dollars on the table." With Disney's Mestres and Cinergi's Vajna agreeing to split the development costs evenly, Stern made Gasmer an offer he knew his clients could not refuse: one million dollars, with an additional commitment to commission the Batchlers to write another script, to be decided upon at a later date. Gasmer, however, was unable to reach his clients, who were *en route* to a weekend-long writers' group seminar in Cambria, some 220 miles north of Los Angeles.

"Friday, the day the auction was coming to a close, was the day we were scheduled to drive up the coast to meet everyone for the weekend," the Batchlers recall. "Because this was back in 1993, we didn't have a cell phone, and had to stop every fifteen minutes or so, pull off the road, and find a pay phone to check in with Alan to see how things were going. We know his inability to get hold of us was somewhat frustrating to the people bidding — at one point an exec told him, 'Get your clients to a phone and get them to stay there!' — [so] eventually, we stopped at a small courtyard motel outside Arroyo Grande and stayed on the phone for about an hour, responding to the final bidding, until the deal was done." Giddy with excitement, the Batchlers celebrated in style, treating the other members of their writers' group to dinner. "That weekend [we] started a tradition that we have maintained ever since: that a writer with a sale takes the rest of the group out to lunch or dinner. Unfortunately, that particular weekend we may have had the sale but didn't have the cash in hand, [so we] had to borrow money from one of the other writers to actually hold the celebration dinner."

The facts remained, however: the Batchlers had a seven-figure commitment from a major studio. Their names were now known by some of the most powerful people in Hollywood. And their script was on the fast-track at Disney.

While the feeding frenzy surrounding *Smoke and Mirrors* was not uncommon, what happened next was unusual to say the least: within three weeks, the script had achieved 'go movie' status. Immediately after the option deal was signed, Ricardo Mestres had secured the services of producer, director (and amateur magician) Frank Marshall, who had helmed the Disney hits *Arachnophobia* and *Alive*. Although Marshall had recently signed a deal with Paramount Pictures, he retained the freedom to direct a picture elsewhere, and *Smoke and Mirrors* was immediately elevated to the top of his own personal script pile. Meanwhile, Vajna managed to interest Sean Connery (who had just starred in Cinergi's *Medicine Man*) in the lead role of Robert-Houdin, a move which was certain to attract other A-list stars to the film's other principal roles: Colette, Robert-Houdin's glamorous wife, and Darcy, the dashing American who accompanies the pair on their trip into the desert. Jay Stern, who had acquired the hot property for his studio, was already reflecting on the success which *Smoke and Mirrors* had brought him: a promotion to Vice-President. Meanwhile, the Batchlers were understandably dazzled by the green light already shining on their script. Alas, the title *Smoke and Mirrors* proved to be prophetic.

Firstly, Sean Connery allegedly slowed the pre-production process by requesting rewrites, as is customary with A-list actors, to tailor the script to his own style. Lee and Janet Scott Batchler churned out several subsequent drafts, the last being a 132-page fourth draft dated January 1994. "We were very involved with the development of the project during its Sean Connery phase," say the Batchlers. "Sean was attached within days of the script being sold, as were Frank Marshall and [producer] Kathy Kennedy. We met with Sean to get his notes, and spent months working with Frank and Kathy. [They] were great to work with in every respect and we think the world of them. We did three rewrites while working with Frank Marshall and Kathy Kennedy on the project. We were really focused at that point on getting the script ready for production," they add. "We were very happy with the fourth draft of the script, which was the culmination of our rewrites. The original script is powerful for reasons of its clean, uncomplicated approach to the storytelling — it's just a great ride, start to finish. [But] we personally feel the fourth draft deepened the main characters and added several plot elements that actually improved on the original while retaining what was important."

Sean Connery did not share their enthusiasm, however; although he remained attached to the project, he insisted upon further rewrites, by which time the Batchlers had been hired by Warner Bros' Bruce Berman to write *Batman Forever*, the third instalment of the studio's most profitable franchise. In their place, Cinergi and Disney hired *Alive* and *Congo* screenwriter John Patrick Shanley to rework the story; the inevitable result was that Connery's rewritten role diminished the supporting roles, Darcy and Colette, making them more difficult to cast. By the time Shanley turned in his draft, Frank Marshall had departed to direct *Congo* for Paramount, leaving *Smoke and Mirrors* without a director. Connery and Shanley parted company with the project soon afterwards, at which point John Fasano (*Another 48 HRS*) and Douglas Ray Stewart (*An Officer and a Gentleman*) took turns at the script. Since screen credit and remuneration tends to be apportioned depending on each screenwriter's contribution, however, both Fasano and Stewart may have been inclined to change elements which might otherwise have fallen under the caveat of "If it ain't broke, don't fix it." Thus, the script began to move further and further away from the one which had excited Disney in the first place, and closer to 'Development Hell'.

Then, in late 1994, Cinergi development executive Brett Fain brought in a young writer named Ted Henning, whose script for an unproduced pirate adventure, *Caribbean Blue*, suggested that he might be suitable to mount a salvage operation. "He was a very smart guy and very [committed] to creating a version of the script that the company could actually make," Henning observes of Fain. "Each had some interesting aspects, but none was shootable — none would make a great movie," Henning says of the previous drafts, all of which Fain showed to him. "They all lacked a sense of fun that we felt was imperative for the movie to connect. [The producers] wanted Indiana Jones meets *Lawrence of Arabia*. Most of the scripts were the latter with none of the former — though one was so confusing I couldn't figure out which line it fell on." Henning dismissed Stewart's draft as "unreadable", but liked Fasano's take on the material. "It was really detailed," he says. "He'd done all this research; you could tell. He brought in the *hashashim*, a really violent cult in Algeria in Northern Africa, which gave us the word 'assassin'." (In fact, the *hashashim* were mentioned in the Batchlers' very first draft, as Darcy describes them to Colette: "An order of fanatics devoted to the art of political murder. That's where our word 'assassin' comes from.") "He brought some incredible detail to it," adds Henning, "but I think he got bogged down in the detail. I went back to the Batchler draft and started from there, working very closely with Brett to create a tight, fun epic that would stay as true to the story as possible while connecting with the largest audience possible, to warrant the $100 million-plus the movie would cost to make."

The nature of their producer-writer collaboration was unusual: instead of taking Fain's notes and delivering a script a few months later, Henning would write ten or fifteen pages at a time, and then go over them with Fain to see if the script was going in the right direction. "It was a really close [working relationship] which a lot of screenwriters wouldn't like," he says. "But Brett was a really smart guy. He had been through all the permutations, and had a really good sense of it." Both knew that the script's biggest flaw was structure. "The movie is about Houdin going to Algeria, and then what happens over there, so you have to set him up in France, put him in some situation where he's vulnerable, and then get him on the boat. [The Batchlers] didn't get him on the boat until page fifty." (While this may be true of their subsequent drafts, the Batchlers' first draft has Robert-Houdin and Colette on the boat by page eleven.) Although Henning and Fain liked the Batchlers' script, both felt that it lacked focus, that Robert-Houdin's character arc was weak, and that it failed to realise the potential of the Robert-Houdin/Darcy/Colette love triangle.

"Structurally, we got it down," Henning says. "We also made really strong decisions about Houdin's arc," he adds, noting that, in all subsequent drafts, Robert-Houdin's name was further simplified to 'Houdin' — presumably for the convenience of the same audience who could not be trusted to pronounce 'Jean-Eugene'. "We started him off as this powerful magician who was on top of the world, and we just flushed him down the toilet. He was disillusioned; he had killed someone with a magic trick [when] something had gone terribly wrong. In real life, it actually happened — I think his son or daughter was killed — and he basically then switched over to science and became a big debunker, and tried to find the reality of his world, because up to then he'd been living the illusion of celebrity. So when we found him [in the story], he hadn't been out of the lab in six months, and his girlfriend [rather than wife] Colette was at the end of her rope, so when he is asked to go to French-occupied Algeria, she says, 'If you don't go, I'm leaving you.' He figures he's going to debunk this guy as a fake, and then leave. Of course, as soon as he gets there, things start happening to draw him deeper and deeper into it, until finally he reaches that place which you reach in all movies, where our hero gets to decide whether he's gonna give up and go home, or carry on and kick some ass.

"The other main character in it is Darcy, an American in the French Foreign Legion, who has given up his life because his wife was killed, and is fearless basically because he doesn't care if he lives or dies," Henning continues. "So Houdin is in his fifties, and he's got this beautiful French girlfriend, but all of a sudden there's this strapping Mel Gibson-type [love rival] who is brave and silly. So when Houdin is finally faced with 'shit or get off the pot', the *real* reason he decides to shit is that Darcy's going like, 'Hey, you leave, I'm in bed with her five minutes later.'" After several drafts, Henning and Fain had a script which they felt was working. Commenting on the 116-page draft dated 30 April 1997, online script reviewer 'Stax' described the story as follows: "Houdin travels to Algeria (accompanied by Colette) for the purpose of demonstrating first-hand to the natives how Zoras' sorcery is performed. Guiding and protecting Houdin and Colette on their dangerous journey is a detachment of French Foreign Legionnaires, led by the swashbuckling Captain Trey Darcy and his Spanish second-in-command, Corporal Augustino Bartolote.

"The group's journey through Algeria is fraught with peril, as Zoras makes several sudden appearances (using actual magic?) to try and scare them off. During the course of this adventure, the one-handed Darcy (yes, that's right, he fences with a wooden prosthetic!) and Colette discover a growing romantic attraction to one another despite their respective obligations to Houdin. This rivalry for Colette's affection, and his confrontations with Zoras, reinvigorates Houdin's long-dormant vitality and his faith in himself and in the magic arts. Exposing Zoras' trickery to his fellow tribesmen, Houdin succeeds in becoming a marked man. Houdin and the expedition must then flee the wrathful Zoras and his army of rebels. This draft culminates with an Alamo-like siege at a legendary desert fortress between Zoras' forces and the cornered Legionnaires." (For the record, the Batchler drafts climaxed in precisely the same way.) Overall, Stax saw *Smoke & Mirrors* (in Henning's drafts, an ampersand replaced the 'and') as "a fact-based adventure chock full of romance, wizardry, David Lean-style vistas, and Golden Age of Hollywood production values."

Despite the Batchlers' assertion that Zoras' men are Berbers, not Arabs, Stax had concerns about the fact that the heroes are essentially Colonialist occupiers, fighting Algerian natives — who, in reality, took 180 years to rid themselves of the oppressive French and win back their homeland. Henning's answer to this moral quandary was to make Zoras so bloodthirsty and mad as to distance him from the other Arabic figures in the story, and ennoble the Colonial heroes. As a by-product of this, Stax observed, "Zoras is pretty one-note heavy in this story. He's mainly a vessel for special effects, just as most of the other Arab characters are mere window dressing." Stax felt that the romantic rivalry between Houdin, Colette and Darcy was handled well, however. "Darcy is a man of honour who finds himself drawn to the lover of the man he's charged to protect, and who he finds lacking in how to treat a woman right. Darcy then becomes torn between his feelings and his obligation to duty. Subsequently, Houdin realizes what he stands to lose if Colette forsakes him for Darcy. This realisation helps Houdin snap out of being such a Grumpy Old Magician. (There are a few good jabs where people mistake Houdin for Colette's father.) If Darcy is a man of action then Houdin is a man of thought who instead relies on his wits and experience. Both men turn out to be more alike than they figured, and they eventually form an alliance to battle Zoras."

Despite her status as the object of affection of both male leads, Stax noted, "Colette is thankfully no mere damsel in distress. Her attraction to Darcy and her reasons for staying with Houdin are well drawn. But the very nature of being a magician's assistant means Colette is relegated to being a supporting player... Overall," he concluded, "the dialogue here was sharp and playful but became far too tongue-in-cheek by Act Three. By then, characters were speaking in comic book-like dialogue balloons. It was one quip after another, and the puns deteriorated in quality as they grew in quantity." Despite such reservations, Henning recalls that the reaction to the script was largely favourable. "Brett was happy," he says. "Andy [Vajna] liked it but wasn't excited about it, [probably because] he had not gotten any feedback from the stars... and then Cinergi fell apart. Andy went off on his own and Brett left, and that was pretty much all I heard from it."

By this time, *Smoke & Mirrors* had accrued several million dollars' worth of negative costs against it, meaning that if anyone took it over — another studio, for instance, or a producer — they would have to repay Cinergi's investment, including the considerable sum they had since paid to buy it outright from Disney. Nevertheless, in 1999, a buyer emerged: Joel Douglas, son of screen legend Kirk and older brother of Oscar-winning actor-producer Michael Douglas, for whom he had co-produced *Romancing the Stone* and *The Jewel of the Nile*. Joel had formed a partnership with actor/director-turned-producer Kevin Brodie (fiancé of Joel's sister, Joann Savitt), funded by Initial Entertainment Group, one of the principals of which was David Jones, brother of Michael's fiancée Catherine Zeta-Jones. The plan was to tailor *Smoke & Mirrors* as a vehicle for Michael and Catherine; in addition, it was widely reported that Kirk Douglas, recovering from a stroke he suffered in 1995, might take a small role as a sultan named Bou-Allem, whose son, Rachid, accompanies Houdin during the latter part of the story.

Despite the fact that the Douglas-Brodie partnership had secured a two-year option from Andy Vajna, they had apparently been shown only the original Batchler draft, and were unaware of any other. Thus, they hired another A-list writer, who spent six months and a great deal of money rewriting the Batchlers' script — with disastrous consequences. "Michael and Catherine obviously wanted to do *Smoke & Mirrors* — it was a great movie for them to do together — but they were at their wits' end, because they had spent all this money, and the script was, by all accounts, unreadable," says Henning. "I never saw it — I don't even know who the writer was — but they were, like, 'This is horrible.'" As a last resort, the producers called Brett Fain, who asked if they had read Henning's draft — the one he felt was filmable. "They read it and called me and said, 'This is exactly what we're looking for.'" Henning agreed to meet with them to discuss yet another rewrite. "There are very few people in Hollywood I respect," he says, "but with Michael — from *Fatal Attraction* to *Wall Street* and *Falling Down* — his movies have had social impact; social resonance. So when I went over to their house in Century City, it was pretty trippy — you know, having 'Gordon Gekko' open the door in his slippers, and Catherine really pregnant." They spent several hours discussing story and character, following which Henning embarked on another rewrite.

This draft, 110 pages in length and dated August 2000, was described by on-line script reviewer Stax as "leaner, less campy and [with] better dialogue than either his 1997 rewrite or the Batchlers' script... retaining the basic structure and scenes from the Batchlers' version while improving the content of those scenes, how they're played out, and the overall behaviour of the characters." While Stax also felt that this draft had "less panache" than the 1997 version, "the 2000 draft is less giddy and the last act's no longer a tirade of pithy one-liners and sight gags." Stax also liked the development of the Houdin/Colette/Darcy love triangle. "*Smoke & Mirrors* is now driven forward by a trio of heroes rather than just by Houdin; Darcy and Colette are no longer mere sidekicks," he observed. Darcy, in particular, had been developed beyond what he saw as the "swashbuckler cliché" of earlier drafts, although he was still demonstrably more of a man of action than Houdin's more cerebral protagonist. Houdin, meanwhile, had become "less verbose and theatrical, more withdrawn and cold now, rather than snooty." Stax also felt that a good balance had been struck between making Colette a woman of her time and retaining an independent streak that's familiar to modern audiences. "She's just plucky and passionate enough without seeming out of step with 1856 Algeria." Stax further noted that the "cartoonish" portrayal of the Arabs had been toned down, and even the principal villain, Zoras, had been improved. "While he's still a secondary (and even sketchy) character, Zoras [is] less of a hokey super-villain now. His dialogue was less theatrical and his presence more enigmatic."

"Supposedly everyone liked it," Henning says of this draft, "and before long the film was in pre-production, with location scouts and set designers working around the clock. That's when things got sort of bogged down." Indeed, it was several months before *Smoke & Mirrors* secured an A-list director, during which time Douglas and Zeta-Jones co-starred in their first film together — Steven Soderbergh's *Traffic* (though they shared no scenes) — were married, and celebrated the birth of their first child. Then, in February 2001, it was announced that the director of *Smoke & Mirrors* would be John McTiernan (*Die Hard*, *The Thomas Crown Affair*), whose version of *Basic Instinct 2* had recently fallen apart when Sharon Stone declined to approve Benjamin Bratt as a suitable co-star. On 22 May 2001, industry bible *Variety* reported that the film might start shooting as early as the autumn: "The fact-based story... has been a high-profile affair since 1993, but reported interest from the likes of Mel Gibson and Sean Connery turned out to be its own version of smoke and mirrors. The dedication of Douglas and Zeta-Jones, who last paired in *Traffic*, is real. Douglas' brother Joel and Zeta-Jones' brother David are producing with Kevin Brodie, and if the film's producer, Initial Entertainment Group, can pull together the financing for the ambitious film and lock down the A-list principals, the movie will be no illusion."

According to Henning, McTiernan's involvement sparked a new wave of difficulties for the production. "He instantly set the world on fire," he says. "He started making all these demands, like he wanted to have Leslie Dixon, his pet writer, work on it. She'd written *Pay It Forward*, which didn't make her seem like the best person to rewrite *Smoke & Mirrors*. Besides, they'd already gone through an eight- or ten-year multi-million dollar rewrite cycle and they were happy with the script. They didn't want to start yet another development cycle on it where [the new writer] would want to change everything." Nevertheless, eager for the project to move forward, Douglas and Zeta-Jones invited Dixon to stay with them at their holiday home in northern Majorca, to which the writer allegedly responded by saying she would not be able to meet them for two weeks — a move which Douglas and Zeta-Jones took as a snub. Shortly afterwards, in June 2001, McTiernan left the project, citing what *Variety* described as "insurmountable business differences". As the Batchlers put it: "John McTiernan never was that involved with the project. The trades often announce things before they are nailed down. Almost immediately after McTiernan's involvement was announced, his deal fell apart for business reasons and was never finalized, so he quickly departed from the project before doing any work on it." By this time, the Batchlers had been brought back into the mix, after a delay of almost a decade. "We met several times with Joel Douglas, and it was agreed that our original scripts would be the basis for the film," they recall. "They were also scouring our other two drafts for nuggets that might be of use. Our interactions with Joel were all very amiable and supporting of our original vision. However, Michael had already decided that a playwright friend of his from England — his 'pocket writer', as it were — should do a dialogue polish for him and Catherine."

Adding to the problems plaguing the production was a rival project, *The Magician's Wife*, which recalled the duelling Robin Hood films of the early 1990s and, more recently, competing disaster movies based around volcanoes (*Volcano* and *Dante's Peak*) and comets/meteors (*Deep Impact* and *Armageddon*). According to British industry trade publication *Screendaily*, Alliance Atlantis' *The Magician's Wife* was adapted by *E.T. The Extra-Terrestrial* scribe Melissa Mathison from a novel by the late Brian Moore, based on the same historical events as *Smoke & Mirrors*. Budgeted at $25 million, the film was set to star Academy Award winner Geoffrey Rush (*Shine*, *Quills*) and Kate Winslet (*Titanic*), under the direction of François Girard (*The Red Violin*). The similarities were no mere illusion: set, like *Smoke & Mirrors*, in 1856, Moore's novel concerns Henri, formerly France's greatest magician, now content to spend his days tinkering with mechanical devices (much to the annoyance of his long-suffering wife Emmeline) until a French colonel convinces Henri to put on a magic show in French-occupied Algeria, in order to convince the natives that a *marabout* (living saint) with alleged magical powers is no more powerful a magician than Henri himself, and thus avert a holy war.

Nevertheless, barely a few weeks passed before *The Peacemaker* and *Deep Impact* director Mimi Leder — whose most recent film, *Pay It Forward*, had been scripted by Leslie Dixon — stepped into the breach. "She met with Michael and Catherine," says Henning, "she loved the script, she loves working with new writers, [she] definitely wanted to work with me... but of course I never met her and a few months into it she was lobbying to bring in her own writer." Perhaps understandably,

Leder also wanted to hire other crew members, despite the fact that several key personnel — including, Henning says, a multi-Oscar-winning production designer — had already been hired. At this point, the budget was pegged at under $100 million, but when Leder returned from a location scouting trip to Morocco (at the production's expense, of course), she submitted a budget proposal a full fifty million dollars higher. This seemed excessive, notwithstanding the fact that the script featured three star-driven roles, took place in Paris and Algiers in 1856, included an Indiana Jones-style set piece in the desert palace of Sulieman the Great, and several other expensive scenes, including an ocean voyage and — in Henning's most recent draft — a musical set piece. "We wrote in a song for Colette, who's supposed to be a cabaret singer," Henning explains. "There's a scene where Houdin is with Colette and all the sheiks, and they start bidding black camels for her. And she's like, 'Three black camels, are you kidding?' So she gets up and does this dance number where she kind of shows the sheiks — and also Houdin — what she's worth."

The actress' jones for song and dance numbers would have to wait until her Oscar-winning turn in *Chicago*, however. As location scouting in Morocco was going on in autumn 2001, the tragedies of 9/11 threw another giant wrench in the machinery. "The planned shoot in Morocco fell apart," the Batchlers recall. "Some location scouting was done in Arizona, but the project couldn't be put back together in time for its planned early 2002 start date. Michael and Catherine are still attached," they add. "However, Initial Entertainment Group, the company which bought the rights on their behalf has itself been bought out by another company, Intermedia, which complicates matters. And North Africa remains a difficult place to shoot." With no studio willing to gamble $150 million on a period film — *The Mummy* had cost half that sum — the project remains in limbo at Intermedia, co-producers of *Terminator 3: The Rise of the Machines*, amid reports that John Milius (*Apocalypse Now*) has been tapped to write yet another new screenplay.

Despite almost a decade of disappointment, Lee and Janet Scott Batchler — who have since scripted the Modesty Blaise movie *My Name Is Modesty* for Miramax's genre division, Dimension Films — remain optimistic about the prospects of *Smoke and Mirrors*, and do not yet consider that they are 'looking back' on the experience. "For one thing, in half the meetings we take, someone still comments on what a great script it is, how much they loved it, and how they wish it would get made. For another thing, the fact that the movie hasn't been made means that no one has ruined a frame of it yet. We still expect this movie to be made someday — and *then* we will get to 'look back' on the experience. At this point," the Batchlers conclude, "while we have ten years to look back on, we are still looking forward as well."

# MONKEY BUSINESS

**An infinite number of monkeys with typewriters could hardly concoct a more bizarre story than the evolution of the *Planet of the Apes* "re-imagining"**

"I thought it was gonna be fantastic, like *Star Wars* or *Lord of the Rings*. The movie they actually made was a bad *Twilight Zone* episode."

— *would-be* Planet of the Apes *producer Don Murphy*

I n 1962, the publication of Pierre Boulle's novel *La Planète des Singes* ('The Planet of the Apes') caused something of a sensation in his native France. Not just because the novel — in which three astronauts crash-land on a planet populated by intelligent apes — was an inspired and dramatically different science fiction fable with a seam of socio-political satire running throughout, but because, at the time, Boulle was considered one of France's most gifted 'serious' writers. His previous novels such as *Face of a Hero*, *A Noble Profession* and *The Bridge on the River Kwai* — the film adaptation of which had won him an Oscar in 1958 — were all rooted firmly in the real world. Boulle's single, extraordinary idea — that of an "upside-down" world where apes were a highly evolved species, and men little more than their pets — was triggered by a visit to the zoo, where the apes' mimicry of human mannerisms set him thinking about the relationships between the two species. It was his sole contribution to the field of science fiction; indeed, Boulle protested that the book hardly belonged to the genre at all.

Shortly after the book's publication, a French literary agent brought it to the attention of Hollywood producer Arthur P. Jacobs, aware that Jacobs was looking for "something like *King Kong*" that he could turn into a major motion picture. "He told me the story," Jacobs later recalled, "and I said, 'I'll buy it — [I] gotta buy it.' He said, 'I think you're crazy, but okay.'" As Jacobs would discover after some three and a half years of rejections, the agent's belief that *Planet of the Apes* was unfilmable was an opinion shared by many, Boulle included. "I never thought it could be made into a film," the author later admitted. "It seemed to me too difficult, and there was a chance that it would appear ridiculous."

Even Jacobs' friend Charlton Heston, who had committed to the lead role within an hour of hearing the producer's pitch on 5 June 1965, doubted that the film would ever be made. "The novel was singularly uncinematic," said the actor. "All Arthur had was the rights to the novel and a portfolio of paintings depicting possible scenes. There wasn't even a treatment outlining an effective script," he added, despite the fact that *Twilight Zone* creator Rod Serling had admitted spending "well over a year, and thirty or forty drafts" trying to translate Boulle's novel to the screen. Nevertheless, the Oscar-winning star of such epics as *Ben-Hur*, *The Ten Commandments* and *El Cid* stuck with the project through months of Development Hell, "trudging studio to studio with [Jacobs'] paintings and being laughed at: 'No kidding, talking monkeys and rocket ships? Gedouttahere!'" He even brought an A-list director, Franklin J. Schaffner, on board when Blake Edwards, Jacobs' original choice, moved on after spending more than a year attached to the project. Yet even the combined track record of Jacobs, Heston and Schaffner, who had directed Heston in *The War Lord*, could not get the movie made.

The problem, it seemed, was the one Boulle had foreseen: that there was every chance that a film featuring a principal cast of talking apes might appear ridiculous to a cinema audience. Finally, Jacobs convinced 20th Century Fox's head of production, Richard D. Zanuck, to let him spend $5,000 on a make-up test, which was filmed on a jury-rigged set on 8 March 1966. "Rod Serling wrote a long, nine-page scene, a conversation between Taylor and Dr Zaius," Jacobs recalled of the test, directed by Schaffner, and featuring Heston as the misanthropic astronaut Taylor and his *Ten Commandments* co-star Edward G. Robinson in full ape make-up as the orang-utan science minister Dr Zaius, with a young James Brolin and Linda Harrison — who would later be cast as the mute beauty Nova — as the sympathetic chimpanzees, Cornelius and Zira. "We packed the screening room with everyone we could get ahold of," Jacobs added, "and Zanuck said, 'If they start laughing, forget it.' Nobody laughed. They sat there, tense, and he said 'Make the picture.'"

The make-up test had also impressed John Chambers, a former prosthetics designer turned Hollywood make-up artist whose innovative creations had been seen in *Star Trek* (Mr Spock's ears), and John Huston's film *The List of Adrian Messenger* (completely disguising the likes of Frank Sinatra, Tony Curtis and Robert Mitchum for their cameos). "The make-up was crude," he remarked of Ben Nye's work for the test, "but they had a semblance of what they wanted. That's how the concept was started." Chambers was required to solve a number of problems before filming could begin. Should the evolved apes look like Neanderthal Man, like animals, or somewhere in between? How could the three subspecies in the script — and the various gorilla, chimpanzee and orang-utan characters — be differentiated? How could masks be made to express the actors' own facial movements, and handle the voice projection required for sound recording? How could the make-up be applied and removed quickly enough to make filming practical?

While Chambers struggled to solve the make-up problems, the film-makers continued to reshape the script, initially with Serling, and later with Oscar-winner Michael Wilson, a once-blacklisted screenwriter — originally uncredited on *The Bridge on the River Kwai* and *Lawrence of Arabia* due to his suspected Communist allegiances — who knew all about senseless prejudice. Wilson's experience at Joseph McCarthy's HUAC hearings lent authenticity and added poignancy to the tribunal scene, the simian equivalent of a typical 'kangaroo court'. With each new draft, the story drifted farther from its source novel, largely because Boulle's depiction of the simians as a technologically advanced race with cars, buildings and helicopters — all re-scaled for primates — required a far larger budget than Fox would allow. "The early designs were of a very high-tech civilisation, which meant you had to design all kinds of special vehicles and buildings and so on," Heston explained. "And Frank [Schaffner] said, 'I don't have enough budget as it is. Why don't we say it's a very primitive society, and they use horses and wagons and very primitive buildings?' And that's what we did." Production designer William Creber based his revised concept drawings for the simian community on what he described as "a troglodyte city" carved into mountains in Turkey.

The greatest alteration, however, was the relocation of the book's action from an alien planet with its own simian civilisation, to a devastated, post-holocaust Earth of the far future, 2,000 years after a nuclear war has wiped almost all traces of mankind from the face of the planet, allowing simians to become the dominant race. The terrible truth would be revealed to Taylor in the last shot of the film, when his journey into the 'Forbidden Zone' leads to the discovery of the wrecked Statue of Liberty, half-submerged in the desolate wasteland which is all that remains of New York City, circa 3955 AD. Although the credit for this devastating idea has been attributed to — or appropriated by — just about everyone involved with the picture, Jacobs claimed that it came to him during an informal development meeting with Blake Edwards at a Burbank delicatessen. "As we walked out, we looked up, and there's this big Statue of Liberty on the wall of the delicatessen," he said. "If we never had lunch in that delicatessen, I doubt that we would have had the Statue of the Liberty at the end of the picture." Jacobs further claimed that Boulle thought the twist was "more inventive than his own ending, and wished that he had thought of it when he wrote the book." Boulle remembered it differently. "I disliked, somewhat, the ending that was used," he said, referring to perhaps the greatest *coup de théâtre* in the history of cinema. "Personally, I preferred my own."

Premièred on 8 February 1968, *Planet of the Apes* was a critical and commercial smash, grossing a staggering $26 million — more than four times the production budget of $5.8 million. "It not only grossed enormous numbers, it created a new film genre: the space opera," Heston said later. "Fantasies set in outer space had long been a staple of the comic strips and Saturday-morning kiddie TV, but had been disdained by Hollywood," he added, possibly explaining the studios' initial reluctance to green-light the project. *Planet of the Apes* endured one of the most prolonged and difficult development periods of any film, only to become one of the biggest successes of the year — and a virtual lifesaver for 20th Century Fox, which, less than a year earlier, had lost a fortune, even by today's standards, on the epic costume drama *Cleopatra*. The following year, as the first of four sequels was going into production, *Planet of the Apes* received two Academy Award nominations, famously beating out the monkey make-up of *2001: A Space Odyssey* to earn a special Oscar.

Although a number of reasons were cited for *Apes'* across-the-board appeal, it was obvious that the film worked on at least two distinct levels. "Whether by design or accident, [it] had this double appeal," explained Maurice Evans, who ended up playing Dr Zaius in the film, and returned in the first sequel. "The appeal to youngsters [was] as a pure science fiction film, but it had a message to deliver which apparently communicated very clearly to the adult audience." But had Schaffner set out to make a sci-fi action adventure with an intriguing premise and an unbeatable twist, or a Swiftian satire with a polemical commentary on the politically turbulent times of the late 1960s? "I had never thought of this picture in terms of being science fiction," Schaffner asserted, echoing Pierre Boulle's opinion of his original novel. "It was a political film." Indeed, *Planet of the Apes* can perhaps be viewed as symbolically similar to its most famous image, the Statue of Liberty itself: an uncomplicated political message delivered to a mass audience via a populist medium.

The first sequel, *Beneath the Planet of the Apes*, was released in 1970, followed by another in each of the following three years: *Escape From the Planet of the Apes*, *Conquest of the Planet of the Apes* and *Battle for the Planet of the Apes*. Two television series followed: *Planet of the Apes* in 1974 and the animated *Return to the Planet of the Apes* in 1975, by which time the entire concept seemed to have been driven to extinction.

Nevertheless, barely two decades later, Zanuck's "Make the picture" evolved into a different imperative: to *remake* the picture. Yet the film which *Batman* director Tim Burton was to bring to the screen in 2001 originally began not as a remake — or a "re-imagining", as the spin doctors in 20th Century Fox's marketing department euphemised — but as a sequel. In 1988, a twenty-one year-old film-maker called Adam Rifkin made a low budget teen flick entitled *Never on Tuesday*, with cameos by Nicolas Cage, Charlie Sheen and Emilio Estevez. Although barely released and seen by few, the film so impressed Fox president Craig Baumgarten that he invited the young *auteur* to pitch anything he wanted to make. Instead, Rifkin pitched something he wanted to *remake*. "I had always been a huge *Planet of the Apes* fan," he says, "and when Craig asked me if I had any ideas for the studio I immediately pitched him on bringing back the *Apes*. Having independent film experience, I promised I could write and direct a huge-looking film for a reasonable price, like the sequel to *Alien*." Although made for a paltry $18 million, James Cameron's *Aliens* looks like it cost five times that sum, and became a huge success for the studio.

Instead of pitching a story which Fox might then ask him to turn into a screenplay, Rifkin took the unusual step of pitching the trailer: "It would open on a barren desert, sand to the horizon. Then a dot would appear in the distance — very *Lawrence of Arabia*. A craggy narrator would begin telling the cryptic tale of a long forgotten race, decimated by turmoil, strife, war. All the while the dot is getting closer. It's a shrouded man on horseback. Wearing all black, scarves hide his face from the buffeting sand. Closer and closer he rides, the narrator's words growing in intensity. Finally, as the storyteller's words apex with some corny, critical, euphemistic phrase, like "... and now, from out of the sand, they're back!" the Horseman at that moment would ride into close-up. His horse would rear just as he pulled off his scarf to reveal the face of a gorilla, bellowing a deafening war cry. The camera would then ascend up over the ape's head to reveal an army of thousands of apes on horseback charging over the horizon.

Rifkin says that Baumgarten commissioned him to write what amounted to a sequel, "but not a sequel to the fifth film, an alternate sequel to the first film. I had pretty much decided that all anybody really remembered was some random imagery from the first film," Rifkin explains, "particularly the end scene on the beach. All the other films were just a blur. Fox agreed, and that's why it was decided to branch the franchise off in the direction that we did." Rifkin describes his version as "*Spartacus* with apes. The film would open on the last scene from the first film where Charlton Heston was screaming up at the Statue of Liberty, then fade to black. A card would read: '300 years later'. When we would fade up, the ape empire had reached its Roman era. A descendant of Heston would eventually lead a human slave revolt against the oppressive Roman-esque apes. A real sword and sandal spectacular, monkey style."

"The legend throughout the humans is this one man who came from space," Rifkin elaborated to *Creative Screenwriting* magazine, "so

our descendant takes on that cause." At the same time, a power struggle has erupted within the ape empire, with gorillas and chimpanzees
hovering on the brink of civil war for dominance of the planet. "The
general of the gorilla army stages this *coup d'état*, slaughters a bunch of
orang-utans, and takes control of the ape empire politics. In a way," he
added, "*Gladiator* did the same movie without the ape costumes."
Rifkin says that 20th Century Fox loved the draft. "Fox was dead set on
making this movie, and fast. Their marketing department went nuts
for the idea of bringing back *Apes*, which just fuelled Craig's determination to get it into production as fast as possible." The studio's only
request was to shorten the draft by ten or so pages, a decision he says
was based more on budget concerns than creative ones. "As soon as I
was to turn in the cut-down script we were to commence official pre-
production. Needless to say, I was thrilled. I couldn't believe it." Rifkin
was set to direct, with Academy Award-winning make-up man Rick
Baker working on the apes, Danny Elfman (*Batman*) composing the
score, "and possibly Tom Cruise or Charlie Sheen to play the young
slave. Both were hot young actors at the time and were pretty much
neck and neck as far as who would turn out to be the bigger star. I can't
accurately describe in words the utter euphoria I felt at knowing that I,
Adam Rifkin, was going to be resurrecting *The Planet of the Apes*," he
adds. "It all seemed too good to be true. I soon found out that, of
course, it was."

Days before the film was to commence pre-production, Craig
Baumgarten was "quite unexpectedly and unceremoniously replaced"
by what Rifkin describes as "a succession of new studio heads. Though
the new heads of the studio didn't specifically kill the project, the
momentum certainly shifted from active pre-production to active
development. Many new drafts were commissioned and it seemed for
a while like the simple *Spartacus* parallel that I had originally intended
was beginning to lose its focus and shape." One bone of contention was
that, like the original film, Rifkin's script ended on a pessimistic note.
"[Fox wanted] a happy, harmonious ending between apes and humans,
this 'we can all finally live together' happy ending, which I always
thought was a bad idea," Rifkin told *Creative Screenwriting*. "I thought it
was a little corny, because you want a hopeful ending for the characters
you care about, but you still want there to be the tension between the

apes and the humans for all the [proposed] sequels."

As the script went through draft after draft, the hope of Rifkin being allowed behind the camera seemed to fade. "Eventually the script evolved to a place where, though different than the original idea, I actually liked it again. Somehow, through all this development, ideas hatched that otherwise would have never been thought of. I was excited again. But alas," he says, "it wasn't meant to be. Eventually, as is so often the case in studio development, my *Planet of the Apes* just died on the vine. There was no grand deceitful moment, or imposing closed door meeting that put the final nail in its coffin. Trends shift, culture changes, new ideas replace old ones and what once seemed like a great idea to a studio and its marketing department now seemed like old news." Although he would obviously have preferred to have seen the project through, Rifkin (whose career has since included writing *Mouse Hunt* and directing *Detroit Rock City*) says he has no hard feelings: "It was my first studio job, and was a valuable personal and professional experience all the way around. It enabled me to join the Writers Guild and opened other Hollywood doors as well. All in all it was a wonderful project to be a part of, if only for a brief moment."

It was to be several years before Fox resurrected the idea of remaking *Planet of the Apes*, this time when Don Murphy and Jane Hamsher, who produced Oliver Stone's *Natural Born Killers*, became involved. Says Murphy, "I called [Fox executive] Peter Rice, who was and is a good friend of mine, and said, 'I have to do this. What do I gotta do?' And he said, 'You gotta find a director. Why don't you find somebody interesting, like Sam Raimi?' I said, 'Well, that's interesting, but I don't know how to get to Sam Raimi, and I'm not sure he's the right guy anyway.' And he said, 'Well, fuck, why don't you walk down the hall and ask Oliver?' So I walked down the hall and asked Oliver... and he didn't say 'No.'" He didn't exactly say "Yes," either. According to the account in Jane Hamsher's book *Killer Instinct: How Two Young Producers Took on Hollywood and Made the Most Controversial Film of the Decade*, Stone may not have known what he got himself into. "I imagine the conversation going something like this," Hamsher wrote. "'So, Oliver, *Planet of the Apes*,' says Don. 'What about it?' says Oliver. 'Do you like it?' says Don. 'Um, sure,' says Oliver... 'So, if I could get us involved, you'd like that, huh?' says Don. 'Huh? Sure, Don, whatever,' says Oliver." According to

Hamsher, Rice responded by saying that he would only be interested if Stone would direct. "What we don't want is an expensive executive producer." Murphy said to leave it to him.

Before long, a top-heavy meeting was arranged at the offices of Stone's production company, Ixtlan, with everyone present from Fox president of production Tom Jacobson, and going down through the ranks of vice presidents all the way to Rice — on whose shoulders the whole experience (not to mention his future career) was resting. What Stone said first caught everyone by surprise. "I watched the original movies again a couple of nights ago, and they were awful," he told a stunned boardroom. "I'm only here because of Don Murphy. You should talk to him." As Hamsher recalled, "[What followed] was the most dreadful silence I've ever heard in a room. Oliver had clearly gotten wind of all of Don's shenanigans in the process, and was now hanging him out to dry." Murphy apparently did his best to encourage the executives on the basis of marketing potential merchandising tie-ins, McDonald's Happy Meals and the like, but it was abundantly clear that there was no *idea*, no pitch, to back up the generalisations and jargon. "The collective embarrassment level in the room was quantumly higher than anything I've ever registered before in my life," Hamsher went on. "When suddenly, Oliver seemed to tune into something."

Stone — who had mixed politics and science fiction in the television series *Wild Palms*, and written an unproduced adaptation of Alfred Bester's sci-fi novel *The Demolished Man* — had apparently become intrigued by the prospect of time being circular, not linear, with no difference between the past and the future. "What if there were discovered cryogenically frozen Vedic Apes who held the secret numeric codes to the Bible that foretold the end of civilization?" he wondered. His interpretation of *Planet of the Apes* would, as he later told *Empire*, be "a sci-fi movie that deals with the past versus the future. My concept is that there's a code inscribed in the Bible that predicts all historical events. The apes were there at the beginning and figured it all out." Nevertheless, he added evasively, "I don't want to say too much, except that the stars will be hairy."

According to Hamsher, Fox thought almost as much of Stone's ideas as Stone himself did. Thus, wrote Hamsher, "Oliver Stone got Fox to take exactly what they didn't want on the project — an expensive executive producer. They called the next day and offered him a million dollars to do just that." When the project was announced in *Variety* in late 1993, Hamsher sounded more confident than she felt about Stone's approach. "Oliver's notion is kind of in the Joseph Campbell-mytho [sic] vein," she was quoted as saying. "It's about what a separate, parallel planet might be. He's reinvented the story with a contemporary scientist going back in time to this simian universe." Although news that Oliver Stone might *direct* a new *Planet of the Apes* spread like wildfire, Murphy says that was never the intention — "he may have led Fox to believe that, so we could do the deal, but no" — and that he only ever intended to executive produce the film. Nevertheless, Hamsher asserts that Stone was enthusiastic about the project. Murphy agrees: "I think Oliver saw there was a very exciting story to be told and a very exciting concept in a very exciting world." Soon the director was working closely with British-born screenwriter Terry Hayes, who had scripted two *Mad Max* sequels and *Dead Calm*, on a brand new screenplay.

Entitled *Return of the Apes*, the script opens in the present day with a plague that causes human infants to be stillborn — within six months, there won't be a live birth on the planet, signalling the end of the human race. Geneticist Will Robinson discovers that the plague is a genetic time bomb embedded in human 'mitochondrial DNA' 102,000 years earlier. Hoping to save mankind, he uses a unique form of genetic time travel to journey back to a time when Palaeolithic humans were locked in a battle for the future of the planet with highly-evolved apes, one of whom plans to defeat the humans with the plague that will ensure ape dominance over Earth. Will and Billie Rae Diamond, a pregnant colleague who follows him back in time, soon discover that a young human girl named Aiv is the next step in *Homo sapiens'* evolution, and they embark on a race against time to protect her from the virus, thus ensuring the survival of the human race 102,000 years hence. Hayes' ending is bittersweet: Billie Rae ultimately gives birth to a healthy baby boy, Adam, whose future coupling with Aiv (pronounced 'Eve') will effectively found the human race; however, Will and Billie Rae are unable to return to the future. ("I never worked out how to get back," Will confesses. "Give me some credit," Billie Rae retorts. "I'm a scientist — I knew that.") The closing image riffs on the ending of the original film, as Will builds a replica of the Statue of

Liberty's head, "to make sure we never forget where we came from."

According to Hamsher, Fox chairman Peter Chernin subsequently described *Return of the Apes* as "one of the best scripts he ever read." Yet Dylan Sellers, one of the lesser executives steering the project through Fox, thought it could be improved. "What if our main guy finds himself in Ape land, and the Apes are trying to play a game like baseball, but they're missing one element, like the pitcher or something," he suggested. "And when our guy comes along, he knows what they're missing, and he shows them, and they all start playing." In a style which is customary in such meetings, everyone agreed that it would be a great idea, while secretly having no intention of including it, or anything like it. In the meantime, two 700-pound gorillas became attached to the project: one was Australian director Phillip Noyce — who had helmed Hayes' *Dead Calm* and the Jack Ryan blockbusters *Clear and Present Danger* and *Patriot Games*; the other was Arnold Schwarzenegger, the kind of star the studio needed to justify the film's considerable budget. Although he appeared better suited to the Charlton Heston role in a more straightforward remake of the original — a suggestion reinforced by his interest in reprising the Heston role in a mooted remake of *The Ωmega Man* — Schwarzenegger loved Hayes' script; furthermore, he would only work with 'A-list' directors, and Noyce was one of them. "At one point," Murphy recalls, "I was in the biggest meeting I've ever been in, with Peter Chernin, the head of the studio, Arnold Schwarzenegger, Phillip Noyce to direct based on a Terry Hayes first draft; me and my ex-partner Jane to produce and Oliver Stone to executive produce, and that was all looking pretty damn good."

Sellers refused to give up his baseball scene, however, perhaps aware that he ought to put his stamp on the project, for better or worse, in order to justify his involvement in the process. (This tendency among executives best exemplified by the cliché, "This script is perfect. Who can we get to rewrite it?") Thus, when Hayes handed in his next draft — *sans* baseball — Sellers fired him, a move Hamsher described as "incredibly stupid", not least because Hayes and Noyce had remained friends since they collaborated on *Dead Calm* several years earlier. As a result, Noyce moved on. Understandably, Fox became frustrated by the distance between Fox's approach and Hayes' interpretation of Oliver Stone's ideas — as Murphy put it, "Terry wrote a *Terminator*, and Fox wanted *The Flintstones*" — and, perhaps feeling that they were not getting the full value of their million dollars from Stone, decided to take back the reins. Suddenly, says Murphy, "it turned into a whole political thing, and before you knew it we were going nowhere." Several events occurred in rapid succession: Stone went off to pursue projects of his own; Tom Rothman replaced Tom Jacobson as head of production; a drunken Dylan Sellers crashed his car, killing a much-loved colleague and earning himself jail time; and Murphy and Hamsher were paid off.

"After they got rid of us, they brought on Chris Columbus," says Murphy, referring to the writer of *Gremlins* and *Home Alone*, and director of *Mrs Doubtfire*. "Then I heard they did tests of apes skiing, which sounded pretty ludicrous to me." Having recently failed to get a film based on Marvel Comics' *Fantastic Four* off the ground at Fox, Columbus teamed up with that project's screenwriter — *Batman* scribe Sam Hamm — for a new, kiddie-friendly version of *Planet of the Apes*. As Hamm told *Creative Screenwriting*, "What we tried to do was a story that would be simultaneously an homage to the elements we liked from the original series, and would also incorporate a lot of material from [Pierre Boulle's novel] that had been jettisoned from the earlier production. The first half of the script bears very little resemblance to the book, but a lot of the stuff in the second half comes directly from it, or is directly inspired by it."

Hamm's script borrowed Hayes' device of the baby-killing virus, this time brought to Earth by an ape astronaut, whose spacecraft crashes in New York harbour. Nine months later, babies throughout the world are being born prematurely aged, dying within hours of their birth, and it is up to Dr Susan Landis, who works for the Center for Disease Control, and Alexander Troy, a scientist based at Area 51, to use the ape's spacecraft to return to the virus' planet of origin, hoping to find an antidote. Instead, they find an urban environment, similar to that described in Boulle's novel, with apes in three-piece suits armed with heavy weapons, helicopters and the other trappings of civilisation — all used to hunt humans. Landis and Troy discover the antidote and return to Earth, only to find that in their seventy-four year absence, the apes have taken over the planet. Once again, Hamm puts an ironic twist on the Statue of Liberty ending, revealing a statue whose "once-proud porcelain features have been crudely chiselled into the grotesque likeness of a great grinning ape."

Although Arnold Schwarzenegger remained attached to the new script, Fox was still not convinced that this was the version they wanted to make. And when Columbus subsequently quit the project following the death of his mother, James Cameron began talks (during the filming of *Titanic*) about the possibility of writing and producing — but not directing — a new version, drawing on elements of the original film and its first sequel, *Beneath the Planet of the Apes*. "Schwarzenegger... is talking with Jim Cameron on 20th Fox's *Planet of the Apes*," *Variety* columnist Army Archerd wrote in January 1997. "Arnold tells me Stan Winston has already created amazing apes... and although [Cameron]'s banner, Lightstorm Entertainment, does not have a 'formal arrangement' with 20th on *Apes*, it's anticipated he will produce it. He loves the project and the franchise."

Given their history together — two *Terminator* films and the megahit *True Lies* — it seemed more likely than ever that Schwarzenegger would remain aboard, but in the wake of *Titanic*'s critical and commercial success, Cameron began to re-think his future. "I'm forty-four," he said in November 1998. "I make a movie every two or three years — it should be something that I create. I've always done that, with the exception of *Aliens*. *The Terminator* was my creation, so were *Titanic* and *The Abyss*. With the amount of time and energy that I put into a film, it shouldn't be somebody else's [idea]. I don't want to labour in somebody else's house." Of his possible interpretation, "I would have gone in a very different direction," is all Cameron would say. With Michael Bay, Roland Emmerich and a pre-*Lord of the Rings* Peter Jackson all declining a proffered place in the director's chair, *Planet of the Apes* was back to square one.

By the summer of 1999, the studio which had revived the science fiction genre in the early nineties with *Independence Day* and *The X-Files*, was busy ruling the planet with *Star Wars Episode I: The Phantom Menace*, and the prospect of a new *Planet of the Apes* reared its head once again. At around this time, American-Armenian producer-director twins Allen and Albert Hughes (*Menace II Society*, *Dead Presidents*) became intrigued by the idea of making a new version of *Apes*. "The original movie is about race in America," Albert told *Empire* later. "[Ours] would have been more socially significant and would have been more reality-based [than the 2001 version]." Added Allen, "We wanted to take the premise and revamp certain elements. But *From Hell* had a green light and we hadn't worked in five years. I think they didn't really want us to do *Planet of the Apes* anyway." ("I don't think the Hughes brothers had anything more than a conversation with Fox," says Don Murphy, who produced *From Hell*, which was written by Terry Hayes.)

In the meantime, the studio hired screenwriter William Broyles Jr, who marooned Tom Hanks in space in *Apollo 13* and on a desert island in *Cast Away*, to write what amounted to a third story about a man stranded far from home. As Broyles told *Creative Screenwriting*, "[Fox president] Tom Rothman called and said, 'Look, would you like to do *Planet of the Apes?*' And I said, 'No.' And then he called back and said, 'Well, you could really do whatever you wanted [with the project].' And I said, 'No.' Then I went outside. I was looking at the stars and thought, 'You know, this could be fun!' Because with this kind of imaginative science fiction, you can deal with themes that are hard to deal with in a more realistic movie. And there was no producer. There was nobody to tell me anything I had to put in or not put in. It was an interesting act of faith on Fox's part just to give me a blank piece of paper and say, 'Go for it.'" Aside from a projected release date — the summer of 2001 — there were, he said, "zero parameters. That was the fun thing about it. [They said,] 'Don't read any of the earlier scripts. Don't feel limited by the previous series. Just follow your imagination.' It was a completely blank slate." At one point, Broyles called Rothman, demonstrating the extent of his departure from previous versions with a single question: "Does it have to be apes?" He was only half joking.

Broyles sent Fox an outline and a chronicle of the fictional planet which would be the setting for his version, before beginning to work on a first draft. Entitled *The Visitor*, and billed as "episode one in the Chronicles of Aschlar," it was conceived as the first of three movies in a whole new cycle. Although it was pointedly not set on Earth, in other respects his story — in which an astronaut crash-lands on a world of civilised apes and enslaved humans — remains faithful to the basic structure of the original, although Broyles ups the ante by having a powerful chimpanzee named General Thade (an anagram of 'death') plotting the genocide of the human race.

A subsequent draft grabbed the attention not only of original *Planet of the Apes* producer Richard D. Zanuck, who signed on to produce the new version, but also director Tim Burton, fresh from the sleeper hit *Sleepy Hollow*. "I wasn't interested in doing a remake or a sequel of the original *Planet of the Apes* film," Burton said later. "But I was intrigued by the idea of revisiting that world. Like a lot of people, I was affected by the original. It's like a good myth or fairy tale that stays with you. The idea of re-imagining that mythology [was] very exciting to me." This "re-imagining" would, he said, "introduce new characters and other story elements, keeping the essence of the original but inhabiting that world in a different way." Despite more than a decade in Development Hell, Zanuck instantly knew that Burton was the right director to bring *Planet of the Apes* to a new generation of movie-goers. "When you say '*Planet of the Apes*' and 'Tim Burton' in the same breath, that idea is instantly explosive, like lightning on the screen," he said. "All of Tim's films are highly imaginative and highly visual. I can't think of a more perfect pairing than Tim Burton and *Planet of the Apes*. It spells magic to me." Better still, Burton was available, the year he spent developing *Superman Lives* for Warner Bros having ended in the collapse of the project.

Under Burton's direction, Broyles wrote another draft which, the writer says, was much closer to the finished film. "Some of the more complex themes of time and destiny that I had in the original draft [were lost]," he explained. "But the heart of them is still there. They were the same things, just more complex versions of them. Riddles of time and destiny that I had to the third power are now just to the second power." When budgetary concerns began to intrude — Burton famously stated that, as scripted, Broyles' version "would cost $300 million" — Fox brought in Mark Rosenthal and Larry Konner, who had previously scripted another ape-related remake, *Mighty Joe Young*. "[Broyles] came up with the characters pretty much as they are," said Zanuck, "but his script was impractical in many respects. It had monsters in it, all kinds of other things. We wanted to go back to the basic element — the upside-down world." Rosenthal and Konner worked with Burton throughout pre-production, and share the final writing credits with Broyles. "I have a lot of respect for the work they did," Broyles said of Konner and Rosenthal, "and think that given what I'd done and given what Tim wanted, they navigated the right course."

This is more than can be said for astronaut Leo Davidson (Mark Wahlberg), who escapes the planet of the apes and returns to Earth, only to find that apes now rule the planet. "The ending, I'm hoping, will be viewed in proportion to the rest of the movie," Broyles said, "not as some huge, big pay-off, but as fitting with the story itself. We always hoped for something like that, and I did a version of it which they then expanded on." What it did not do, however, was make much sense. "Can I explain the *Planet of the Apes* ending? No," admitted Tim Roth, who played General Thade. "I've seen it twice and I don't understand anything." "I thought it made sense. Kind of," Roth's co-star Helena Bonham Carter (Ari) told *Total Film*. "I don't understand why everyone went, 'Huh?' It's all a time warp thing, isn't it? He's gone back and he realises Thade's beat him there. Everyone's so pedantic," she added. "You start bringing logic to an ape film, it's always dodgy."

By all accounts, including his own, the production of *Planet of the Apes* was a bruising experience for Burton, largely because the set-in-stone release date, 27 July 2001, meant that everything from pre-production to editing and effects work was rushed. "Tim had three months to edit the film where he'd normally spend a year, so there were a lot of elements that were shot that were missing," Estella Warren (Daena) told *Arena*. Yet problems began long before shooting started. "I'm fascinated by the studio technique that sort of leaves you bloodied, beaten and left for dead right before you're supposed to go out and make a great movie for them," Burton told *The Independent* newspaper. "They give you a script," he added, "and you do a budget based on that, and say, 'This movie would cost $300 million to make,' and then they treat you like a crazy, overspending, crazy person! It's like, 'Well, you gave me the script!'" Asked by the same interviewer whether he'd like to make a sequel, Burton's response was simple: "I'd rather jump out of the window." Nevertheless, despite withering reviews, the film grossed a record-breaking $68.5 million on its opening weekend, with a total worldwide gross in excess of $300 million. For one summer, just as the tagline suggested, *Apes* really did 'rule the planet'.

Despite the thirteen years, manifold drafts and numerous directors which elapsed between the unproduced Adam Rifkin version and Tim Burton's interpretation, Don Murphy denies the notion that the film was in Development Hell. "I suppose it was, in a way," he allows, "but it really wasn't. What happened was they tried to reboot it with Rifkin. Then some years later they tried to reboot it with us. Our reboot led them to believe they had something big there, and that led to trying to get other directors interested. Looking back," he adds, "at the time we may have been a little bit over our heads. It became a really big thing pretty freaking fast. Everybody started to try to grab onto it. And we were soon out! I would do things differently today, but... that's just the way it is." Like many, Murphy was disappointed with the final film. "I thought it was gonna be fantastic," he says, "like *Star Wars* or *Lord of the Rings*. The movie they actually made was a bad *Twilight Zone* episode."

## CAST INTO MOUNT DOOM

### Paths not taken on the road to Peter Jackson's
### *The Lord of the Rings*

"When Gandalf is vanquished, the text is 'He fell beyond time and
memory'... we puzzled about how you put that on film."
— *director John Boorman on his proposed adaptation*

"In a hole in the ground there lived a hobbit." With these words,
impulsively scribbled on a piece of paper by thirty-eight year-old
Oxford languages professor John Ronald Reuel Tolkien, the greatest fantasy epic in the history of literature was born. Although *The
Hobbit*, as the resulting story would eventually be titled, was written
largely for Tolkien's own children, it found its way to publisher Allen &
Unwin, and appeared in 1937. It sold well; well enough that Allen &
Unwin asked for a sequel. Thirteen years later, 'J.R.R.' Tolkien — a
noted perfectionist and self-professed procrastinator — was ready to
deliver it. "My work has escaped from my control," he wrote to his publisher in 1950, "and I have produced a monster: an immensely long,
complex, rather bitter, and rather terrifying romance, quite unfit for
children (if fit for anybody)." Its title was *The Lord of the Rings*.

It was another four years before Allen & Unwin finally published
the book, an epic saga set in a fictional world called Middle-Earth.
Between 1954 and 1965, the book — divided, much to the author's
annoyance, into three parts entitled *The Fellowship of the Ring*, *The Two
Towers* and *The Return of the King* — sold moderately well, particularly
for a thousand-page trilogy of hardcover doorstops which, unable to fit
into any existing genre, had invented one all of their own. By 1965,
when Ace Books (home of Philip K. Dick and Tolkien-inspired fantasist
Ursula K. Le Guin) and Ballantine published rival editions of the book,
American youth had been caught up in hippie culture. *The Lord of the*

*Rings* seemed to capture the zeitgeist, and the quiet Oxford don suddenly found his story about hobbits, elves, dwarfs and wizards selling hundreds of thousands of copies per month, and becoming — almost overnight — required reading for a generation of psychedelic explorers. With a vast readership stretching from middle England to the Midwestern United States, one would have expected Hollywood to come knocking on the door of his study, the cigar smoke of a producer mingling with that of Tolkien's beloved pipe as he signed away the film rights to his masterpiece. In fact, Hollywood had been ahead of the curve, with Hugo award-winning science fiction fan, writer and magazine editor Forrest J Ackerman — the man credited with being the first to abbreviate science fiction to 'sci-fi' — approaching Tolkien as early as 1957.

Ackerman made his appeal in person, flying to London and taking the train to Oxford. "I had no sooner landed in London than an hour later I was in the drawing room of Professor Tolkien," Ackerman recalls. "There were two young lady fans who went with me. The Professor talked to us with a pipe in his mouth, and holding his head kind of down, and a very thick accent, and when the two girls and I got back on the train we were saying, 'What did he say? Did you understand anything?' We only understood about one word in five!" Nevertheless, he adds, "He gave me permission for a year to try to find a movie producer for it."

Ackerman's ambitious plan was to make a live-action film, rather than the animated one which Tolkien would have preferred. "I should welcome the idea of an animated motion picture, with all the risk of vulgarization," Tolkien wrote to his publisher Rayner Unwin on 19 June 1957, "and that quite apart from the glint of money, though on the brink of retirement that is not an unpleasant possibility." Referring to an earlier bowdlerization of the book for a dramatised reading performed on British radio, he added, "I think I should find vulgarization less painful than the sillification achieved by the BBC." Although a writing associate of Ackerman's, Morton Grady Zimmerman, set to work on a treatment for the proposed film, while production designer Ron Cobb began scouting suitable locations in California, Ackerman found it difficult to interest the few producers he knew in such an ambitious undertaking. "I had gone to school with James Nicholson, who was the president of American International Pictures, and I thought perhaps that he would be interested," he says, "but the scope was too great for him. I no longer recall just who else I approached, but nobody obviously was prepared to produce it at that time."

In April 1958, Tolkien admitted in a letter to Unwin that he was "entirely ignorant of the process of producing an 'animated picture' from a book, and of the jargon connected with it." He had recently received Zimmerman's synopsis of the book, described as a "story-line", and while Tolkien claimed ignorance of the adaptation process, he did know the difference between a film 'treatment' and what he saw as ill treatment. "This document, as it stands, is sufficient to give me grave anxiety," he wrote, adding that Zimmerman seemed "quite incapable of excerpting or adapting the 'spoken words' of the book. He is hasty, insensitive, and impertinent," he went on. "He does not *read* books. It seems to me evident that he has skimmed through the [*Lord of the Rings*] at a great pace, and then constructed his [storyline] from partly confused memories, and with the minimum of references back to the original."

Tolkien, a lifelong philologist, was principally peeved with the constant misspelling of Boromir as 'Borimor,' but there were other slights, and overall Tolkien felt "very unhappy about the extreme silliness and incompetence of Z and his complete lack of respect for the original." Nevertheless, there was one redeeming feature about the whole affair, and it was an obvious one. "I need, and shall soon need very much indeed, money," he wrote, referring to his encroaching retirement, and promising to restrain himself, "and avoid all avoidable offence." In a letter to Ackerman circa June 1958, Tolkien begged understanding of "the irritation (and on occasion the resentment) of an author, who finds, increasingly as he proceeds, his work treated as it would seem carelessly in general, in places recklessly, and with no evident signs of any appreciation of what it is all about." Although hardly an avowed cinemagoer, Tolkien understood the medium well enough to note that "the failure of poor films is often precisely in exaggeration, and in the intrusion of an unwarranted matter owing to not perceiving where the core of the original lies." His commentary on Zimmerman's synopsis was thorough in scope and condemnatory in tone. "He has cut the parts of the story upon which its characteristic and peculiar tone principally depends, showing a preference for fights; and he has made no serious attempt to represent the heart of the tale adequately: the journey of the Ringbearers. The last and most important part of this has, and it is not too strong a word, simply been murdered."

Bryan Sibley, author of a later (and widely acclaimed) BBC radio adaptation of *The Lord of the Rings* and the official 'making of' books for Peter Jackson's trilogy, believes that some of Tolkien's criticism may have been unfair. "The problem was that, because Tolkien was not a regular moviegoer, he didn't understand the problems of dramatisation," he told *Starlog*. "One of his chief criticisms of [the] treatment was that he had arranged the books in chronological order. It's actually something that you have to do if you're going to construct a screenplay out of what is essentially a novel." Nevertheless, despite the considerable efforts of Ackerman et al to convince Tolkien that his story was in safe hands, the proposed adaptation withered on the vine, and no firm agreement was ever made. "I think it was just as well," Ackerman admits, "because it could never have been given the grand treatment that Peter Jackson has afforded it." Ackerman did manage to produce another adaptation of the book, however. "I edited 200 issues of *Famous Monsters of Filmland*," he says, "and the man who produced those issues saw a value in Tolkien. As I recall he had me do a one-shot comic book [based] on it. I had already created a [comic strip] character called Vampirella, so he had me create a one-shot on a portion of the Tolkien [stories]." There was another, more surprising consolation for Ackerman, albeit tangential: "I had a cameo in one of Peter Jackson's films, long before he became famous," he says, referring to the director's early splatter flick *Braindead* [aka *Dead Alive*].

The prospect of a film version of *The Lord of the Rings* did not arise again until the late 1960s, by which time the book had become one of the publishing sensations of the decade. This time, it was another 60s phenomenon — The Beatles — who became linked to the project, a move apparently instigated by John Lennon. "We talked about it for a while," Paul McCartney told Roy Carr, author of *The Beatles at the Movies*, "but then I started to smell a bit of a carve-up because, immediately, John wanted the lead." According to Carr, however, Lennon was interested in the role of Gollum, with McCartney, George Harrison and Ringo Starr opting for Frodo, Gandalf and Sam respectively. Whether related to The Beatles' ambitions or not, United Artists successfully acquired the rights to film *The Lord of the Rings* in the autumn of 1969, for the sum of $250,000.

It was around this time that Heinz Edelmann, designer and art director of The Beatles' animated film *Yellow Submarine*, became interested in pursuing the idea of an animated adaptation. At the time, Edelmann was doubtful that stories of action, suspense and thrills could be depicted as straight animation, and proposed to make the film "as a kind of opera, or a sort of operatic impression", more closely related to Disney's *Fantasia* than, say, *The Sword in the Stone*. He intended to approach it "As one does an operatic version of any book," he told *Outré* magazine, "[to] sort of try for a distillation of the mood and the story, but not follow every twist of the plot." For instance, "One could have packed 300 pages of wandering into a five-minute sequence set to music."

Edelmann has said that his version of *The Lord of the Rings* would not have been stylistically similar to *Yellow Submarine*: "The artwork would have been completely different: much less colour, and unrealistic, but without the *art nouveau* touch *Yellow Submarine* has." Neither did Tolkien's original illustrations for the book, which were all based on medieval art, appeal to Edelmann, who saw the story more in terms of an Akira Kurosawa film. "If you look at all the fantasy films done in the last thirty years," he said in 2001, "there is a strong Japanese ethnic influence in the staging, in the buildings, and especially in the costumes. I think at that time we might have been the first to think in those terms. *The Lord of the Rings* is such a classic right now that almost no artistic freedom is possible. Back at that time, when it was new and Tolkien was still alive, it would have been a contemporary version, and I think that would have given us much more artistic freedom." Nevertheless, he added, "I would have loved to have done it. Sometimes I do still think about it, but it would have been an awful amount of work. Maybe it's better that it has remained just a concept."

Ultimately, United Artists decided that animation was not the best way to proceed, and in June 1970 announced that John Boorman, the young British director who had come to Hollywood's attention three years earlier with his gritty thriller *Point Blank*, would helm a live-action version. Boorman had originally wanted to make a movie about the legend of King Arthur, but when United Artists offered him the chance to turn Tolkien's fantasy tale into reality, he leapt at it, bringing aboard Rospo Pallenberg to work with him on the script. They conceived of several approaches, from a straightforward adaptation, to what Pallenberg later described as "like a Fellini movie in a never-land, or in a big studio, like [Baz Luhrmann's] *Moulin Rouge!* — sort of all fake." In the end, a more straightforward approach prevailed, with the studio hoping to combine all three volumes of the book into one film — an endeavour which proved challenging to say the least. "At the time, they produced long movies with an intermission," Boorman explained. "[The script] is 176 pages with an intermission on page eighty-one, after the Fellowship goes down the rapids, and you have a sense that they have reached a great landscape as the river widens." After the intermission, "we accelerated as we continued the story, and dropped things out. We were propelled by what we liked, and invented as we went along."

Among the script's inventions was the opening, in which the camera would invade J.R.R. Tolkien's own study, disturbing him at work, followed by a brief history of Middle-Earth, conducted by what Pallenberg described as "a kind of Kabuki play in which the story of Sauron and the creation of the rings was explained to a gathering in Rivendell." Pallenberg wrote new scenes for several characters, including a love scene between Frodo and Galadriel (husband Celeborn was not featured). He also claimed a particular affinity and sympathy for the dwarf, Gimli, for whom he wrote a new scene in which Gimli was buried in a hole and beaten to utter exhaustion in a bid to recover his unconscious ancestral memory, and thereby remember the word necessary to enter Moria and discover other insights about the ancient dwarf kingdom. "I had a rather fanciful idea involving these orcs that are slumbering or in some kind of narcotic state," he added. "The Fellowship runs over them, and their footsteps start up their hearts. John liked that a lot." Another original idea was a unique duel between Gandalf and Saruman, inspired by African magicians who duel with words (an idea subsequently explored, incidentally, in Neil Gaiman's *Sandman*). "It was a way of one entrapping the other as a duel with words rather than special effects flashes, shaking of staves, and all that," he explained. "I tried to keep away from that a lot, and Boorman did too."

At the time, the possibility remained that The Beatles might be involved, perhaps even playing the four hobbits, a prospect which Pallenberg relished, despite the fact that it would have been difficult to apply roles to each of the group's members. "It was presented to me as, 'Let's see if we can try and keep the four hobbits on sort of an equal basis — [though] obviously, Frodo was the protagonist — so we did that," Pallenberg added, opining that Paul McCartney would have been his ideal Frodo. "They were the emotional anchor to the whole piece. We also anchored a lot of the film on how the ring corrupts, and we were fascinated by Tolkien's idea of 'stewardship of the land'."

New Zealand director Peter Jackson, who would bring a live-action *Lord of the Rings* to the screen thirty years after Boorman's aborted attempt, sympathised. "When you're faced with adapting the twelve hundred pages of *The Lord of the Rings* it's obviously an incredibly daunting task," he told the makers of *The South Bank Show*. "It's daunting in several ways. One [is that] just as a book, it's very dense and there's a lot of characters and it has... layers, [so] that you can scrape away one layer and there's more information below, and you can scrape that away [and] there's more information, which is exactly what makes it such a wonderfully beloved book. To somehow translate that particular aspect of the book into film, it's virtually impossible. What you *can* do is you can take the story, you can take the characters, and you can make a movie that presents on film the moments that people remember from the book. Tolkien did a lot of things in his story that if you were a film-maker you would choose not to do — it's as simple as that," he added. For example, "His villains are very difficult to put onto film. Sauron, his ultimate evil in the story, is unable to take physical form by the time the events of *The Lord of the Rings* take place, and he manifests himself as a giant flaming eyeball. Now, you know, to have a movie in which your principal villain is a flaming eyeball is not a decision that you would make if you were writing an original screenplay..." Added Boorman, "[We] used to get the giggles about some of the issues. There was one I remember clearly when Gandalf is vanquished. The text is, 'He fell beyond time and memory', and we puzzled about how you put that on film."

Perhaps the biggest hurdles for Boorman to overcome in the

process of adapting the book were the technical challenges. Making the hobbits appear smaller than life would have been accomplished with oversized props and locations, and forced perspective. Flying creatures were excised from the story, so that instead of having the Nazgul chief swoop in on a flying steed, it rides a horse with no skin — just exposed, bleeding flesh. "I still have this feeling that the dazzle can take away from the fundamental drama," Pallenberg suggested. "We always tried to do things on the cheap, simply. When you saw a castle in the distance, it could have been made out of anything — even gleaming, high-voltage transmission towers. You saw those in the distance between the trees, and then suddenly you were inside it. John Boorman is tremendously clever at that." Nevertheless, Boorman had other ideas which might not have proved so cost-effective, including a model of Middle-Earth so large it would have displayed the curvature of the Earth, and filled an entire studio. Principal photography would most likely have taken place in Ireland (which would have opened up tax incentives for the production), with interiors being shot at Ardmore Studios. Said Pallenberg, "As I drove around, taking breaks from writing, I saw all sorts of places. I remember there was one view that he could pass off as the Shire — it looked down towards a little village that was called Anamoe, I believe."

The Boorman/Pallenberg script ended poignantly, as Gandalf, Frodo, Bilbo, Galadriel, Arwen and Elrond sail away from Middle-Earth in a ship. A rainbow appears, prompting Legolas, who is watching from the shore, to remark, "Look — only seven colours. Indeed the world is failing." Although it sounds like Tolkien, the line is Pallenberg's own. "From a physics standpoint it's incorrect to say that there could be more than seven colours," the writer points out, "but what it's saying is, 'We live in a diminished world.'" The end of Boorman and Pallenberg's year-long endeavour was no less poignant: no sooner had they submitted the script to United Artists than the studio decided it was too risky, too costly or simply not commercially viable, and put it on the back burner. Boorman and Pallenberg had not wasted their efforts, however. A decade later, in 1981, they used the knowledge they had gained during their year of development on the unrealised Tolkien project as the basis for *Excalibur*, the film about King Arthur which Boorman had set out to make before United Artists persuaded him to consider *The Lord of the Rings*.

By the time of Tolkien's death in 1973, word of Boorman's stalled production had reached Ralph Bakshi, a Brooklyn-born animator best known as the film-maker who brought *Fritz the Cat* to the big screen. Says Bakshi, "I was a Tolkien fan, and I thought *Lord of the Rings* was not only one of my favourite fantasies, but one of my favourite novels. I was doing my own stuff at the time, and I knew Disney were talking about doing it, but the Tolkien family wasn't happy with their approach, because Disney wanted to make it a musical, tone it down, and make it more palatable for young kids." Interestingly, both Disney's archives and legal department dispute the notion that the studio ever pursued an animated feature based on the books. "Then I heard that John Boorman was going to do it live-action for United Artists, and had somehow condensed the three books into one script, which I thought was ridiculous," Bakshi continues. "So I went to Mike Medavoy at United Artists and told him it should be done in animation, in two or three parts. He said, 'We've spent $3 million on this script we don't understand. I don't know if we're gonna make it.' So I walked across the lot and talked to Dan Melnick at MGM, who loved the idea and immediately wrote a cheque to buy it from United Artists."

One might think that Bakshi, whose animated features *Fritz the Cat* and *Heavy Traffic* had both received 'X' ratings, was the last person to whom J.R.R. Tolkien's estate would give their blessing for the first feature film based on his most famous work. Not so, he says. "They had no contractual approval, but I said, 'Unless they give me the okay I'm not doing it.' So I went to see Tolkien's daughter and spent two days discussing how and why I was going to make the film. I said I couldn't do everything, but the scenes that I *could* do would be pure Tolkien, both in dialogue and depiction, and she loved that. She took me to the studio where Tolkien wrote *Lord of the Rings*, and gave me her blessing, and I got to work." Chris Conkling wrote the first draft of the screenplay and delivered it on 21 September 1976. This was subsequently revised (in a second draft dated 3 May 1977) by Peter S. Beagle, with the third draft (credited to Conkling, Beagle and Bakshi) being completed on 21 September 1978, exactly two years after the first. In the meantime, however, Dan Melnick had left MGM, and *The Lord of the Rings* was not a project his replacement wanted to pursue.

Undeterred, Bakshi approached Saul Zaentz, who had financed *Fritz the Cat* (and had produced Best Picture Academy Award-winner *One Flew Over the Cuckoo's Nest,* and would later produce another, *Amadeus*). Zaentz agreed to back the film, which would be divided into two parts. In adapting the books, Bakshi made good on his promise to remain faithful to the spirit, if not the letter, and elected to employ the controversial 'rotoscoping' technique — essentially tracing over live action footage — to ground the fantasy in the kind of "nasty realism" he found omnipresent in Tolkien's work. "His fantasy is grounded in *totally* realistic terms," he explains, "and to get that kind of realism I knew I would effectively have to do a live-action picture in animation. I thought rotoscoping was the answer. After all, [Walt] Disney used rotoscoping on every film he did — Snow White and the Prince, every realistic character, every song and dance number in every Disney film was rotoscoped [from performers] in full costume — but he kept it a secret. So it was not a cheat, it was a *choice*. Besides," he adds, "if we'd done it in animation, we'd still be animating the picture today!" Even so, making the film was, he says, "a logistical nightmare. I recorded the voices in England, then I filmed the live action scenes — seventy-five to 200 setups a day, to get it done in time — using mostly different actors, fully costumed, playing back the pre-recorded dialogue to them so that the movement and timings would match the recordings. Only *then* did I go back to my desk to begin animating this two-and-a-half-hour picture! It was the hardest, most devastating and nerve-wracking two and a half years of my life."

The worst was yet to come. When the film ended half way through the second book, *The Two Towers*, audiences and critics cried foul. Bakshi says he always intended to make a second film, but by the time the first film was released, the film's backers had reneged on their agreement to produce a follow-up. "They screwed me royally, because they never put 'Part One' on the screen," he says of United Artists, who had declined to produce the film but wound up distributing it. "They were supposed to make two films, but they chickened out." Although two animated television specials were produced in the late 1970s, based on *The Hobbit* and *The Return of the King*, neither was related to Bakshi's version. Bakshi took solace in the fact that the film was a favourite of the Tolkien family, and has subsequently enjoyed a critical reappraisal.

"I got a letter from Tolkien's daughter saying she loved the movie, but I was pretty despondent for years, until I started to go online [at www.ralphbakshi.com], and got thousands of emails from people around the world saying they loved the movie. I feel much absolved." Nevertheless, Bakshi was upset that no one involved in Peter Jackson's adaptation contacted him during the production of those films: "I sat with the book with no illustrations, so every decision about what a goblin or hobbit or wraith has to look like was coming out of my own imagination and my experience of reading Tolkien, and my fear of making a mistake with the Tolkien fans. And he doesn't even call me and thank me. Not that I'm bitter — I just find it ungentlemanly."

It was during 1996 that the first rumours began to circulate concerning a proposed adaptation by Peter Jackson, whose diverse output as a director ranged from the splatterfests *Bad Taste* and *Braindead*, to horror comedy *The Frighteners* and the award-winning drama *Heavenly Creatures*. It was not until 1998 however that Miramax Films came forward to negotiate with producer Saul Zaentz (who still retained the movie rights to the saga) and underwrite a two-movie adaptation of *The Lord of the Rings* with Jackson as writer, producer and director. When Miramax got cold feet about a production of this scale, New Line Cinema stepped in, agreeing to back not two but *three* films — a risky project which has since paid off handsomely. "That was the key to it," Jackson told *Dreamwatch* magazine. "Without someone committing to the three movie idea, I think it would always have remained unfilmed." The director has said that his own (commercially successful, universally lauded) adaptation "presents the characters that people love, and... the themes that were important to Tolkien in the book. But there's no way ever that a movie could come close to capturing the sort of level of detail and complexity [present in the novel]. It's an interesting dilemma, I guess, because *The Lord of the Rings* is so beloved that [although] you have to make a film that fans are wanting to see... you really cannot make a film for fans, [or] for readers. You would become homogenised and diluted."

Boorman acknowledged as much in reference to his own failed adaptation. "It's a huge uphill struggle to make [films like] that and, as someone who's tried to do it, I have the greatest admiration and sympathy for Peter Jackson. It's glorious in that you know that's what movies should be about — taking these huge risks and making something as wild and unfilmable and impossible as *The Lord of the Rings*."

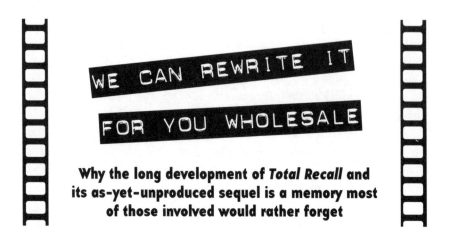

# WE CAN REWRITE IT FOR YOU WHOLESALE

**Why the long development of *Total Recall* and its as-yet-unproduced sequel is a memory most of those involved would rather forget**

"Ron [Shusett] said, 'You've done the Philip K. Dick version,' like I had done something terrible. And I said, 'Well, yeah.' And he said, 'No, no, we want *Raiders of the Lost Ark* Goes to Mars.'"

*– original* Total Recall *director David Cronenberg*

In 1990, Austrian action superstar Arnold Schwarzenegger and Dutch director Paul Verhoeven teamed up for what would become one of the biggest science fiction films of all time — *Total Recall*. Schwarzenegger, the star of such films as *Conan the Barbarian*, *The Terminator*, *Commando*, *Predator* and *The Running Man*, played Douglas Quaid, a man whose dreams of Mars come to life when he takes a virtual holiday, only to be embroiled in a desperate race to save the red planet — a scenario which may or may not be a product of his imagination.

For a film that would gross $250 million worldwide (in 1990 dollars) despite its restrictive R rating, thereby becoming the highest grossing film of its year of release, *Total Recall* had an inauspicious beginning. The film was loosely based on a 1966 short story entitled 'We Can Remember It For You Wholesale', written by American science fiction author Philip K. Dick (1928-1982). Dick's novel *Do Androids Dream of Electric Sheep?* had previously been the basis for Ridley Scott's *Blade Runner*, which despite being a critical and commercial failure, had revived interest in Dick's writing, and led to a number of his other stories being optioned for the cinema. 'We Can Remember It For You

Wholesale', however, had been snapped up almost a decade earlier. "I think it was probably 1974 that I optioned this story," said Ronald Shusett, at the time a struggling producer with only the throwaway suspense flick *W* (aka *I Want Her Dead*) to his credit. "Phil Dick was then not a known author at all. He was still a struggling pulp writer, [as he was for] most of his career until *Blade Runner* got made."

Shusett first encountered the twenty-three-page short story in the pages of the April 1966 issue of *The Magazine of Fantasy and Science Fiction*. "This was the first story which knocked me right out, which I knew would make an incredible movie, [albeit] an incredibly expensive movie." Shusett's enthusiasm is perplexing. In the story, clerk Douglas Quail visits Rekall, Inc for a false-memory implant of a secret agent's trip to Mars, only for the process to uncover his true identity: not only a secret agent recently returned from Mars, but someone whose death will lead to the invasion of Earth, thanks to a deal he struck with aliens as a child. Shusett paid $1,000 for the rights, and invited screenwriter Dan O'Bannon (*Dark Star*) to help him turn it into a script. "Ronny Shusett walked into my apartment sporting a filthy old Xerox copy of Dick's [story]," O'Bannon told *Cinefantastique*. "He said, 'Dan, I was wondering if you'd take a look at this story and tell me if you think this would make a good movie.' I said, 'I know that story and I think it would make a *terrific* movie.'" Thirty pages into the script, now retitled *Total Recall* at Shusett's suggestion, O'Bannon realised he had exhausted the story. "Dick's story is short," he said. "It ends very abruptly. You cannot take that particular story and simply inflate it up to a full-length piece." O'Bannon realised that the story was effectively a first act, and that the second and third acts would have to be invented from whole cloth. "Shusett liked what I did and asked, 'Where does it go from here?' And I said, 'We take him to Mars.'"

The resulting script opens with the protagonist, Quail (the name was eventually altered to Quaid to avoid references to the then-Vice President, Dan Quayle), dreaming of a Martian pyramid of which he has no conscious memory. "Quaid, Earth's top secret agent, went to Mars and entered this [alien] compound. The machine killed him and created a synthetic duplicate. He is that synthetic duplicate," O'Bannon explained, "[and] he cannot be killed because he can anticipate danger before it happens." The fact that this duplicate is invulnerable leads the government of Earth to a radical solution: "Earth wants to kill him but cannot. That's why they go to all this trouble to erase his brain to make him think he's nobody. It's the only way they can control him." At the climax of the script, Quaid puts his hand on the Martian machine, at which point he achieves 'total recall', discovering his true identity: a Martian machine. "He is, in effect, the resurrection of the Martian race in a synthetic body. He turns and says to all the other characters, 'It's going to be fun to play God.'" How O'Bannon would have externalised Quaid's discovery is uncertain; Shusett, in any case, wanted a more dramatic climax. "Shusett and I never saw eye to eye on the end of the movie," O'Bannon admitted, adding: "The end that they filmed, in my estimation, is lame."

O'Bannon and Shusett enjoyed a more fruitful collaboration on *Alien*, the success of which gave Shusett a development deal at Disney, where he set to work on *Total Recall* once again. When Disney eventually passed on the project, Dino De Laurentiis' company DEG stepped in, with plans for Richard Rush (*The Stunt Man*) or Lewis Teague (*Cujo*) to direct. Yet the difficulties with the script's third act remained — problems which De Laurentiis hoped his next choice would solve: Canadian director David Cronenberg, fresh from the success of *The Dead Zone*. "At that time I was not a Philip Dick fan," Cronenberg admitted to Serge Grünberg. "I knew about him but I had stopped reading sci-fi when I was a kid — probably sometime in the 1950s. That was when I started reading guys like Burroughs and Nabokov. So I missed the beginning of Philip K. Dick's reign as one of the supremos of sci-fi. It was the script of *Total Recall* which Dino gave to me which got me interested." (Now, Cronenberg has a collection of Dick first editions.) The script, which Cronenberg said was written by Dan O'Bannon and Ron Shusett, "had this very wonderful beginning which was pure Philip K. Dick — and then they didn't know what to do with it. So I was intrigued because it felt very close, it felt good. And as I say, I had no preconceived ideas of Philip Dick."

Cronenberg spent a year writing and rewriting his own version of the script on a Xerox 860 word processor. "It's a good thing I had a computer because I did about twelve drafts in about twelve months," he says. "I was constantly fighting with Ron Shusett, and meeting with him, and then at a certain point I was sitting in a room full of people, and Ron said, 'You know what you've done — you've done the Philip K. Dick version,' like I had done something terrible. And I said, 'Well, yeah.' And he said, 'No, no, we want *Raiders of the Lost Ark* Goes to Mars.' So I said, 'Well, Jeez, I wish we'd all had this discussion twelve months ago — it wouldn't have wasted all our time.'" Says Shusett, "I didn't want to do it as serious as *Blade Runner*. I thought it needed to have a *Raiders* tone; not quite so humorous, but certainly closer to that than Cronenberg's approach, which was the exact tone of Steven Spielberg's *Minority Report* [another film based on a Dick story, of which more later]." Cronenberg confirms that De Laurentiis shared Shusett's view. "I went to Dino and I said, 'Dino, I think we have to stop because we're obviously talking about two different movies, and we might as well acknowledge it now. I don't want to make your movie. It seems that you don't want to make my movie. We should stop.' He was rational but he was telling me he was going to sue me. I was surprised he even cared, but it was like he had done a deal with me and ... so I basically said that I would make another movie with him. I mean I obviously wanted to work with him, but that project was clearly not the right one."

"Cronenberg quit for a number of reasons," Shusett told *Cinefantastique*. "First of all, he and I were having a number of creative disagreements, which started about the time of Richard Dreyfuss' involvement, because DEG didn't want to do it as it was written for [him]." Dreyfuss, already an Oscar winner and star of two Steven Spielberg hits, *Jaws* and *Close Encounters of the Third Kind*, had asked Cronenberg to mould the character of Quaid to his 'everyman' persona, rather than the action hero described in the O'Bannon-Shusett version. "Cronenberg started to feel that the movie should take on a whole *new* approach, different than either of the previous ones," Shusett explained. "I disagreed with him. I wanted to go either with our earlier approach... [or] the one Dreyfuss, Cronenberg and I had evolved. But suddenly David was against his own ideas." Indeed, Cronenberg recalls that, several years down the line, De Laurentiis offered him the project again, his way. He declined. "It's dead for me now," he said. "I can't get back into that now. I just can't go back to working with Ron and fighting the same old battles and doing all that stuff." (Evidently, there were no hard feelings: De Laurentiis would subsequently produce

Cronenberg's *Dead Ringers*.)

So how would Cronenberg's *Total Recall* have looked? "First of all, I really wanted to cast William Hurt," he says, "and the difference between Bill Hurt and Arnold Schwarzenegger probably tells you everything. I was doing something that I thought was faithful to Phil Dick and also to my own sense of the complex understanding of what memory is and what identity is. Obviously it would have been sci-fi and you would have gone to Mars, but it would have been like *Spider* Goes to Mars," he adds, referring to his 2002 film starring Ralph Fiennes as a man struggling to piece his memories together, "as opposed to *Raiders of the Lost Ark* Goes to Mars. In a way, *Spider* really is an examination of memory and how it is a created thing, not sort of a video documentary of your past but something that you're constantly upgrading, altering, changing, shifting and editing — to the extent that your memories are your identity and you're also messing around with your identity, which certainly in *Total Recall* was something that I'd really gone into in great depth."

In 1991, *Cinefantastique* writer Bill Florence summarised one of Cronenberg's drafts, noting that his version diverged most significantly following Quaid's arrival on Mars. "Quaid takes a cab driven by Benny... to the cab depot, where he finds Melina, the chief cabbie. She gives him a job as a cab driver, and he quickly avails himself of his own transportation to visit Quato [Kuato in the final film], a memory manipulator [who] has a malformed head growing out of his body ... called 'The Oracle'." (Given Cronenberg's fondness for physical mutation in his films, it is perhaps unnecessary to say that the idea of mutants on Mars, and of Kuato's malformed congenital twin, were originally Cronenberg's inventions.) When The Oracle dies while attempting to bring Quaid's secret past to light, Quaid visits Pintaldi, a face changer, whose manipulations of Quaid's facial structure reveals him to be Chairman Mandrell, dictator of Earth. After a failed assassination attempt, Quaid/Mandrell confronts Mars Administrator Cohaagen, who convinces him to infiltrate Mars Fed, who suppressed his true identity, and gives him a signal generator to track his location. "When the generator explodes — meant to kill Mandrell, but killing Benny the cab driver instead — Mandrell returns to the cab depot," Florence continued, "where an EIA doctor tries to convince him he's dreaming, a scene almost exactly like the final film's Dr Edgemar sequence... In the climax of Cronenberg's script, Mandrel and Cohaagen find themselves alone on a robot-controlled tour bus, moving over the Martian desert. Cohaagen reveals that Mandrell never really existed, that Quaid is just a minor government functionary selected to fill the role of chairman. Cohaagen planned to take over, using Quaid's Mandrell image." A fight ensues, Quaid/Mandrell defeats Cohaagen, and assumes his place as Chairman Mandrell, with Melina at his side.

According to Ron Miller (*Dune*), engaged as production illustrator by DEG during the period of Cronenberg's involvement, it was more than just the story that might have been different: Miller recalls Martian creatures called 'Ganzibulls', created by Shusett, but retained in Cronenberg's drafts. "They were creatures that lived in the sewers of the Mars city, called Venusville," he told *Cinefantastique*. "In Cronenberg's version, they were mutant camels. In Ron's original script, the Martian colonists used camels as pack animals, and the camels wore oxygen masks... Cronenberg elaborated on the camels idea by having the monsters in the sewers be mutant camels." Miller also remembers working with art director Pier Luigi Basile (*Conan the Destroyer*) at DEG's studios in Rome, where "nothing much happened. We just drew all day for weeks on end. Cronenberg finally was hired, and he gave us more direction, more purpose. Bob Ringwood was going to do the costume design for the Cronenberg version, so he was there, on and off, for a couple of weeks and did a few sketches."

Cronenberg was mostly unimpressed by the finished film. "I thought it was a bad movie," he told Serge Grünberg, "although there were one or two moments that were true Philip Dick moments in it — they were good. But they weren't good because it was Schwarzenegger still: first of all as an actor for that kind of role, and secondly as that character. The whole point of that character was that he was a unique, shy, mild character. They tried to compensate by making him a construction worker, but they gave him this beautiful Sharon Stone wife." This, of course, was a deliberate move on the part of director Paul Verhoeven (who would soon make Stone a star in *Basic Instinct*), who understood that Quaid's low-grade employment was as far as possible from secret agent, while his beautiful wife was designed to keep him satisfied with his otherwise average lifestyle. As Verhoeven explains,

"With Arnold Schwarzenegger in the main part, [an audience] would not want him to dream. So to a large degree by choosing Arnold, there was a preference in reality." Nevertheless, Cronenberg had other reservations: "I thought it was very visually tacky and messy," he said. "Verhoeven didn't do a good job with all the effects and the mutants and all of that stuff... They went for the action stuff purely and that was it: it was an action gimmick. So I didn't really like the movie and I didn't think much of it. But by the time I saw it, I didn't care. I was over it."

Although Cronenberg was the first director involved with *Total Recall*, his would certainly not be the last name to be stencilled on the director's chair before Paul Verhoeven's was allowed to dry. "As I recall it was seven directors," says Shusett, "most prominently Richard Rush, who'd [directed *The*] *Stunt Man*. He and Dino couldn't agree, because [Richard] liked our third act of *Total Recall* — Mars gets air — and Dino didn't. Richard Rush said, 'It's wonderful, Dino, it'll work perfectly.' And Dino said, 'Rick, I can't go with you as director. I don't even want to go to Mars.' And *I* said, 'Well, you can't take that out, it's in my contract.' Dino said, 'It'll never get made,' and I said, 'Fine, I'd rather never make it.' I said, 'Mars is in it, and Mars gets air, it's the first ending that's worked, Dino. Show it to another director.' So one day I get a call from Dino, he says, 'Ron, I love you so much I could kiss you on the mouth! You saved me! You're so goddamned stubborn, you saved me! I showed this script to Bruce Beresford... [and] I say, 'Take out Mars, take out air.' He says, 'Dino, you full of shit!'"

Beresford soon found himself in Australia in pre-production, with the then-hot *Dirty Dancing* star Patrick Swayze in the lead of what Shusett has described as a less gritty, more fun, 'Spielbergian' version. The next thing Shusett knew, however, "Beresford called us and said, 'The movie's off — Dino's gone bankrupt. He's fired eighty people and they're tearing down the sets as I look out the window.'"

It was at this point, around 1987, that Shusett's co-screenwriter Gary Goldman first encountered the project. "I was asked to do a polish," says Goldman. "I read the script, liked it, but turned down the job because I had just started working with Paul Verhoeven on my own project, an out-of-body action movie that I co-wrote and was producing, entitled *Warrior*. This was set up at Warner Brothers, and I wanted to work with Paul, whose work I had long admired, and who had just come off *RoboCop*, which I loved." Although the pair worked together for several months, they were unable to reach a point where Verhoeven was ready to direct *Warrior*. In the meantime, Arnold Schwarzenegger — who had been circling *Total Recall* for several years — learned that his *Conan* collaborator Dino De Laurentiis was in financial difficulties in Australia, and that the production had all but collapsed. Schwarzenegger called De Laurentiis and asked if his company would sell the rights to Dick's story. When De Laurentiis agreed, Schwarzenegger called Carolco co-owners Andrew G. Vajna and Mario Kassar, for whom the actor had made *Red Heat*, and suggested that they buy it. Says Schwarzenegger, "Within a few hours, they owned the movie," paying a record $3 million for the rights, including pre-production costs. Next, Schwarzenegger claims to have cornered Dutch director Paul Verhoeven — hotter than hell following the success of *RoboCop* — at lunch, and insisted that Verhoeven take a look at *Total Recall*.

Incredibly, Verhoeven was the director Ron Shusett had originally wanted when he was trying to set the film up at Disney: "In 1981, eight years before I got the movie financed, I wanted Paul to direct it," he reveals. "I'd just seen *Soldier of Orange*, and I said, 'That's the guy I want.'" At the time, Verhoeven was living in Holland, not Hollywood, but Disney dutifully sent him the script. "His agent said she gave it to him but that he doesn't like science fiction. Then about seven years later he fell in love with science fiction and made *RoboCop*." When Verhoeven did eventually read the script, adds Shusett, "he didn't even have to finish reading it before he had committed to it. He said he'd got as far as the scene in the hotel where Edgemar says, 'You're not really here, you're asleep in the chair at Rekall,' closed the script, called his agent, called Schwarzenegger, and said, 'I'm in!'" Adds Goldman, "I told Paul the ironic story that I had turned down the chance to re-write *Total Recall* in order to work with him. He asked my opinion of the screenplay. I told him. He said that we saw it the same way, and that he would try to get me the job to rewrite it. And he did."

By this time, there had been dozens of drafts — Verhoeven remembers "about thirty" — variously credited to Shusett and O'Bannon, Shusett and Jon Povill (*Star Trek: The Motion Picture*), and Shusett and Steven Pressfield (*Freejack*). "Paul read all the drafts," says Goldman, "and then he gave me the ones he wanted me to read. The story of the first half was almost exactly as it is in the movie, but there was general agreement that the second half of the movie wasn't working — that is, everything after the Dr Edgemar scene. I had to adjust everything in order to make the second half work adequately. I also had to reconfigure the movie to fit Arnold, [because] in the short story and in all previous drafts, Quaid (named Quail) was a mild-mannered guy who suddenly discovered that he was a high-powered secret agent."

According to Goldman, several fundamental decisions determined most of the changes. Firstly, Verhoeven wanted to make the movie as if Dr Edgemar might be telling the truth in the hotel room; that from the point that Quaid undergoes the procedure at Rekall, everything you see is Quaid's fantasy. "Everything we have seen before, in the last forty-five minutes, is all fantasy," Verhoeven explains. "It's a dream. Which is disturbing to the audience because they don't want that, of course. They want an adventure story, they don't want a fake adventure story. So they are on Arnold's side trying to believe that it's all true, while [Dr Edgemar] is trying to tell him that it's not true." As Edgemar asks rhetorically, "What's bullshit? That you're having a paranoid episode triggered by acute neurochemical trauma? Or that you're really an invincible secret agent from Mars who's the victim of an interplanetary conspiracy to make him think he's a lowly construction worker?" Quaid, of course, shoots Edgemar, thereby choosing to continue the fantasy — if, indeed, it *is* a fantasy.

Thus, Goldman had to reconfigure the story so that it could work both ways: as if it were really happening; and as if it were Quaid's Rekall trip gone wrong. "That's the great thing about the movie," says Schwarzenegger, "that from the beginning it always works on two levels and the audience has to guess what is reality and what is not." Says Verhoeven, "As much as possible we kept these two realities alive, so that everything could be explained one way or another. And of course with Arnold being a superhero, people would always hope and think that it's real, but there's strong doubts about that if you look at the movie for a second time." To illustrate this, Verhoeven points to the scene where the Rekall salesman Bob McClane tells Quaid the nature of his chosen vacation: "You are a top operative under deep cover on your most important mission," he tells his eager customer. "People are trying to kill you, left and right. You meet this beautiful, exotic woman... by the time the trip is over you get the girl, kill the bad guys and save the entire planet." In other words, says Verhoeven, "McClane tells him everything that's going to happen in the movie! It's counter to every normal narrative — you would not tell anyone where it's going. [But here] you get the whole story completely formulated for you. In the next scene," he adds, "we are given several clues, [such as] the woman that he wants to be implanted in his dream — because he can make a choice; he can choose the woman — of course the woman he describes is the woman he has a kind of fantasy image of that he dreams about, which is this girl, Melina. He describes her as well as he can, and he gets her!"

Having solved this problem with dazzling narrative acrobatics of which Philip K. Dick and David Cronenberg might have been proud, Goldman tackled another problem. "At the point that Quaid gets his memory back, I thought there was nothing interesting left in the movie — suddenly it just became this ordinary action picture. I wanted the whole movie to be as interesting as the beginning. So I invented the idea that Quaid wants to get back to being his authentic self, but he finds out that his authentic self [Hauser — the agent working for Cohaagen] is evil." In other words, Quaid is not merely Hauser without some key memories, but a separate individual. "At the end of the movie, you find out that Hauser's in on it," says Shusett, "that he helped erase his own brain so that Quaid would not recognise his intent to assassinate [the rebel leader] Kuato. And then Hauser says, 'Well, I hate to ask you but it's my body — I was there first, and I want it back. Maybe we'll see each other in our dreams.'" Says Goldman, "This was a very fresh idea at the time. To my knowledge, it was without precedent." In the new version, Quaid must decide if he wants to be technically authentic, but evil, or be true to his artificial self, and good. "He has to make a very interesting moral choice, and this takes him straight into Phil Dick territory," Goldman explains. "Quaid is an artificial human, like the replicants in *Blade Runner*, except that it's not his body that is artificial, but only his mental programming. The artificial person, Quaid, is more human than the authentic human, Hauser.

"It's also psychologically accurate, I think, to say that no one (except in a Hollywood movie) would give up his/her identity, just to become authentic. Identity is life itself. It's an interesting idea to be offered a choice to have a better life, but not to be oneself." The hard part, says Goldman, was making this work — even Verhoeven was not convinced it could work, until Goldman came up with the idea for the second video message from Hauser, which he receives after Quaid is captured by Cohaagen in Kuato's lair. "That part of the narrative, that little twist, was something that Gary Goldman added to the story, because that was never there before," Verhoeven agrees. "Now Quaid will be forced to become the person he doesn't want to be, because he has to make a moral choice. The last thing that he wants is to go back to being Hauser."

"Paul Verhoeven had great instincts, great ideas, and intellectual courage," says Goldman. "I am sure that all of my good ideas would have been rejected by any studio and almost any other director. In Hollywood, ideas are anathema, and the bigger the budget, the more forbidden they are. The authorities are not very educated, but they can smell an idea at a hundred paces — and, like a giant in a fairy tale, they will sniff out the idea and rip it out. Only a powerful director can protect an idea. And Carolco was the perfect place to work, because Mario and Andy gave their directors almost complete freedom."

Goldman says that he and Verhoeven were "generally interested in having as much fun with 'mindfucks' as we could. This included introducing as many big surprises as possible. For example, the idea that the whole plot was about using Quaid to lead them to Kuato, because Kuato was psychic and would detect any traitor. Plus we knew that, at that time in Hollywood, for reasons of political correctness, African-American characters had been typecast as good guys. So I decided to make Benny the bad guy, as it would catch audiences by surprise. Paul wasn't afraid of being politically incorrect — in fact, you could say that his whole career is based on being politically incorrect. He does it with a vengeance. I would say that I have the same bent, but don't take the same relish in it. But we're both interested in seeing things clearly, and seeing through popular clichés and delusions and hypocrisies. It was this same disposition that made us really embrace Phil Dick's challenge to consensual reality, and to push it as far as we did. And to leave the movie on a note of doubt, but with a sense of humour."

Ironically, Goldman was not a fan of Dick's work at the time, having had very little exposure to it. Nevertheless, he says, "I am generally faithful to all the writers who come before me, from source material to earlier screenwriters. I try not to get involved in rewriting projects unless I like what's already there. And then my *modus operandi* is to bring out the existing values, and try to complete and perfect them. So, I was being faithful to the ideas in the first half of the screenplay, which were the same as the ideas in the first half of the short story. Phil himself tended to combine and garble his many ideas, and he rarely worked out any idea in a complete and consistent way. He just kept flitting about to the next idea." Shusett agrees: "His work is very tough to translate into a screenplay because it has such brilliant set-ups that it's hard to match his level of brilliance in the pay off. That's why most of his best work is short stories, and even those stories don't have a third act."

Goldman admits that the second half of the movie, beginning as Quaid arrives on Mars, was largely a concession to Hollywood plotting, and therefore retained most of the structure of the version Bruce Beresford had planned to shoot. "I didn't think I had the liberty to make big changes because I was under the impression that Arnold, the studio and Paul were all ready to make that story. So I mainly concentrated on fixing and improving what was there. I would have preferred a more consistently realistic view of the future and more believable science, in regard to gravity, physics, and atmosphere. But we were making an Arnold Schwarzenegger movie, and that guided the tone and many of the decisions. Even so, we tried to make the movie a bit less jokey and more rigorous than Arnold's previous movies."

Having completed his first rewrite, Goldman and Verhoeven met with Schwarzenegger, Shusett, Vajna and Kassar. "Arnold and Ron had discussed our draft, and they felt that our climax lacked emotion," Goldman remembers. "This was a valid observation because Paul prefers a dry emotional tone, and he really didn't take very seriously the subplot about Martian liberation. He saw the movie as an intellectual puzzle. But faced with opposition from the star, I saw the need for a compromise, and fortunately an idea came to me in the meeting, and I proposed the idea about Cohaagen shutting off the air. This gave us a nice cruel action to justify the suffering of the poor mutants. I made these changes, and we went into production." Adds Shusett, "All of a sudden all the pieces came together, and instead of going to Australia we went to Mexico."

Unusually, Verhoeven invited Goldman to Mexico for the entire shoot. (Shusett was also present throughout the shoot, but his was a right automatically afforded him by his additional status as a co-producer.) "I think we were a very writer-friendly group," says Verhoeven, "because they were part of everything. They could see the dailies and have as much input as they wanted." Adds Goldman, "It was a rare privilege for a Hollywood screenwriter, who is usually unwelcome on the set. If a screenwriter is present, it is usually an emergency script doctor who is brought in to 'fix' a problem. [But] Paul has great respect for screenplays and screenwriters. He works tirelessly on his screenplays, and then he shoots them word for word. He almost never improvises, and he prevents the actors from deviating from the text. If something wasn't working on the set, he would call for me and ask me to write something new. Ron Shusett and I liked and respected each other, and we worked together on the rewrites while we were down there. We spent a lot of time making small revisions, but ultimately I would say that we changed less than one per cent."

Both writers admit that there are a few things they dislike about the finished film. "Too much foul language," says Goldman; "too much noisy shooting, too much violence and death, [it's] a bit too long, and you don't really care about the mutants. And the bulging eyes at the end went on too long," he adds, referring to Quaid and Melina gasping for air in the Martian atmosphere. "I think that hurt us a lot because it was like a runner stumbling at the finish line. A lot of these things could have been fixed if we had had one test screening, but — alas — we didn't. There was no time." Shusett agrees: "Paul and Gary and I always regretted not having time for a preview, because you can't get any perspective on what you're doing. We were worried about *Dick Tracy* because it had all those stars — Warren Beatty, Al Pacino, Dustin Hoffman. We didn't want to open the same week, so we paid editors 'golden time' so we could go out a week earlier than *Dick Tracy*, but that robbed us of any preview. If we had just had a week to calm down, look at what we'd just cut — there was too much machine-gun fire, mostly, and those faces bulging... I wouldn't have shot anything differently, I just would have re-edited the third act a little tighter, and then

I think it would have hit the jackpot instead of it being seventy-five or eighty per cent the movie I was hoping it would be. Having said that, we were lucky to get that close."

"I think that we captured Phil's serio-comic tone better than anyone else has." Goldman says. "That's really what sets his work apart, in my opinion — his irreverent, alienated, kitchen sink, neurotic view of the future. Also, Paul Verhoeven is a truly brilliant man with a Doctorate in mathematics from the University of Leiden. Although his movies can be crass, Paul is a truly independent and deep thinker. It's important not to confuse style with substance. Paul likes to be crass and offensive, on top of being incisive and precise. Paul, like Phil defined himself, is a 'crap artist', making great art from shit. It's a mistake to think that a good Phil Dick movie is necessarily dark, moody and elegant, like *Blade Runner*." Above all, Goldman doubts that anyone but Verhoeven would have had the courage to make a movie which questions the supposed reality the audience has just experienced. "He made that decision, and I executed it," he says. "I doubt that anyone but myself would have thought up the idea that Quaid doesn't recover his memory and become authentic again; [that] he is not the same as Hauser — Hauser is bad — and Quaid must choose his artificial identity over his real one. I think these are powerful extensions of Phil's set-up and themes." Overall, he adds, "I loved working with Paul, Ron, Mario and Andy, Arnold, and Sharon Stone. It was a perfect experience from beginning to end, and I don't expect to be so lucky again." Certainly, Goldman would not be so fortunate with his subsequent association with *Total Recall 2*.

Today, the box office performance of *Total Recall* — a $25.5 million opening weekend, and overall global earnings of ten times that figure — would virtually guarantee a sequel. In 1990, however, Hollywood was a very different place, as Goldman explains: "There has been a big change in the thinking about sequels since *Total Recall* came out. When we finished *Total Recall*, none of the major players wanted to make a sequel. They all felt that the franchise wasn't well suited to a sequel. They also held the previously accepted idea that sequels were commercial debasements that serious artists did not indulge in." But the artistic and commercial success of James Cameron's *Aliens* had been an exception, and later his *Terminator 2: Judgment Day* would further change this way of thinking. At the time, however, Shusett's and Goldman's interest in a sequel to *Total Recall* fell on deaf ears.

Then Goldman optioned another Philip K. Dick story, 'Minority Report', with a view to directing it himself as a low-budget feature, and approached Verhoeven to ask if he would attach himself as executive producer — thus throwing the weight of his name behind the project, even if he was not directly involved. "He read the short story, liked it, and agreed to help me out. Then he asked me if I had thought about how well the story worked as a *Total Recall* sequel. Although it had nothing to do with the themes of the movie, there was something about the tone and driving narrative that made it seem perfect for a sequel." Better still, it did not repeat anything from the original film, allowing Goldman to take the franchise in a totally new direction, but one which would be thematically consistent with the original. "This is what appealed to Paul," he says. "The possibility of doing a sequel that seemed original, not repetitive or derivative."

In Dick's story — eventually filmed in 2002 by Steven Spielberg, with Tom Cruise, Colin Farrell and Samantha Morton — certain human beings are born with telepathic powers, shunned by ordinary citizens but embraced by the government as the foundation for a new anti-crime organisation called the Pre-Crime division, which uses the telepaths (known as 'pre-cogs') to predict illegal activities before they occur, and arrest the would-be criminals before any crime is committed. The plot revolves around a particular Pre-Crime detective forced to go on the run when the pre-cogs spit out his name as a future murderer. (In this respect, the story shares many elements with Alfred Bester's *The Demolished Man*, another long-term resident of Development Hell.) As Verhoeven explains, "There was an introduction [in *Total Recall*] that the mutants were perhaps clairvoyant — that they can see certain things — and that was used in the idea for the second one where [Quaid] becomes the head of this company that can look into the future and protect citizens by eliminating criminals before they do the crime." Thus, the mutants would become the 'pre-cogs' of Dick's story, the film rights to which Goldman now owned.

"I had to make a tough decision between continuing with my plan to direct a small movie from 'Minority Report', or to become the writer-producer of a *Total Recall* sequel based on 'Minority Report'," Goldman says. "At the time, I was still working closely with Paul and Carolco. We had worked together on *Basic Instinct*, which had turned out to be the biggest movie of the year worldwide, and I had done a rewrite on *Crusade* which had gotten the project out of Development Hell and into pre-production [see chapter 6]. It seemed like the *Total Recall* sequel was a sure thing to speed into production, and become another big hit. So I decided that it was too good an opportunity to pass up." Thus, 'Minority Report' became the basis for *Total Recall 2*. At this point, Goldman and Verhoeven discovered that Ron Shusett had a contractual right to write the first draft of any *Total Recall* sequel, and that they would therefore need his permission to proceed. Luckily, Shusett and Goldman remained friends from their time in Mexico, when they had co-written revisions on the set. Goldman proposed that they write the sequel together, on the proviso that Goldman would then be attached to co-write all future *Total Recall* sequels. Says Shusett, "We worked on it together and immediately clicked, and it became a wonderful sequel. Arnold was going to star in it, and Paul Verhoeven was going to direct it. Then right after we wrote it, Carolco went bankrupt." Indeed, Carolco's financial situation was so serious it reneged on its contractual payments to Shusett and Goldman. As a result, ownership of the underlying rights — both the short story and the first draft — reverted to the writers, allowing them to move it to 20th Century Fox.

By this time, Verhoeven was busy shooting *Showgirls*, and Goldman says he lost interest in the sequel. Not so, says Verhoeven: "Somebody whose name I won't name, without warning, took it away — somebody who had me on their pay list, like a Judas. So in some subversive ways, I think, it left Carolco [and] it came into the hands of Jan De Bont." At this stage, Verhoeven's fellow Dutchman was a celebrated cinematographer, yet to direct the runaway hit *Speed*. Says Goldman, "Jan and the studio discussed acquiring the *Total Recall* franchise from Carolco, and continuing to develop 'Minority Report' as a *Total Recall* sequel. Ultimately, they decided not to continue as a sequel, so we removed all the *Total Recall* elements and used the first draft as the foundation for further work." From that point on, 'Minority Report' was developed as a free-standing movie, based only on the Dick short story. As Quaid might have put it, "Consider that a divorce." Says Shusett, "We were really devastated, because we had proved tangibly to everybody, including Paul and Arnold, that it would make a great sequel. But my spirits rose when Fox bought it as a non-sequel, a free-standing movie."

Even after its estrangement from *Total Recall 2* and development as a separate entity, *Minority Report* suffered a further five years in Development Hell, with Jan De Bont eventually jumping ship, as Shusett recalls: "He was very hot from *Speed* and he'd followed up with *Twister*, but then *Speed 2* and *The Haunting* bombed out, and gradually Fox lost faith in him. We wrote a new draft for him in '95, but they couldn't find an actor that liked his draft that Fox was in favour of too. It was years later — '98 or '99 — that Spielberg came in and read a draft he didn't like. But when we personally got our draft to him, and persuaded him to read it, he did like it. And then he used an amalgamation of some of their draft and some of our draft and his own ideas, and because he's Steven Spielberg, his version was better in many ways, and he made the best film of all." Shusett — who, like Goldman, earned an executive producer credit on Spielberg's film (Jan De Bont gets an associate producer credit) — admits to being surprised that the director's take on the material was so dark, "even darker than our last draft. It was so dark that I think summer audiences weren't ready for it. We should have released it in the winter, and then I think they might have expected it, and been able to handle it. It was too dark a movie for people expecting summer fun with a *Total Recall*/Phil Dick name on it, and our names connected to it — they thought it would be like *Total Recall*. And instead it was more like *Blade Runner* and they weren't ready for that." Indeed, although *Minority Report* grossed an impressive $350 million worldwide, it fell far short of expectations generated by the first teaming of Steven Spielberg and Tom Cruise, especially on a sci-fi project. "It got wonderful reviews, and everybody thought it would do $500 or $600 million [worldwide]," Shusett points out, "but it only made $350 million — and only $130 million in America, when there are movies making $200, $300 million [domestically]."

In the meantime, Carolco had sold the *Total Recall* TV rights to DFL Entertainment for $1.2 million, resulting in the short-lived Showtime series *Total Recall 2070*. The sale led Shusett and Goldman to believe that the possibility of a *Total Recall* sequel was dead forever, since studios rarely buy into a script or film, much less a franchise, unless all rights are available in all media. Nevertheless, at a subsequent bankruptcy hearing for now-defunct Carolco on 14 January 1997, Dimension Films, the recently-formed genre division of Disney subsidiary Miramax Films, paid $3.15 million for the theatrical sequel, prequel and remake rights to *Total Recall*. "I heard later that they were surprised that the TV rights had already been sold off," says Goldman. "They thought that was part of the package of rights that they acquired." (Indeed, pressure from Dimension may have been behind DFL's decision to ditch its original concept for the TV series — a direct continuation of the movie, featuring Quaid on Mars — for an Earth-based format using new characters, which ironically owed more to *Blade Runner* than *Total Recall*.) In what Carolco bankruptcy counsel Howard Weg described as "lively bidding", Dimension had outbid DFL Entertainment, 20th Century Fox (which retired from the bidding when it reached $500,000) and Live Entertainment, whose final bid of $3.14 million was narrowly exceeded by Dimension, which had recently produced its first *bona fide* hit, *Scream*. "This is the perfect franchise opportunity for Dimension," said co-founder Bob Weinstein, "[and] franchises are what Dimension is all about." (He wasn't kidding: since 1997, Dimension has made two sequels to *Scream*, three *Scary Movie*s and resurrected the long-dead *Halloween* franchise.)

Weinstein went on to say that he intended to contact the film's original cast, but not its director Paul Verhoeven, whose most recent film was the costly flop *Showgirls*. "We're going to our Miramax stable of directors," Weinstein stated. "We have discussed story ideas, we have a concept, and we're going forward with this film within the next year." Weinstein dismissed suggestions that a sequel to the $80 million *Total Recall* would be expensive by definition, noting that significant profit participation on *Scream* made the $14 million-budget hit possible, and that the same financial structure — forgoing an upfront fee in return for a share of the back end profits — would make *Total Recall 2* viable. Nevertheless, purchasing the rights, particularly for such a colossal sum, was a curious move for Dimension, since under the terms of a deal with corporate parent Walt Disney Co, the average budget of its films must be $12.5 million. Thus, if one film's budget exceeds this sum, another must fall under it by the same amount. As a result, they hoped to generate a screenplay as cheaply as possible, and were delighted when a writer already under contract to Miramax offered his services.

Shortly after graduating from New Hampshire's Dartmouth College, Matthew Cirulnick had signed with United Talent Agency on the basis of a script he had written, and which was subsequently read by executives at Dimension Films. Cirulnick had just turned twenty-two when he signed a three-picture deal with Miramax, the first of which was the urban drug drama *Paid in Full*, eventually released in October 2002. "Immediately after turning in that script, Miramax informed my agents that they wanted to activate the second picture in my deal," says Cirulnick. "My agent gave me an open writing assignment list, and — lo and behold — on the list I see *Total Recall 2*. So I flip out. I remember to this day the font, I remember the way it looked, because when I saw those words I was like, 'I'm getting this job.' I was born in '76, so I was watching *Total Recall* on tape when it came out and it was one of my favourite films. But my agents laughed at me and said, 'Young buck, you're just starting out, they've had some big guys on this job,' blah blah blah, and that fired me up, because I thought, 'I can't control how old I am or my credits, all I can control is the quality of the words on the page. I can't control whether or not a movie gets made.' So I said, 'Look, I'll put my writing up against whoever's writing, and let's see what happens. I gotta take a shot.'"

At the time, Dimension was set to close a deal with Bob Gale, who co-wrote the *Back to the Future* films with Robert Zemeckis. "I can't say for certain what the reasons were for my agents not going after the job aggressively," says Cirulnick, "but the bottom line is that what I was getting for the entire script for the second picture of my deal would have been the commission my agents would get on Bob Gale!" When Dimension failed to make a deal with Gale, Cirulnick did not wait to be asked. "Luckily for me, one of the executives on *Paid in Full*, Jesse Berdinka, was also one of the executives on *Total Recall 2*, so I had my agent hit Dimension, and I hit Dimension personally, and I locked myself in a room and came up with an idea for *Total Recall 2*. I pitched the junior executive, then I pitched the president [Cary Granat], then I met with Bob Weinstein, Andrew Rona, Cary Granat and Jesse Berdinka, and gave them my pitch — and Bob was like, 'Okay, you got it. Go.'"

There was just one problem: unbeknownst to Dimension, Ron Shusett's contract for *Total Recall* meant that they were obliged to hire him to write the first draft of any sequel. Shusett, in turn, was obliged to bring Goldman aboard, due to the agreement the pair had made. Having learned of their obligations, Dimension could simply have asked Shusett and Goldman to turn Cirulnick's concept into a script; instead, they invited the pair to pitch their own ideas. "They didn't even give us Matt's idea," says Shusett. "They said, 'We have some ideas, but what idea do you have?' So we told them our take." Dimension had an idea aside from Matt's which, by coincidence, was uncannily similar to the one Shusett and Goldman pitched. "We had, almost eerily, the same approach to doing the sequel — a different one than Matt had in mind. So they said, 'Okay, we'll pay you to do it,' and they did. They were very good to their word," he adds. "They didn't low-ball us." Announcing the deal in May 1998, *Variety* further noted that Arnold Schwarzenegger had attended a four-hour development meeting with Weinstein and Granat, and was said to be "actively involved" in the development of the film.

"We stuck fairly closely to their set-up that launches the story, but from there we were free to go where we wanted," Goldman explains. "They knew what they liked in the original movie: they wanted to keep it as a popcorn movie with lots of cool stuff, but they also liked the 'is it real or is it Memorex?' theme — the 'mindfucks'." Dimension's hope, he says, was to keep the ambiguity alive as long as possible by alternating between the theories. "It was a high wire act," he explains, "where we would confirm that it was real on Mars, then use a narrative device to make it seem like he was on Earth or still in the Rekall chair, and then use an even more clever device to put him back on Mars. Even though this was our favourite theme too, Ron and I actually had to restrain them from overdoing it. They were real students of the movie, and we were flattered, but they didn't quite understand the simplicity and subtlety of how we achieved our effects in the first movie. We took direction from them, but resisted decisions that we felt were mistakes. Eventually, they came to trust us when we said you can easily overdo the complications — and we arrived at a workable balance."

The Shusett-Goldman draft opens amid celebrations for Mars' independence, with Quaid and Melina honoured by President Gloria Palomares for their part in the struggle. Just as Quaid is about to give a speech, however, a double stabs him and takes his place... He wakes to find himself next to Melina. Only three weeks have passed since the events of *Total Recall*, and he is still among the Martian rebels — independence for Mars is still a dream. They tell him of 'Project Whisper', a form of mind control being planned by President Saarinen's government, and suggest delving into his mind to see if Hauser knows anything about it. Reluctantly agreeing to submit to the operation, he falls unconscious... only to wake up at Rekall Incorporated, his wife Lori and Bob, the Rekall salesman, at his bedside, and Dr Edgemar very much alive. They convince him that he has not left Rekall since he began his vacation, yet events on Mars appear to have transpired largely as they occurred in Quaid's Rekall trip — Mars has air, Cohaagen is dead — a suspicious development which Dr Edgemar attributes to real-world news programmes filtering into Quaid's virtual adventure. "So, Mr Quaid," Edgemar tells him, "like all vacations, this one too comes to an end. And as usual, we feel a little sad returning to the daily grind." Quaid returns home with Lori, only to be told that during the six months he was comatose at Rekall, she began a new relationship with her personal trainer. ("Harvey Weinstein had a [professional] relationship with Sharon Stone, and they wanted to try to get her back into the franchise," Goldman explains.) Dejected and financially dependent on Rekall, Quaid finds a job on the construction site of a Seattle-based 'space elevator' — one of Arthur C. Clarke's proposed constructs tethering an orbital space station to the Earth, allowing payloads to be transported cheaply to and from space.

Meanwhile, an imminent presidential election draws Quaid's attention to an electoral campaign by Gloria Palomares, the President from his dream, denounced by her opponents as a "mutant lover" for promising to hold a referendum on Mars' independence if she is elected. Torn between his feelings for Melina (whom he now believes to be a construct of Rekall) and Renee, one of Mrs Palomares' campaign volunteers, Quaid becomes involved with her political campaign, but is betrayed and framed for an explosion which wrecks the space elevator. Imprisoned for six months in a space prison known as the Pasternak Institute for the Criminally Insane, he manages to escape, and rejoins what remains of the rebels, who tell him of Melina's death. Posing as Hauser, Quaid heads to Vladivostock, where he is shocked to meet up with his own mother, whom he thought long dead. Mrs Hauser, evidently a Saarinen sympathiser, sees through Quaid's deception, but although she threatens him, she knows that if she kills Quaid, her beloved Hauser will die too. Through his mother, Quaid discovers that Project Whisper is a planet-wide programme designed to keep the electorate voting a certain way, thus keeping the next government — Saarinen's — in power forever. After a gunfight with a dozen Lori clones and his own mother, Quaid succeeds in destroying Project Whisper, an act which creates a vacuum (allowing a popular scene from *Total Recall* to be reprised) and ultimately leads to the election of Mrs Palomares and independence for Mars. He is about to make a speech when he sees Dr Edgemar sitting in a front seat — but the next instant, he is gone. Did his eyes deceive him? Or is he still back at Rekall, dreaming of Martian independence?

"[Dimension] liked the screenplay," Goldman says. "We did one fairly minor polish, [then] Dimension was ready to make the movie. They told Arnold that they were ready to make the movie. They let him know that they would pay him his price. Ron, Arnold, and I were all at William Morris Agency. Five or six agents there read our script and loved it. I would say that there was a consensus that this should be Arnold's next movie." Schwarzenegger, however, didn't agree. "He said [the script was] too complicated. In general, Arnold never seemed to appreciate the complications in the original, or to grasp that the essence of the franchise was the complicated mindfucks." Adds Shusett, "He had seen the outline, and gave [Dimension] the okay to pay us, but sometimes when you see things in script form, some things feel different than on a ten-page outline. He said, 'No, I don't like this, I don't want to do it.' Bob [Weinstein] said, 'He just turned down the best script that's ever been offered to him,' which coming from Bob, who can be very tough, is a real compliment. He said, 'I always considered the first *Total Recall* [to be] one of the five best science fiction movies ever, and now you've topped it with this one, he won't do it.' Dimension was very disappointed, and we were too. At that point," he concludes, "it just went into limbo."

In the meantime, rumours had been circulating that *Star Trek: The Next Generation* actor Jonathan Frakes — who had directed the $150 million-grossing hit *Star Trek: First Contact* and had already been hired to helm the next instalment of that franchise — had been in talks about directing *Total Recall 2*. In March 1998, Frakes confirmed that, of the various projects being developed by his Geopp Circle production company, *Total Recall 2* was the closest to realisation. "I'm very jazzed about that," he told Ian Spelling. "If it all works out and Mr Schwarzenegger is available, we'll get going with pre-production of it at the end of [*Star Trek: Insurrection*]. They wouldn't have gone this far if Schwarzenegger weren't interested," he added. "Miramax bought it because he wants to play the character again. Wouldn't it be cool if it all happens?" Speaking to the *Calgary Sun* later in the year, Frakes added: "Arnold is serious because I've already received a draft of a screenplay." Frakes expressed concern that the budget of the script might prove too rich for Miramax's blood. Nevertheless, he added, "Apparently, Sharon Stone wants to return as well — and it's possible because there is a lot of time travel in this draft of *Total Recall 2*."

Goldman, however, recalls a different version of the story. "Jonathan Frakes was involved in the early stages," he says. "Dimension had been in talks with him before we got involved. We had one meeting with Frakes, but we never heard any more about him. The reason was that Bob Weinstein started working with Arnold, and Arnold's vision of the picture was different than Bob's. To get Arnold, it was clear that the sequel couldn't be medium budget, as envisioned by Bob... and that Arnold would not consent to work with anyone but an A-list director or rising star. So Frakes was tabled." In August 1999, Frakes was quoted as saying that *Total Recall 2* was still on Dimension's list of movies, and that they were "waiting for Mr Schwarzenegger's hands to free up. We've got a script from the writer of the original, and we're giving some notes on it," he added. "It's a very big, wonderful, expensive script. I'm waiting for Miramax to get up on the dime and actually go ahead." By February 2000, however, Frakes confirmed to *Starburst* that the project was dead — at least for the time being — blaming Schwarzenegger's over-loaded schedule. "*Total Recall* is an old movie now and it looks like one," he added. "I shouldn't say this, obviously, because I'd love to do that film, but they blew smoke up my ass four years ago, and nothing's happened since. I'm not holding my breath."

"Instead, Arnold made this movie *The 6th Day*, which was in essence a *Total Recall* sequel in everything but name," says Goldman. In *The 6th Day*, directed by Roger Spottiswoode (*Tomorrow Never Dies*) and released in November 2000, Schwarzenegger plays a commercial pilot who discovers that he has been cloned, a story which might be summarised by paraphrasing *Total Recall*'s tag-line: 'They stole his life, now he wants it back.' "The 'A' plot line of one of our [sequel ideas] was good and bad Arnold — Quaid versus Hauser," says Shusett, "so that was passé because he'd done a movie [*The 6th Day*] where there were two Arnolds. So we came up with a new [concept]; they came up with part of the idea, we came up with the rest of it, and they gave it to Arnold and he *still* said, 'No, I don't want to do it.'" At this point, the exasperated Dimension went back to Matt Cirulnick, giving him a copy of the Shusett-Goldman draft — which he dismisses as "an assault on the English language" — and one piece of guidance from Andrew Rona. "He said, 'What we'd really like is for the story to end on the same note of ambiguity that the first one did.'" Cirulnick remembers. "And that's why I really fell in love with getting this assignment, because how do you sequel-ise something that ended on an ambiguous note without ever resolving what that was? So that was the challenge... I was going to answer it and then not, answer it and then not, and basically leave you at the same point. What was also great was that this was my own original story — I didn't use anything from the previous scripts, except the cloned Sharon Stones."

The resulting thirteen-page treatment was greeted with enthusiasm by Rona and Berdincker. "We went down to the Tribeca Grill and just cut up the outline. They're two great executives," Cirulnick adds, "and their notes were specific. They gave me strong direction, helped me make the cuts that needed to be made, and I got commenced." Cirulnick's first draft, dated 20 April 2000, follows the treatment in most respects — although Quaid's discovery of a Martian colony living deep beneath the surface was omitted. Cirulnick's ninety-six-page 'revised first draft', dated 8 May 2000, opens with a spectacular action sequence, as Hauser and fellow 'ReKall Unit' agents York Brogan (described to put the reader in mind of Ving Rhames), Chris Park ("think Jet Li") and Quaid's paramour Maggie Thomas (a Parker Posey type) foil the hijacking by terrorists of a Saturn-bound cruise ship, which culminates with the terrorists' turbinium bomb being diverted into the sun. As the successful mission ends, Hauser/Quaid wakes to find himself at ReKall, where doctors Bob, Edgemar and Jaslove explain that he suffered a schizoid embolism during his original ReKall trip, and has been effectively comatose for ten years. Here Cirulnick borrows a few elements from the earlier Goldman-Shusett draft: the explanations for Quaid's assimilation of real-world developments into his dream (the news was on) and his lack of muscle atrophy ("newest thing, Doug — magneti-pulse muscle stimulation"), Lori's break-up and affair with her personal trainer (although Cirulnick plays the brush-off as a taped vid-phone 'Dear John'), and Quaid's subsequent employment on the construction of a space elevator, which, this time, is described as a 'space bridge' and is tethered to Mars, which trillion-aire industrialist Hugo Strickrodt is preparing to open to the public.

Commencing work at the construction site, Quaid is surprised to meet York Brogan, now calling himself 'Jones Seni' and denying all knowledge of his association with Quaid or Hauser. Quaid is more cautious approaching 'Sue Richards' (shades of *Fantastic Four*), a nerdish neighbour who resembles Maggie. When Quaid's flashbacks cause an accident on the space bridge (itself a flashback to the Goldman-Shusett draft), Quaid injures his arm, peeling away a piece of false skin to reveal scars he suffered in his hijack-foiling fantasy. Now convinced that starting the reactor which gave Mars its atmosphere and foiling the Saturn cruise ship hijack are real memories, not implanted ones, Quaid is pursued by ReKall's Colonel Ladson — Hauser's commanding officer in his hijacking memories — who is anxious that Quaid may be about to achieve 'total recall' and discover the truth: that he, York Brogan, Chris Park and Maggie are part of a secret cadre of NorthBloc Intelligence operatives so elite even *they* do not know who they are or what they do — or have done — for the government. Employing ReKall technology, each operative has dual identities, both stored on digital disk: one disk contains their birth and upbringing through each of their missions logged and catalogued in detail — this is their real, or 'Alpha' life. The second disk contains their lives up to a point — their real childhood is used, but at some key juncture a new 'program' has been written, with a normal, run-of-the-mill 'Beta' life, the identity these elite agents possess when off-mission. Thus, the agents are only restored to their true selves (for Quaid, the Hauser persona) when they are on-mission; as soon as their missions are completed, they resume their Beta lives with no knowledge or memory of their agency activities.

"That way," Brogan tells him, "should we want to betray the agency, or should anyone get their hands on us, we'll be useless."

Quaid learns all this from a digital recording of York Brogan (echoes of the cement factory scene from *Total Recall*), who urges him to break Chris Park out of the Pasternak Institute for the Criminally Insane, where he has been held since his memory implant failed to take. (Quaid is also shown footage of his own mission history, among which Cirulnick slyly includes images from such Schwarzenegger films as *Predator*, *True Lies*, *The Terminator* and *Commando*.) Meanwhile, things on Earth are hotting up — literally — as the turbinium bomb appears to have swollen the sun until it swallows up Mercury and threatens to burn all life on Earth to a cinder. Global warming accelerates on a catastrophic scale, as giant holes appear in the sky, through which deadly heat rays scorch the Earth (a cinematic cataclysm subsequently explored in *The Core*). Meanwhile, Quaid helps Chris to escape, the pair head to Mars (disguised as a fat Samoan and his Japanese wife), where Brogan and Maggie appear to be in Strickrodt's employ, the latter also (much to Quaid's chagrin) in his bed. Maggie explains that she and Brogan are on a ReKall mission to infiltrate Strickrodt's inner circle. Through her, they learn that the hijacking was a set-up, and that Strickrodt used them to send the turbinium bomb into the sun, hoping that the devastation of life on Earth would lead its inhabitants to flock to Mars. Quaid and his team counter with a plan of their own: using explosive charges planted in its turbinium core, they intend to blow up Mars, hoping that the resulting "gravity gap" causes the Earth to shift into the vacuum previously occupied by Mars, thus saving the planet from the expanding sun.

Before they can implement their plan, however, Dr Jaslove shows up (à la Dr Edgemar's second act appearance in *Total Recall*) and tells him he's still at ReKall Incorporated, where he has been in a coma ever since the accident on the space bridge — the point at which he 'discovered' that his secret agent fantasies were true. His fellow agents, his mission to Mars and Earth's impending destruction by an expanding sun are all products of his imagination! Dr Jaslove shows him vidphone images of Earth, his own comatose body and Lori at his bedside, and tells him that if he does not snap out of his delusion, he will suffer a fatal embolism. Quaid refuses to believe, vowing to continue his mission, but as his 'fantasy' continues, Ladson floors him with a further revelation: that even his 'true' identity, Hauser, was merely the invention of a military supercomputer (provoking the potentially classic Schwarzenegger line, "Then if I'm not me, or Hauser... who the hell am I?"). Refusing to believe any of this, Quaid secures the planting of the turbinium charges and blows up Mars, the fragments of which circle Earth in a ring similar to that of Saturn while Earth assumes the position of the destroyed planet. No sooner has the explosion occurred, however, than Quaid wakes up at ReKall, where the news announcer is commenting on Mars' destruction, which has shifted Earth's orbit and saved it from the swelling sun. "Scientists say the Mars explosion was an unexplained phenomenon, and may be the result of the Sun's growth, which pressurized Mars' turbinium core," the anchorwoman announces. "Earth's a little worse for wear, but she'll live — and hopefully like her makeover!" Quaid — either denied the credit for saving the planet, or recovered from his schizoid embolism, depending on which version of events he and the audience chooses to believe — is reunited with Maggie/Sue at the spacebridge, where they kiss in front of the awe-inspiring view of Earth, complete with its ring of Martian debris — an exact reprise of the Melina/Quaid clinch at the end of *Total Recall*.

"I turned in the script," says Cirulnick. "They dug it, Jesse [Berdinka] dug it, my agents dug it. Everything was cool. I was all fired up. I kept calling and calling, 'Hey, what's happening?'" Eventually, Cirulnick heard that Schwarzenegger had read the draft, and that a meeting had been arranged between Bob Weinstein, Andrew Rona and the star. "My understanding is that meeting took place," says Cirulnick. "I never found out specifically what happened — all I know is after that I got a call from Miramax who asked me would I be interested in rewriting the script to shrink the budget down. Maybe they wanted to cut money out of the below-the-line stuff to give more money to Schwarzenegger. It began to look like they couldn't make a deal with Schwarzenegger, and it may have had something to do with Miramax not thinking that his stock was high enough for the fee he was asking. After that," says Cirulnick, "Andrew Rona told me that they were beginning to talk about other people — Vin Diesel's name was mentioned — but it never happened. I think at the time Vin Diesel was paid $20 million to do *xXx*, so I guess he wasn't going to be that much cheaper than Schwarzenegger."

Although Cirulnick half-expected to be asked to rewrite it for another actor, his agents advised against it: "They said, 'Look, if it's not going to go with Schwarzenegger, don't write any more on the project. You want to have written the script for Schwarzenegger, not some other guy. It's a dynamite sample, but don't get too wedded to it.'" For most of 2001 and 2002, Miramax suffered a series of flops and financial disasters, including the expensive collapse of *Talk* magazine, ballooning costs on Martin Scorsese's *Gangs of New York* and MGM's abrupt exit from its co-production deal on *Chicago* — from which it did not recover until *Chicago* turned a profit in 2003. So when a comprehensive *Variety* profile failed to mention *Total Recall 2* among the future projects either of Miramax or Dimension, Cirulnick surmised that the project was dead. "I think the monetary issue, the economics of the script and the film, and not being able to make a deal with Schwarzenegger cost the film momentum, and that was it," he says. "I left a man down on the battlefield and there was nothing more that could be done."

Dimension refused to let it die, however, offering Shusett and Goldman a chance to write another draft: "They called us and said, 'Here's Matt's ideas — let's blend [them with] your action set pieces, which we love,' because, as we do in the first one, we had a lot of unusual special effects ideas, some humorous, some bizarre. They said, 'Can you fit these into Matt's plot?' And we said, 'Yeah, we can do that.'" Shusett and Goldman wrote what they describe as "a beat sheet, just five or six pages," showing how a new version, combining Cirulnick's story with their set pieces, might look. "Andrew Rona said, 'This is wonderful, this is great — it's a combination of what Matt had come up with and how you guys see it having to be re-channelled to fit your action sequences. I'll give this to Arnold right now.' And Bob said, 'I'm completely convinced that you guys can deliver on the script. If [Arnold] buys the concept, we'll make the movie.'" Yet again, Schwarzenegger shot down the script.

In the meantime, former Carolco partners Andrew G. Vajna and Mario Kassar reunited to form C2 Productions, one of their first moves being to purchase the rights to continue Schwarzenegger's most successful franchise, launched in 1984 with *The Terminator* and eclipsed in

1991 by Carolco's own sequel, *Terminator 2: Judgment Day*. While James Cameron, director of the first two films and creator of the Terminator concept, passed on the chance to direct *Terminator 3: Rise of the Machines*, more crucially, Arnold Schwarzenegger agreed to reprise his most famous role, with *Breakdown* writer-director Jonathan Mostow at the helm. Around the same time, Vajna and Kassar entered negotiations with Dimension to re-acquire the sequel rights to *Total Recall*. Although that deal reportedly fell apart in early 2003, the $75 million US opening of *Terminator 3* put Arnie back on the box office map, leading Shusett and Goldman to approach Bob Weinstein with yet another concept, presented as a five-page treatment. "The tone will be the original tone," Shusett reveals. "We have a lot of funny new ideas, including six or seven very unique and funny and bizarre set pieces which we wrote in our '98 draft which we're transplanting into this, because we wrote them for Dimension and they still own them and they want us to use them. And the plot will be very complex again, and very much fantasy versus reality. We hope to shock the audience — something that most films would be afraid to do — by having the audience think something completely different as to how they interpreted the first movie. You see that in the first half hour. And that'll be the first shock. And from then it'll go on twisting back and forth towards 'fantasy versus reality', but with a new storyline involving a new leading lady." Shusett confirms that Melina will not be returning — "it will be fifteen years later by the time we get it on screen" — and that even Schwarzenegger is expendable. "The way we've sent it to him is flexible," Shusett notes, "so if Arnold's not available, or he doesn't want to do it, or ends up being Governor of California, it can be done with another actor."

Nevertheless, with *Total Recall* having taken sixteen years to reach the screen, there is still plenty of room for yet further development on what may, or may not, prove to be *Total Recall 2*. Expectant fans can turn to Philip K. Dick for encouragement. "After all," runs the final line of the short story that started it all, "the real one probably would not be long in coming."

# KEEPING UP WITH THE JONESES

**Separating fact from fiction in the development of Indiana Jones IV**

"I was done with the Indiana Jones series, and Harrison got very proactive with both George and [me] and said, 'I want to play Indy one more time.' So he started this. Blame him."

*— Steven Spielberg*

**W**hen *Indiana Jones and the Last Crusade* was released in 1989, director Steven Spielberg, producer George Lucas and actor Harrison Ford insisted that after three blockbusting adventures — two of them in the all-time box office top ten — the whip-cracking archaeologist Dr Henry 'Indiana' Jones Jr was hanging up his battered fedora for good; *The Last Crusade* would also be Indy's last adventure. Five years later, at the Venice Film Festival, Ford reportedly let slip that he was "reading scripts" for a fourth Indy film — and the rumours began. Although it would be a further decade before ideas coalesced, schedules aligned and enthusiasm returned to make a fourth 'Indy' instalment — set for release in July 2005, sixteen years after the last — the intervening period saw no shortage of imitators, from videogames (*Tomb Raider*) to TV shows (*Relic Hunter*) and movies (*The Mummy*). Nor was there any shortage of proposed storylines and scripts for the next film, with a dizzying array — all purporting to be the *real* 'Indy IV' — emerging over the years. Separating the counterfeit artefacts from the genuine article, however, would prove as challenging as any of Indy's adventures...

Lucas first dreamed up the character of Indiana Jones — then conceived as a Cary Grant-type character who used the spoils of his relic hunting expeditions to finance a lavish playboy lifestyle — in 1973, four years before *Star Wars* made movie history. Together with fellow fledgling film-maker Philip Kaufman, Lucas hatched a plot concerning the Ark of the Covenant, an idea which he would subsequently relate to his friend Steven Spielberg while on holiday in Hawaii in 1977. Spielberg, who, like Lucas, grew up on swashbuckling adventure serials, immediately responded to the tales of derring-do, and a unique partnership was forged between the two — then, as now, the hottest film-makers in Hollywood. Although Lucas was famously unable to cast his first choice for the role of Indy — Tom Selleck, who was contractually committed to *Magnum, PI* — a supporting actor from *American Graffiti* and *Star Wars* stepped in to save the day, and on 21 June 1981 *Raiders of the Lost Ark* officially made stars of Harrison Ford and Indiana Jones. When the film grossed $242 million in the US, a total of $432 million worldwide, and was nominated for eight Academy Awards, it was clear that Indy would be back: sure enough, *Indiana Jones and the Temple of Doom* followed in 1984, with the third and supposedly final instalment appearing five years later, grossing $348 million and $418 million worldwide respectively. A television series, *The Young Indiana Jones Chronicles*, followed in 1992; when this was cancelled, a series of made-for-television movies, *The Adventures of Young Indiana Jones*, continued the saga. Together with the theatrical movies, these spanned Indy's life from age ten, travelling with his father, to ninety-three — with an elderly, one-eyed Indy relating stories from his younger days at the beginning of each new episode. (Each episode, that is, except 1993's *Young Indiana Jones and the Mystery of the Blues*, which featured a cameo from Harrison Ford, who took a day off from filming *The Fugitive* to appear as a bearded, fifty year-old Indy in the story's framing sequence.)

Although the television show was finally killed in 1996, enthusiasm for the chronicles of Indiana Jones never died, and on 11 November 1994 — shortly after Harrison Ford set the Indy IV ball rolling at the Venice Film Festival — a story appeared in the London *Daily Mail* claiming that *Speed* star Sandra Bullock would play Indy's "sparky" sidekick in the fourth instalment of the franchise, entitled *Indiana Jones and the Lost Continent*. According to the article, which appeared in Baz Bamigboye's column under the headline "From *Speed* to Ford Escort", *The Lost Continent* begins as one of Indy's students (Bullock) uncovers an ancient artefact which she believes holds a clue to the whereabouts of the lost continent of Atlantis. "When Jones gets wind of his student's find, he prepares to set off on one last quest," the story continued. "However, his plans are scuppered since the girl refuses to allow him to go along without her. The lost continent and its otherworldly inhabitants are ultimately discovered in an air pocket beneath the ocean bed, just as the nuclear testing begins on Bikini Atoll, threatening the lost tribe of Atlantis with total extinction." Nothing further surfaced with regard to this potential storyline — which bore a passing resemblance to a 1992 Indiana Jones computer game, *Fate of Atlantis* — and it has since been revealed as the work of a highly-paid hoaxer who bamboozled Bamigboye into thinking it was the real deal. "Baz Bamigboye was hungry for stories at the time," admits the story's anonymous source. "I'd broken a story about Pierce Brosnan being cast as James Bond, and ever since then, Baz had been hounding me for stories. So finally, I gave him one — mainly to prove to my mum that most of the stories in the *Mail* are made up."

On 21 March 1995, *Variety* reported that a fourth instalment was unlikely to happen any time soon. "While Nazis and various cultists couldn't stop Indy, the lack of a suitable script has pushed back the fourth instalment in the series for the time being," the report said. "Ford, director Steven Spielberg and producer George Lucas hoped to make the Indy pic the actor's next project after *Sabrina* for Sydney Pollack. They turned loose screenwriter Jeb Stuart on a story conceived by Lucas. Stuart... has just turned in his second draft. Early indications are more work is needed [on the script]." Around the same time, *The Last Crusade* screenwriter Jeffrey Boam privately admitted to having been asked to write a script, with subsequent rumours suggesting that the story concerned an attempt to foil a Soviet plot to establish a missile base on the moon, or had something to do with the UFO crash at Roswell, New Mexico — or both. No story details were given when the Lucasfilm Fan Club confirmed to its members that Boam — who wrote several Indiana Jones-style scenes into his script for *The Phantom* — was working on a story which Lucas reportedly liked.

On 29 May 1996, a script entitled *Indiana Jones and the Sons of Darkness* and credited to Boam (from a story by George Lucas) appeared on the Internet, supposedly posted by a light-fingered courier who claimed to have lifted it from Lucasfilm's offices. The script concerned a race by Indy (complete with wife and daughter) to beat the Russians to the remnants of Noah's Ark — a Judeo-Christian artefact which fit nicely into the pattern (Ark of the Covenant, Holy Grail) of previous Indy films, but which had already been the focus of a Lucasfilm-approved novel, *Indiana Jones and the Genesis Deluge*, set twenty years before (and therefore incompatible with) the events of the script. The fact that the script was removed from the web a day after its initial posting, at the specific request of Lucasfilm Ltd, did nothing to stem the tide of conspiracy theories, since they would want the script removed forthwith whether it was genuine or a fake. Nevertheless, after a week of frenzied newsgroup activity, guesswork and/or detective work on behalf of Indy fans, a Lucasfilm spokesperson confirmed to America Online that the script was a work of copyright-violating fan fiction. It would be a further four months before the true story behind the fake script emerged, when ambitious Indy fan and aspiring screen-writer Robert Smith owned up to writing the bogus *Sons of Darkness* script and posting it to the Internet, after having failed to submit it to Lucasfilm through legitimate channels.

Talking to Charles Deemer of the Internet Screenwriters Network, Smith admitted that he had sent the 166-page script to an agency which initially promised to submit it to Lucasfilm, but then went back on its word. Smith got no further when he called to plead his case to Lucasfilm itself — unsurprising, since no legitimate production com-pany accepts unsolicited material. "About a year later it occurred to me to try and get Lucasfilm's attention by posting my Indy script on the Internet," Smith continued. "I knew I'd have to take a radical approach, so I concocted a courier theft story and posted it to all the film discus-sion groups. In a matter of days the site 'hit' counter jumped from 0 to 300 and snowballed from there on." A week later, Smith received his first 'cease and desist' order by e-mail. "I got Lucasfilm's attention, but I felt it wasn't enough. So with the help of some brave friends of mine, we moved the script to a new site and set up a comments page where readers of the script could leave their two cents' worth. At the same time, the Harrison Ford and Steven Spielberg news groups were all abuzz with chatter of the stolen script posted on the 'net."

Fan feedback was mixed, regardless of whether the commentators believed the script to be genuine or bogus. "I was paid the ultimate compliment by those fans who believed the script was the real McCoy," added Smith. "I thank them sincerely. And to the naysayers I bow to your abilities at sniffing out a forgery." Lucasfilm was not prepared to sit back and watch its copyright violated, however. "Four 'cease and desist' orders later I pulled the plug and shut down," Smith explained. "At that point, I felt I'd rocked the boat sufficiently enough that Lucasfilm had no choice but to deal with me." They did: by sending the police round to his friend's workplace. "To make a long story short, my friend ratted me out and I was obliged to give the constable a call... I assured the constable that I wouldn't do anything like that again (wink) and hung up with the constable's promise that he'd put in a good word for me at Lucasfilm." Smith concluded by apologising for his actions, dissuading anyone else from emulating them, and thanking Lucasfilm for its tolerance. "My Internet fugitive days are over," he said. "In my letters to Lucasfilm I apologised and explained that my actions weren't malicious in any way and that I simply wanted someone to read my script. I guess one could chalk it up to the actions of a desperate screenwriter."

On 24 March 1997, during an interview with Barbara Walters, Harrison Ford was asked if he would play Indiana Jones again. "In a New York minute," he replied swiftly. "It's a question of Steven Spielberg and I finding a slot we have in common." Two months later — while the ever-reliable London *Daily Mail* was 'reporting' that *Indiana Jones and the Sons of Darkness* would feature Kevin Costner as Indy's 'bad seed' brother — Spielberg told *Time* magazine that he expected to direct a fourth Indy movie. In July, during a press conference for *Star Wars Episode I: The Phantom Menace*, George Lucas went further, stating: "We're working on a screenplay for [a fourth] Indiana Jones and it's really now a matter of trying to get Steven and Harrison and all our schedules so that we can actually work on it, because everyone is so busy."

In October of the same year, archaeologists at the website Ain't It Cool News unearthed a sacred find: what appeared to be the first draft of a *genuine* Indy IV script, labouring under the multiple-choice title "*Indiana Jones IV* aka *Indiana Jones and the Monkey King* aka *Indiana Jones and the Garden of Life*," and written by Chris Columbus — who wrote

*Gremlins* and *The Goonies* for Spielberg, and later directed *Home Alone, Mrs Doubtfire* and the first two *Harry Potter* movies. The script put Indy, Marcus Brody (Denholm Elliot's character), an attractive English anthropologist named Dr Clare Clarke, and 'Scraggy', a Portuguese guide, on the trail of a legendary Chinese artefact which may hold the secret of eternal life. "The script had to do with the lost city of Sun Wu-Kung, a stone monkey, a golden hooped staff and 'The Garden of Immortal Peaches'," said Harry Knowles, host of Ain't It Cool. "The only recurring character from the past besides Indy was Brody," he added, "but [in the story] he has been on the other side for quite some time now. Nazis and evil Chinese Pirates are the bad guys. And the script was by far the most 'fantastical' in terms of mysticism and such." Despite the fact that the script was dated 10 February 1995, it should have been obvious from the setting (1937) and the theme (immortality) — if not the absence of Jones' father, a hugely popular addition to the Indy canon, with Sean Connery unlikely to be excluded from future films — that this was very probably a rejected script for the *third* instalment of the Indiana Jones series, not the *fourth*, and more likely circa 1985 than 1995.

A few months after the appearance of Columbus' rejected draft, on 15 January 1998, another website, Dark Horizons, posted what it claimed to be the opening pages of another script, entitled *Raiders of the Fallen Empire*, which supposedly concerned Indy's discovery of the Garden of Eden. Although even the title seemed dubious — for the 1999 video release, *Raiders of the Lost Ark* had been quietly retitled *Indiana Jones and the Raiders of the Lost Ark* to tie it in with its sequels, much as Lucas had appended *Star Wars* with the sobriquet *A New Hope* — confirmation of the script's religious theme seemed to come from a respected theologian in Moscow, Idaho, who claimed to have been hired to fact-check a script with this subject matter. The script segment, amounting to just a few pages, was subsequently withdrawn — not, this time, due to pressure from Lucasfilm, but at the request of the extract's author, who claimed that the whole thing was a misunderstanding. In April, *Cinescape* reported receiving yet another script, entitled *Indiana Jones: The Law of One*, which dealt with Indy's pursuit of a powerful ancient device responsible for the destruction of Atlantis. *Cinescape* judged it "a fake or at the very least a 'spec' script", and a month later, broke the real story in an interview with *Star Wars* producer Rick McCallum. "We finished the script about three years ago," he said. "[But] at the time we finished it, Harrison Ford had two years worth of commitments, Spielberg was just starting DreamWorks and George Lucas and I were in the middle of *Star Wars: Episode I*. The plan is that in the next five years, George and I finish *Episode II* and *Episode III* of *Star Wars* and then we will definitely do another Indy," he added. "Our plan is that viewers can take the forty-four hours we did of the Young Indiana Jones [TV series], where you watch Indy born in 1899, and then you follow him in the movies through the end of the 1950s. We see these movies as a chronicle of the century."

The same month, Ain't It Cool claimed that the title *Indiana Jones and the Lost Continent* was what "they would probably stick with [now that] the 'Area 51' story has been dropped in favour of the new one that follows the lines of the lost city of Atlantis." The report added, optimistically and inaccurately, that "Due for a summer 2000 release, it was written by Jeffrey Boam." Ford himself quickly dismissed such rumours during an appearance on Rosie O'Donnell's talk show, when he repeated his desire to don the fedora once more, but insisted that, despite rumours to the contrary, there was no script. A week later, on 9 June 1998, Ford appeared on Earvin 'Magic' Johnson's talk show *Magic Hour*, stating that he would love to make another Indiana Jones. "We just haven't really settled on a script idea yet," he said. "Hopefully, something will come along." In July, the *Chicago Herald-Tribune*'s Cindy Pearlman quoted Steven Spielberg as saying "The Indiana Jones 4 hat is halfway on my head," while Ain't It Cool went further: "Yes, there will be another *Indiana Jones*," Spielberg said. "We don't have a start date for it because we still don't have a script, but we do have an idea of what type of villain it should be, but it won't be a Nazi. Everyone's on board for the picture but don't look for it for a couple of years." Four months later, a spokesperson for Paramount Pictures told *Empire* magazine that the official position was that "there is no official position. They may all be on the verge of signing contracts, but since no public announcement has been made, officially there *is* no Indiana Jones 4."

On 2 December 1998, a little over a year after Ain't It Cool unearthed Chris Columbus' rejected screenplay, website Indyfan.com was given a synopsis of a script entitled *Indiana Jones and the Saucer Men from Mars*, apparently written by Jeb Stuart (*48 HRS, The Fugitive, Just*

*Cause*) from a story by Stuart and Lucas. "The script, labelled as the final draft and dated 1995, involves an alien artefact which continuously changes possession between Indy, Russian baddies, and saucer men [ie, extra-terrestrials]," the report stated. "Besides being convoluted and unbelievable, the storyline ends in indulgent sappiness, with Indy marrying the lady linguist who accompanied him throughout the adventure. The ceremony is witnessed by Sallah, Marion, Willie, Short Round, and Henry Jones Sr [all well-loved characters from the previous films]."

*Indiana Jones and the Saucer Men from Mars* opens in Borneo in 1949, as Indy manages to keep a stolen idol from falling into the hands of pirates. Later, he meets a beautiful and brilliant linguist, Dr Elaine Mcgregor, who hires Indy to join her at a dig site, where she is captured by the same pirates, and rescued by Indy. Elaine and Indy fall in love and decide to get married, but the wedding is interrupted by the arrival of Elaine's ex-husband, Bolander, who spirits her away to White Sands, New Mexico, where a spacecraft has crash landed, killing its alien occupants. While the Americans and (Communist) Russians engage in a race to discover the secrets of the alien ship's fuel supply — a stone cylinder covered in hieroglyphics — Indy finds himself at the test site of an atomic bomb, and later on an out of control aircraft which he and Elaine escape as *another* alien spacecraft appears to retrieve the cylinder. They subsequently hide out in a hot-wired pickup truck at a desert drive-in movie theatre (showing, for good measure, a cheesy '50s sci-fi movie), meet Sanskrit-speaking aliens, get arrested, escape, witness Bolander's incineration by the cylinder and the departure of the aliens, and finally get married, driving off into the sunset with Short Round at the wheel. (Whether this was a genuine Indy script or not has never been established.)

Less than a fortnight later, Ain't It Cool described yet another storyline, this time supposedly taken from a treatment an unnamed writer had submitted to Creative Artists Agency. "Indy, working in Egypt, circa 1947, encounters a mysterious Egyptian at the great pyramids. It turns out that he has escaped from Atlantis and needs to prevent the destruction of the Atlanteans. He is to marry the King's daughter, but his fellow Egyptian has heard of the surface world and wants to raise Atlantis. This second Egyptian is none other than the ancient Pharaoh-

God, Ramses. He is now a mummy and plans to Destroy the Atlanteans, who are alien in origin, and raise the continent through the triggering of a massive earthquake. Indy finds Atlantis at the bottom of the Atlantic Ocean — [apparently] the city was spared because they trapped themselves inside a giant dome. There an Egyptian minority population still thrives. Indy must choose between the rise of the world's greatest archaeological find and the death of the Atlanteans, or to help preserve the marriage of the Egyptian to his Atlantean love by joining him to defeat *Ramses*." The pseudonymous poster, 'KABOOM', was perhaps unaware that the Atlantis theme had been the subject of numerous other rumours over the years, or that Universal was already filming an Egyptian-themed Indiana Jones knock-off entitled *The Mummy* — the success of which, at least, proved the contemporary audience's appetite for an Indy-style adventure. More tellingly, KABOOM's post was accompanied by the following subjective (not to mention immodest) endorsement of his or her story outline: "As you can see, the story is magnificent, with room to add tremendous conflict and spectacular visuals. Imagine when Indy approaches Atlantis and enters the dazzling city! It also introduces an awesome villain and great supporting characters that we will actually care about their fate! I hope they go with this treatment, it would be awesome."

Barely a month passed before another, slightly more credible story emerged. On 12 January 1999, *Cinescape Insider* reported the existence of a script entitled *Indiana Jones and the Sword of Arthur*, credited to Jeffrey Boam, with pages marked 'Property of Lucasfilm Ltd' and 'Final Draft'. (The latter marking casts some doubt on the legitimacy of the script, since professional screenwriters will seldom, if ever, tempt the fates by writing 'final draft' on a script. It could, however, be a reference to the best-selling screenwriting software of that name, though in practice scripts written and/or printed out in this format display no reference to the software with which they are written.) As expected from the title, the script concerned a search by Indy for King Arthur's magical sword, Excalibur, reputedly hidden on Enigma Island, a small isle off the Spanish coast, six centuries earlier. The Nazis are after it too, as are the surviving descendants of the original Knights of the Round Table, who help Indy and his companions — Anthony Brody (Marcus' son) and new friends Arianna Smith (a kind of female Indy, as might be guessed from the name) and Sebastian Collins (a dead ringer for *Frasier* actor David Hyde Pierce, and soon revealed to be the villain of the piece) — recover the sword, only to have it snatched from their grasp by the arm of a woman who reaches up from beneath the Atlantic Ocean to reclaim it forever. (One of the script's more imaginative moments is a battle with Collins, during which Indy loses an eye, leaving him sporting a very fetching eye patch — thus explaining the elderly Indy's appearance in the TV series.) At the end, Indy goes back to teaching, and prepares to embark on his next adventure: settling down with Arianna.

Less than a fortnight after the initial posting, the *Sword of Arthur* script was revealed to be the work of two aspiring screenwriters, Steven Frye and Michael Prentice. "The two of us wrote *Sword of Arthur* back in 1996 as a lark idea," Prentice admitted to Micah Johnson, host of website Indyfan.com. "Neither of us are professional writers, we're just fans who enjoy the Indy series. The whole *Sons of Darkness* fiasco had happened and we felt a better job could be done, so he and I wrote up the story, [while] I went ahead and did a first draft of the script. We hoped maybe something could happen with it, but mainly, we wrote it in the spirit of fun. We just wanted to write a half-way decent story." Prentice went on to say that, in mid-1997, he had been duped into sending the script to an unscrupulous character with purported connections to Spielberg, but who was subsequently found to be selling it as a script by Jeffrey Boam. (For the record, Boam died on 24 January 2000 without ever commenting on the *Sword of Arthur* affair.)

Six months later, on 14 July 1999, Rick McCallum revealed some official Indy IV info at a joint Lucasfilm/LucasArts press conference in London. "We've got a fantastic script, and everyone really wants to do it," he said. "We've now got to wait for everyone to be free," he added. "George is tied up, as you know; Steven is busy for a couple of years; and Harrison is committed for the next eighteen months. But the script is great and age is not a problem. I think we'll get it together in about three or four years." Although no title had been agreed on, McCallum concluded with an elliptical reference to the storyline: "Watch the stars... and watch the desert." Could this have been a none-too-cryptic reference to the widely-circulated *Indiana Jones and the Saucer Men from Mars* script credited to Jeb Stuart? Three days after McCallum's comments, an Ain't It Cool scooper named 'Makman', who claimed to be an insider at a "San Francisco company" — Lucasfilm and several of its subsidiaries are based in San Francisco — announced that the fourth Indiana Jones film only existed as a twelve-page treatment, with the working title *Indiana Jones and the Red Scare*. "It takes place in the early fifties, Indy is retired from gallivanting across the globe," Makman suggested. "He is the department chair of the archeology department at Princeton. Henry Jones Sr is gravely ill and lives with Indy in their modest home just off of campus. Papa Jones has maybe six months to live. He has a live-in nurse. Indy weathered and very much looking his age. He longs for excitement but knows his days are over. He wants to marry, pass on the Jones name. He spends most of his time with his father and a middle-aged history professor named Gladys, who's affection he wins from another colleague at a faculty dinner — a hilarious opening sequence in the true Indy form." The gist of the story, Makman went on, has Indy being retained by President Eisenhower's administration to obtain information about the Russians' retrieval of some dubious artefacts found in Hitler's bunker after the raid on Berlin at the end of the Second World War. "Hitler, as we know, was into the occult and it seems Russia is now in possession of all the documents and oddities found with the Nazi *Führer*. Sallah returns," he/she added, "and Indy's new lady friend is a blacklisted author well versed in the occult and deemed a Communist."

Towards the end of 1999, news came thick and fast. First, Spielberg admitted that he, Lucas and Ford were considering three separate scripts. Secondly, Ford rebutted suggestions that, having recently turned sixty, he was too old to play Indy, being virtually a relic himself — "I'm still quite fit enough to fake it," he told *Entertainment Tonight*. "It's all smoke and mirrors anyway." Lucas told the same show that the script search had been narrowed to two possibilities. "All I'm waiting for is a phone call from Steven and Harrison," he said. "I'm ready to go." A week later, Ford told E! Online that he was "ready when they're ready", suggesting that it was Spielberg who was causing the delay. The director admitted as much in one of the interviews accompanying the 26 October 1999 video release of the *Indiana Jones Trilogy* — featuring the retitled *Indiana Jones and the Raiders of the Lost Ark* — although his reasons for hesitating were laudable: "We don't want the fourth Indiana Jones movie to leave a bad taste in anyone's mouth."

The script appeared to be the sticking point. "If there was a script they all loved, they would kill themselves to clear their schedules," Ford's agent, Patricia McQueeney, told *USA Today* columnist Jeannie Williams. "They love [Indiana Jones] so much, but they can't seem to get their heads together on a script they are all enthusiastic about." Interviewed in the London *Sunday Express* around the same time, however, Rick McCallum suggested that work had been completed on the script as early as 1999, and that the delay was caused by "everybody having commitments years in advance." Indeed, appearing on the UK morning show *The Big Breakfast* to promote *Random Hearts*, Ford said, "Steven and George will not be available until 2005, and I don't know whether I'll be fit or interested at that point. I hope it could happen before that." Appearing on *Larry King Live*, Spielberg subsequently promised that the film would happen eventually, so long as "Harrison isn't too old to jump, and I'm not too old to yell."

Spielberg, Lucas and Ford continued to keep hopes for a fourth film alive, not least because the question came up so often. "I want it to happen," Ford announced during the taping of his appearance on *Inside the Actor's Studio* on 15 February 2000. "There is no script yet that everybody is *really* happy with. George is a bit preoccupied with that *other* movie," he added, referring to the ongoing *Star Wars* saga, "but Steven and I are very ambitious to do it. But we all realize it has to be great." A month later, at a Director's Guild of America honouring Spielberg with a Lifetime Achievement Award, Spielberg admitted that the question he was asked most often is "Dad, when are you going to make a new Indiana Jones film?" and delighted Indy fans everywhere with a promise: "Indiana Jones is coming back soon." How soon was difficult to say: with *A.I.* due to begin shooting in July 2000, followed by *Minority Report* in April 2001, Spielberg's definition of "soon" appeared to grow less and less distinct.

Around the same time, an intriguing new development occurred in the saga of Indiana Jones IV. On 15 February 2000, eight days after Spielberg underwent kidney surgery, the Coming Attractions website posted a rumour, "completely unconfirmed and graded as an 8 on the rumour-mongering scale," that M. Night Shyamalan, acclaimed writer-director of *The Sixth Sense*, had been approached by Spielberg to discuss the possibility of writing an Indiana Jones script. (Shyamalan had been inspired to become a film-maker himself after seeing *Raiders of the Lost Ark* at the age of twelve.) Coming Attractions' effort to distance itself from the rumour appeared to have been unwarranted when, on 22 June, *Variety* published a story entitled "Arnold & Indy: They'll Be Back" which appeared to confirm that Spielberg, Lucas and Ford were "in the process of drafting" Shyamalan to pen the new script, although, even if he accepted the assignment, Shyamalan would not be available to start work until he wrapped production of his next film, *Unbreakable*. A week later, the MovieHeadlines website called Lucasfilm's Jeanne Cole to clarify the story, which turned out to be only partially correct: Shyamalan was apparently only one of several writers being considered; no deal was in place, but the project was being actively worked on, being one that Spielberg, Lucas and Ford were all enthusiastic about. In November, MovieHeadlines quoted Shyamalan as saying that he would "have to think about" writing Indy IV. "There are a lot of things on my plate." It was not until July of the following year that Ain't It Cool finally laid rest to the rumours by quoting Shyamalan as follows: "I was never contacted formally to do the project. I did publicly express interest, but nothing really ever came to fruition. I have talked with all of them besides George," he added, "and it sounds exciting. They have their ideas and I, of course, as a fan, have ideas of how they should do it."

Other, less high-profile fans continued to have their ideas, however. In mid-2000, a forty-two-page treatment entitled *Indiana Jones and the Tomb of Ice* began circulating on the Internet, its format somewhere between a script, a treatment and a work of prose fiction (stage directions, scripted dialogue and scene transitions are juxtaposed with sections of reported speech). Set in 1949, the story follows Indy, his father and pretty palaeolinguist Abigail Shaw to northern Siberia, where Russians have discovered what appears to be King Arthur's mortal remains, along with his magic sword, Excalibur. The sword proves to be merely the tip of the iceberg, however, as Indy and Abby discover when they reach northern Siberia and discover the titular tomb, which is none other than Valhalla itself, and guarded by an army of Viking ghosts. Unlike *Indiana Jones and the Sword of Arthur*, another script which used Excalibur and the legend of King Arthur as its basis, there was little doubt that *Indiana Jones and the Tomb of Ice* was a work of fan fiction — albeit one for which, somewhat mysteriously, no one has since claimed authorship...

In October 2000, in an interview posted on the Internet Movie Database, Ford said he was "looking forward" to doing a fourth Indy. "It's a great character that I've enjoyed playing in the past and I would like to revisit him," he said. "I think the movies are great entertainment and Steven Spielberg and George Lucas and I have spent a lot of time discussing how we would like to proceed with the next Indiana story. We're still hammering out the details," he added, "but I'm pretty confident we're going to do another Indy, although it might be at least a year or more before our respective schedules allow us to do it. I'd personally love to work with Sean Connery again. I think audiences would enjoy seeing us back together." Asked if Indy would age gracefully, he responded, "I think we have to show that he's suffered some wear and tear over the years. That's going to make his character that much more interesting. For me, adding some flaws and layers is what is going to make Indy even more interesting. We can address issues like whether his character's virtues are based on his youth or on other aspects of human nature like his wisdom, his toughness, his resourcefulness, his integrity. A lot of work went into creating Indy and giving him a certain history and identity, and I think it will be extremely fascinating to expand on that. It's something that I think the public would enjoy watching."

In a February 2001 interview with *The New York Times*, screenwriter Stephen Gaghan (*Traffic*) revealed that he had received a call in January asking if he was interested in writing the next Indiana Jones movie. By July, however, Kathleen Kennedy was telling the *Calgary Sun* that there had been a lot of discussion "but to be honest there is no script because there isn't even a writer in place. It sounds like a slam dunk to do another Indiana Jones," she went on, "but you have to get everyone available and committed and then you have to get a screenplay that excites everyone. In reality that could probably take years." Even more alarming was the fact that the gross participation of the 'Big Three' could run to $150 million, leaving Paramount Pictures with little more than small change for financing the film. (20th Century Fox had found itself in a similar position with the second *Star Wars* trilogy, for which it was paid a small percentage for distribution of films which Lucas had financed himself.) Nevertheless, at a party for the 2002 Golden Globe awards, a different triumvirate — Spielberg, Ford and Kate Capshaw (*Indiana Jones and the Temple of Doom* actress and now Mrs Spielberg) — confirmed to Fox News reporter Roger Friedman that Indiana Jones would return in a new adventure. "We have a title, but we're not ready to announce it," Spielberg said, adding that Capshaw's character, Willie Scott, would also return — and not via a flashback. The following day, Spielberg's publicist, Marvin Levy, was doing damage control, insisting that Indy IV would *not*, as Spielberg had implied, be his next picture. Nevertheless, Levy told E! Online, "Right now, Steven's been described as being in 'development heaven'. They do have a story they like and they have a title... [but] they don't have a script." This was an odd admission, given Ford's comment to Fox News the night before: "It was always about getting the right script, and now we have it."

Apparently, they did not. On 23 April, *Variety* mentioned that Tom Stoppard, the acclaimed British playwright and screenwriter whose script for *Shakespeare in Love* won him an Academy Award, and who had worked uncredited on *The Last Crusade*, had been approached to write the next Indy instalment. Barely a week later, producer Kathleen Kennedy dismissed the suggestion , stating that another (unidentified) writer would begin writing in June and submit a first draft by early autumn. It was three weeks before IGN FilmForce broke the news that the mystery writer was none other than Frank Darabont, who wrote numerous episodes of *The Young Indiana Jones Chronicles* television series and several of the feature-length *The Adventures of Young Indiana Jones* TV movies before turning writer-director with such films as *The Shawshank Redemption* and *The Green Mile*. (More recently, he wrote an uncredited draft of Spielberg's *Minority Report*, and directed Jim Carrey in the misfire *The Majestic*.) Speaking to *MTV Movie House* reporter Master P at Skywalker Ranch on 24 May, Lucas would neither confirm nor deny the Darabont rumours. "We're in the process of hiring a writer," he said, "and hopefully we'll be able to start shooting... not next year, but probably the year after [2004]." By the end of May 2002, not only had *Variety* confirmed the rumours regarding Frank Darabont, but a release date had been set: 1 July 2005 — the beginning of the five-day Fourth of July weekend, and a few days short of Harrison Ford's sixty-third birthday.

"George called about a month ago and said, 'Would you be interested in doing this, we're looking for a writer,'" Darabont told *Cinescape* in June, "and I said, 'Yeah, George, I'm there.' It's the only gig I've taken sight unseen." As for the story, he went on, "I have no idea at this point what the movie is about. I'm putting my faith in Steven and George — I will be their writing vessel." The same month, Ford took a more cautious stance in an interview with the same magazine. "It's official that we have an ambition to make the film," he said, "but unless we get a script that we're all happy with, I don't think it's sure that will happen. So, I'm very happy about the fact that we've all committed to a certain idea, and we're developing it and hoping it will be fruitful." Spielberg had soon confirmed to *Dreamwatch* magazine that Darabont had commenced work on the screenplay, based on a "wonderful" story by Lucas, who told the official Star Wars website, star-wars.com, how excited he was to revisit a character he created a generation ago. "Steven, Harrison and I have wanted to do this for some time, and this feels like the right moment."

2003 heralded further Indy IV news, as Spielberg confirmed that Sean Connery — who was then busy playing Allan Quatermain, one of the inspirations for Indiana Jones, in Stephen Norrington's *The League of Extraordinary Gentlemen* — would return as Henry Jones Sr. "Indy's pop will be back for a few scenes," he said, "and it's set in the early 1950s. Harrison is going to be sixty-two years old when the film [begins production], so we had to push the years into the 1950s. I'd like to get Karen Allen back for one soundbite," he added, referring to the actress who played Marion Ravenwood in *Raiders of the Lost Ark*; yet plans to bring back Kate Capshaw appeared to have been derailed by Darabont. "He called me and said, 'I'm not sure we can work her into the script, too,'" Spielberg said. Darabont had other ideas about the direction the script should take. "I absolutely don't want to do things like having him say, 'I'm getting too old for this shit,'" he told the *Alameda Times-Star Online*. "I don't want to be slipping and sliding in clichés. The character is no longer in the 1930s. He has to age honestly. He's got to be in the 1950s." Describing the process of working on the script as "a total blast," he added: "Let's face it, what's not to like about Indiana Jones? I saw the first movie in 1981, five years before I started my writing career. Who knew I would grow up to write the sequel?"

In October 2003, the fans' appetite for a fourth Indiana Jones was further whetted by the DVD début of the trilogy, previously available only on video and laserdisc. Meanwhile, Ford told *US Magazine* that although Indy IV would not begin shooting until the following year, it would probably be his next film. "I'm taking some time off and then I'll get ready for Indy IV in 2004," he said. "We have a great storyline, and it will be as good as any of the others we've made. Maybe even better."

Whether it would be as good, if not better, than those they hadn't made — the rejected scripts and storylines that didn't make the grade, and the amateur creations of well-intentioned fans — remained to be seen. Whatever the fate of Indy IV, it was clear that, from the beginning, it was Harrison Ford who had been cracking the whip. "Harrison's the one who got George and [me] to do it," Spielberg admitted. "I was done with the Indiana Jones series, and Harrison got very proactive with both George and [me] and said, 'I want to play Indy one more time.' So he started this. Blame him."

# THE LOST CRUSADE

## Despite a ten-year crusade by Arnold Schwarzenegger, it may take a miracle to bring *Crusade* to the screen

"The story of the Crusades is the murderous attack
of the Christians on the Arabs and the Jews. Do you think
that's a politically interesting situation?"

*— director Paul Verhoeven, circa 2002*

The era of the Crusades was one of the richest, bloodiest and most controversial in history, and therefore eminently suitable for frequent visitation by Hollywood. The road to the Crusades began on 27 November 1095 in Clermont, France, where a polemical proclamation by Pope Urban II, describing in lurid detail Turkish attacks upon the Christian Byzantine Empire, set in motion what was to become the First Crusade. Soldiers, clergy and commoners alike travelled to the East to wage war on Muslims, and although payment would be scarce and conditions were likely to be harsh, Pope Urban offered a 'Papal Indulgence', which promised anyone taking part in the enterprise the immediate remission of all sins. By the middle of the following year, tens of thousands of Christians were on their way to Byzantium, attacking Muslims (whom they viewed as ignorant heathens) and Jews (judged 'Christ-killers') with equal relish.

Although thousands of civilians joined the Crusaders, the 'official' armies were comprised of three groups: one led by Godfrey of Bouillon, Hugh, Count of Vermandois and Robert, Duke of Normandy; another led by Raymond IV of St Gilles; and a third under the command of the Norman warlord Bohemond. The armies' spiritual leader was Bishop Adhémar of Le Puy, a close confidant of Pope Urban II. Joining forces in Byzantium in early 1097, they set about recapturing the city of Nicaea from the Turks, before dividing into two groups *en route* to Antioch, after which they staved off a Muslim ambush and put the Turks to flight, almost starved to death in Anatolia and, in October 1097, lay siege to Antioch — a seemingly impregnable city which was so large it was impossible to surround. The siege dragged on through the winter and into 1098, and the Crusaders, deep in hostile territory, quickly ran short of food. Many died of starvation and disease (including Bishop Adhémar), and many more went home, but ultimately the Crusaders were victorious. Under the command of Raymond of St Gilles, early in 1099 they set out for Jerusalem, by that time a heavily fortified garrison of Arab and Nubian troops, where another siege took place. In order to break the siege, forces led by Godfrey of Bouillon and Robert of Normandy breached the city wall in the dead of night — and rampaged through the streets, slaughtering everyone in their path...

Nine hundred years after the First Crusade, another began: a campaign by Arnold Schwarzenegger and director Paul Verhoeven, collaborators on the worldwide sci-fi hit *Total Recall*, to make a historical epic. Part *Spartacus*, part *Conan the Barbarian*, the simply titled *Crusade* was to star the Austrian Oak as Hagen, a thief-turned-slave who winds up joining the Christian army to free Jerusalem from the Muslims in 1095, only to discover that each of the rival faiths have more than religious reasons for waging holy war. As Verhoeven recalls of the project's origins: "We were sitting outside Arnold's trailer in Mexico City at Charabusco Studios, while we were shooting *Total Recall*, and he started to talk about a script he had once read about the Crusades. He said it wasn't a good script, but he really liked the idea so much — to make a movie about the Crusades. And it was also one of my favourite times in history." Verhoeven had read a great deal about the period while still living in Holland, and even though he had discussed the possibility of a film with his regular screenwriting collaborator Gerard Soeteman, he did not think they would ever get such a project financed. "But then, when Arnold mentioned it, I said, 'Well, that's very interesting, I think I know exactly who the writer for that would be,' because by then I had met Walon Green."

Born in Baltimore in 1936, Green had begun his screenwriting career as co-writer (with director Sam Peckinpah) on the bloodthirsty western *The Wild Bunch*. His first collaboration with Verhoeven was an unrealised adaptation of *Women* by Charles Bukowski; this was followed by a script for what became Disney's *Dinosaur*, which Verhoeven originally planned to direct using a combination of Phil Tippett's 'stop motion' effects and Dennis Muren's CGI. Says Verhoeven, "Walon wrote a script for *Dinosaur*, and is still mentioned in the credits of the movie, although I never directed it of course. I thought he was a great writer, and I got along with him very very well. He reminded me of my Dutch screenwriter, Gerard Soeteman, in that he's very well read, and he knows a lot about politics and history, and he has a good take on the politics of the Crusades. He seemed to be the perfect candidate for *Crusade*. When I discussed it with Walon," he adds, "he was immediately enthusiastic, and Mario Kassar and Andy Vajna [of Carolco] paid for him to develop a script."

Green's first draft of *Crusade* opens in France as Hagen, a cynical thief in the employ of Count Emmich of Bascarat, is caught robbing an abbey, and brought before the Abbot. Sentenced to hang, he finds himself in jail with a Jewish snake oil salesman named Aron ('Ari'), also sentenced to hang for using the occasion of a visit by Pope Urban II to sell fake cure-alls to the locals. Ari explains that Hagen's booty of gold and silver is all very well, but religious artefacts — the tooth of a saint, the finger-bone of John the Baptist, a fragment of the holy cross — are where the real money is at. Upon hearing that the Pope is always on the lookout for signs from God, Hagen burns a huge cross into his back, thereby tricking the holy fools (including Bishop Adhémar, the Crusade's spiritual leader) into thinking it is a stigmata-like symbol of his piety, and so engineering his emancipation. (This scene may have been inspired by the 'miracle of the lance': Provençal peasant Peter Bartholomew, claiming to have had a vision of Christ and St Andrew in which they told him that the lance used to pierce Christ's side was buried beneath the high altar of St Peter's Church, was allowed to supervise the digging, and the lance was duly found. Although the crusading army's leaders were sceptical that a miracle had occurred, many of the Crusaders were convinced, and they took advantage of the boost in morale to launch a last-ditch attempt to break the siege of Antioch.)

Released from his bonds, Hagen is dispatched to the Holy Land, with Ari in tow, to join the Crusades, where his first action is to rescue a Jewish wedding party from a merciless attack led by Emmich. "We wanted to be honest to history, and as close to what we think happened at that time, and were the motives of the time," says Verhoeven. "And also to point out that the Crusades started out with persecuting the Jews. The moment they [the Crusaders] go on the road, they think, 'These are the killers of God, the theocides, so let's kill them first.' That was all acknowledged in the script." Emmich responds to Hagen's interference by challenging him to a duel in which Emmich is defeated, and scarred for life. Adding insult to injury, Robert, Duke of Normandy, punishes Emmich for his unprovoked attack, and rewards Hagen for his heroics by inviting him to march in his command. Emmich, vowing vengeance, sells Hagen into slavery in Jaffa, where he is rescued from a eunuch's fate by Ari, now posing as a Muslim in the service of local Emir Ibn Khaldun, commander of Jerusalem's forces. The Emir, meanwhile, is trying to marry his beautiful daughter Leila to a Muslim fundamentalist, Djarvat, whose army her father is eager to use to bolster his own. Although she and Hagen have a growing attraction — albeit from a distance both physical and social — and she is suspicious of Djarvat's motives, Leila agrees to go along with the arranged marriage.

When Djarvat's true nature as a bloodthirsty warmonger is revealed, Ibn Khaldun calls off the wedding, but Djarvat kidnaps Leila and demands the Emir's obeisance in return for his daughter's life. Hagen manages to rescue Leila, but after they consummate their relationship, she is captured again, this time by Emmich. Emmich is about to rape her when the alarm is sounded — Muslims are approaching the encampment under a flag of truce, and 'Hagen of the Miraculous Cross' is with them! Ibn Khaldun offers peace in return for his daughter, and a truce is agreed between the Muslims and Christians. Having brokered Leila's rescue, Hagen then feels betrayed when Ibn Khaldun sends her away and, following Emmich's murder of Ibn Khaldun, he finds himself on the side of the Crusaders in the subsequent battle. When the Christians are victorious, the defeated Djarvat offers Emmich a deal: he will allow Emmich to acquire the holiest relic of all — a fragment of the cross on which Christ was crucified — if he is spared and allowed to control the Muslims who survive the slaughter to come. Emmich agrees, on one condition: he wants Leila too, "to wed and bed the true love of Hagen of the cross while he watches and dies." Djarvat's attempt to kidnap Leila is frustrated by Hagen and Ari, but the sepulchre containing the Holy Cross is set on fire — and only Hagen can save it. Hagen rushes in, and emerges from the smoke and flames carrying the cross on his back — a spectacle which brings his destiny full circle, and has Emmich's men falling to their knees. Hagen seizes the chance to kill Emmich, and escape with the holiest of relics and his beloved Leila. At the end, disgusted by the death and destruction unleashed in the name of one god or another, Hagen turns his back on the Crusaders, and places the true cross in the hands of monks who vow never to reveal its location. According to a closing caption, it was never found.

Aside from the spectacle, bloodthirsty battle scenes, action and adventure, the politics of Green's script are intriguing. Although it does not contextualise the period in historical or epochal terms — it does not, for instance, open with a caption explaining what the Crusades were all about — there are political elements to both the story and the characters. The fictional Emmich and his cousin Waldemar are corrupt opportunists, using the religious crusade as an excuse to rape and pillage — vividly illustrated by the attack on the Jewish wedding party, launched on the pretext of having them contribute to the war effort. Pope Urban II seems more concerned with the geographic incursions made by the Muslim Empire than the souls lost to Islam as a result. Robert of Flanders, commander of the Papal guard, is nobler, decreeing that pillage or violence against any but the enemy will be punishable by death. Godfrey of Bouillon, one of the knights leading the Crusade, is as noble as his counterpart Ibn Khaldun, who believes that Christians, Jews and Muslims are fundamentally the same, and hopes that peace may be forged between the disparate religions. Khaldun's new ally, Djarvat, seeks no such accord; he wishes to drive the infidels from the Holy Land as surely as the Crusaders wish to wipe worshippers of Allah from the face of the Earth with the rallying cry of "Convert or die!"

"It was always supposed to be a movie for Arnold," says Verhoeven, "so we were all very much aware what kind of movie we had to make. I knew it would have a certain grandeur, also perhaps a little bit of hyper-reality, but on the other hand we wanted to have the historical events be completely correct, and the political point of view — the evil side of the Crusades, which is undoubtedly there. We wanted to make clear that this was not a great endeavour; that it was all cheating by the

Pope, who basically lured all these fighting nobles from France so they could die somewhere else, instead of having trouble with them! That's what most historians think about Urban II. On the other hand, there was this idiotic thinking in Christian religion that Jerusalem should be in Christian hands, for some unclear reason. Even now people think the city should be part of Christianity — [a view] still subsidised by a lot of fundamentalists in the United States." Before the Crusades, he adds, there was no persecution based on religion in Jerusalem: "Arabs, Muslims, Orthodox Christians and Jewry were all accepted. There was just this evil thought of the Church that because Jesus had lived there, or spent a couple of weeks there, and got killed, that this belonged to Christianity — an even more absurd claim than saying that God promised it to the Jewish population. But as Gore Vidal pointed out, 'God is not a real estate dealer'."

Perhaps unsurprisingly coming as it does from the co-writer of *The Wild Bunch*, the script is as bloodthirsty as it is scatological. At one point, Hagen is bound, sewn into the rotting carcass of a donkey and set upon by hungry hyenas. He narrowly escapes the fate of a eunuch — namely, having his genitalia cleanly severed, the wound cauterised and compressed with a mixture of tar and fresh cow dung. An enemy is killed by having a trident thrown through his face. In a climactic scene, Emmich is severed in two by Hagen's sword, his legs and lower body remaining on his fleeing horse while his upper body falls to the ground. It's hardly PG-rated stuff. Blood and guts, carnage and chaos are seldom far from the screen, a tendency which might have phased lesser filmmakers, but not the taboo-breaking, envelope-pushing director of such ultra-violent films as *Robocop* and *Total Recall*, who later courted a different kind of controversy with *Basic Instinct* and *Showgirls*. "There are touches of lightness and romanticism and there are often funny scenes," Verhoeven says of *Crusade*, "but it's not a happy story. It's cruel and it's violent — my kind of ultra-violence that I've displayed in many movies — but there is also a lightness and tenderness, and I think with Arnold it would have worked for an audience. And the fact that it wasn't made had nothing to do with the disbelief of the producer or anyone else that this movie, with Arnold as a Crusader and an honest political touch, would not reach its audience — we all felt that we would."

Nevertheless, Verhoeven was not entirely satisfied with the early drafts, and *Total Recall* co-writer Gary Goldman was called in to rework it. "They came up with a draft or two, and for some reason Paul wasn't excited about it," says Goldman. "I think he more or less decided there was something wrong with it, or it wasn't good enough for him to be ready to make, so he kind of lost interest in it. He showed it to me at around that time and I remember thinking it was very good, and I told him so, and he thought I was an idiot for liking it." Nevertheless, Goldman found it easy defending his high regard for Green's efforts. "He wrote a very good screenplay," he says. "He has a wonderful feeling for period. It was well written, filled with wonderful ideas. It was a great story, and very cynical — a serious historical epic tailored to Arnold Schwarzenegger."

Moreover, Goldman believes it was a subversive script, hiding an intelligent film in the guise of an action movie, allowing Verhoeven to have his cake and eat it — a trick they had already pulled off with *Total Recall*. "We presented it in the way of *Total Recall*," Verhoeven confirms, "so you can be looking at this movie completely in a non-involved way, just Arnold and adventure: he gets caged, he nearly gets castrated, he finds a girl — this beautiful Arab princess — and he has to kill the bad guys, and then he decides that the best part of life would be to be on his farm with his Arab wife. You could see it on that level. But there were also these other levels: the anti-Semitism, the anti-Arab thinking, prejudices left and right. You could say the movie was also pro-Arab, or certainly not anti-Arab — there are bad Christians and good Christians, bad Arabs and good Arabs, but most of the Arabs seem to be okay, so it doesn't fit into this [attitude of] looking at Arabs as evil people. It wasn't the Arabs that persecuted the Jews, it was the Christians, with a couple of thousand years of anti-Semitic thinking. In the year 1000 this was common thinking. Even the Gospels, especially the Gospel of John, are permeated by anti-Semitic thinking. So I think we wanted to express that without hitting it hard."

"It was a picaresque tale about a roguish serf who gets caught stealing, and the only way to get out of being hanged is to fake a miracle," says Goldman. "He completely cynically endorses the Crusade, and shows the venality of all the European lords who were jockeying for power. It *was* anti-Crusades, but it was more an anti-war statement which basically said the Christians had no business going there. That's not how Hollywood would do it," he concludes, "but at Carolco we were free to do what we wanted." Adds Verhoeven, "If you see other movies about the Crusades, of course it looks great — Christianity is saving the world in Jerusalem, and there is this absolute claim of Christianity that that city should be their property or something. So for the last four hundred years they have desperately tried to get it, and [they believe] that if it's not to be in Christian hands, at least it has to be fully in Jewish hands."

Goldman's final rewrite, dated 24 January 1993, does not differ significantly from Green's. One of the more fundamental changes has Hagen and Emmich — a role for which Christopher McDonald (*Thelma & Louise*, *Requiem For a Dream*) was being eyed — re-imagined as half-brothers, with Emmich as the true heir of a Count, and Hagen as the illegitimate son of the same father (shades of Gloucester's sons in *King Lear*). Not only does this add a Cain and Abel sibling rivalry to the relationship, but the Abbot who catches Hagen stealing also uses it to his own advantage: because he knows Hagen is legally entitled to half the estate of Emmich's father, he agrees to sentence Hagen to death only if Emmich signs a quarter of *his* estate over to the Abbot. Goldman tones down the attack on the Jewish wedding party so that it is disrupted, not decimated, and Hagen saves the bride from being raped by Emmich and his men, rather than intervening too late. Leila is also given something of a makeover. Instead of agreeing to the arranged marriage with a Muslim noble (named Duqaq in Goldman's versions — though in reality 'Duqaq' is a rank, not a name — and with Djarvat demoted to a relatively minor presence), she rejects his proposal, forcing Duqaq to resort to nefarious means to ensnare the woman he loves. Furthermore, in Goldman's version, Ibn Khaldun promises his daughter that in marriage her will is to be her own, to which Djarvat responds, in true fundamentalist fashion, that no woman's will is her own, and further twists the situation to his advantage by suggesting that their faith faces desecration because of a woman's pride. Another key device in Goldman's revisions is that it is Hagen who attempts to broker the peace accord between the Christians and the Muslims, only to have Djarvat's soldiers attack — thus, it appears that Hagen led the Christians into a trap.

Goldman's greatest addition to the script is the spectacular 'Shadow Warrior' sequence, perhaps the most memorable scene in the entire 132-page enterprise. As Goldman envisaged it, in the middle of the climactic battle between the Crusader army and Djarvat's Muslim horde, the setting sun projects a gigantic image of Hagen on horseback onto a wall of smoke, throwing the Muslims into a panic and inspiring the Crusader army to victory. The effect is increased when Hagen throws a sword at a Saracen horseman, who keels over dead with the sword arcing straight up like a triumphant cross, surrounded by a mystical aureole of sunlight. From this point, the battle becomes a slaughter, with even Ibn Khaldun — who survives far longer in Goldman's drafts — falling to Emmich, who drives his men to attack even as the Saracens lower their colours and attempt to surrender. As the surviving Muslims retreat to relative safety within the walls of Jerusalem, the Crusaders lay siege to the city, killing Jews and Muslims with equal vehemence. At the end, Hagen and Leila walk off into the sunset, leaving Ari to ponder which of the three religious faiths he will adopt this week, and the Crusaders to wonder where the true cross is hidden.

Reviewing the same draft for Ain't It Cool, 'Damien Thorn' described it as "the greatest unproduced script of the decade... a brutal action epic laced with literate political dialogue and evil humour (what you'd expect for a slicing cavalier Paul Verhoeven flick), this is foremost a smashingly entertaining story that hurtles forward like all those severed limbs in *Starship Troopers*. Green is known for his ruthless sense of structure and here every scene is loaded with fascinating details that set up the following events with enormous payoff. The Arnold character Hagen is the ultimate part for him — iconic and shrouded in charismatic mystery that reveals a keen intelligence and the sort of presence you can believe would be at the center of an epic shite storm in the medieval Christian world." Thorn also pointed to a few problems — some "ordinary" action sequences, and a third act which was somewhat "perfunctory". He felt that the script might benefit from more political scenes, à la *Ben Hur* or *Spartacus*, and a punchier ending, but concluded that with its play on church politics, mass schizophrenia and sense of entire civilizations out to exterminate each other, it was a worthy and timely event film, "Verhoeven's answer to *Alexander Nevsky, Lawrence of Arabia*". It might not make back its production cost, and would certainly antagonise "every known special interest group on the planet," but was nevertheless the film that Schwarzenegger and Verhoeven "were born to make... [and] the kind of film Universal was fated to produce the moment cameras rolled on *Spartacus.*"

Another Ain't It Cool script reviewer thought the draft somewhat muddled. "*Crusade* doesn't want to take a religious stand, although it does seem to indicate at one point that Hagen has had a Christian vision," the anonymous reader opined. "The result is that we watch three religiously-motivated armies (Christian, Jewish, and Muslim) fight over Jerusalem and its Holy Shrine, and we don't really care about any of them. Truth be told, I found the character of Ari (Hagen's little con man sidekick) far more interesting and complex. It's all terribly violent, even for Verhoeven," the critic concluded, "but at least there's a creative escape from prison."

Working on his rewrite, Goldman took guidance from both Schwarzenegger and Verhoeven, noting that most of the perceived problems were in the script's third act. "We tweaked and tweaked and tweaked until we finally got it to the point where Paul was very happy with it, and they were ready to go ahead and make it," the writer explains. "Some of it was that after trying things and trying things, Paul started to realise how good the Walon draft really was, so he kept the changes that were improvements and got rid of the ones that weren't, pieced together the best parts of each draft, and we ended up with a draft that he was ready to make. I was very excited about it. Walon Green was also very happy with it. He thought the best parts of all his drafts had been chosen all along, which was Paul's doing. Your horror as a writer, or your fear, is that someone's going to ruin your work, but I've always been a very respectful rewriter, and Paul really is a creative rewriter-developer. He's not into starting over. So by the end we were all going ahead."

Carolco put the film into pre-production, with Schwarzenegger being joined by Robert Duvall as Adhémar of Le Puy, John Turturro (though some sources say his brother, Nicholas) as Ari, Christopher McDonald as Emmich and future Academy Award-winner Jennifer Connelly as Leila. "I tested a lot of women, with or without Arnold," says Verhoeven. "I only knew Jennifer from this Disney movie where she flies [*The Rocketeer*], but since then I have asked her several times for other movies — *Starship Troopers* and *Hollow Man* — but she felt they were not good enough, or not her kind of movie." With shooting scheduled to begin in the summer of 1994, however, Carolco began to feel the aftershocks of its production profligacy, with expensive misfires such as Richard Attenborough's *Chaplin* presaging a general downturn in the company's fortunes, despite the box office performance of such high-profile pictures as *Total Recall, Basic Instinct* and *Terminator 2: Judgment Day.*

"We couldn't quite figure out where the money went," says Goldman, "but it had gone by that time. [*Crusade*] was a giant movie, and the company didn't trust the numbers that were being thrown around. They felt that the movie was going to end up costing a lot more than Paul and [producer] Alan Marshall said — which is odd because Paul and Alan are probably the two least political film-makers on that level. Paul is ideologically honest — he takes pride in defining himself as a person who will give you the brutal truth, and you have to handle it. So he doesn't really lie about budgeting, which is a mistake because there's no way to get these movies made without lying, because people won't ever admit up front that they're willing to make the movie for that amount — you have to get them slightly pregnant, or they'll never have the guts to bite, because they'll be held accountable on these decisions." As Verhoeven, who holds a PhD in mathematics, admits, "I was too honest. I was stupid. I should have said that we could do it for a hundred million. We started out with seventy-five or eighty or something, but we didn't really get the budget lower than ninety-five or a hundred because it was too complex." As a result, Carolco began to lose confidence that it could be brought in on budget, and despite the millions of dollars spent getting to this point — including a 'pay or play' deal with Schwarzenegger, which meant that he was owed his full salary whether the movie was made or not — the film was scrapped at the eleventh hour. "We were already building [sets] in Spain," says Verhoeven. "We had to break it all off, and the whole pre-production cost of the not-made movie was about $10 million.

"Carolco went through a terrible time," Verhoeven continues. "They had two big movies [in development] at the same time, [Renny Harlin's pirate epic] *Cutthroat Island* and *Crusade*. Ultimately they realised that in the circumstances they were in financially, they could not do both, they could only do one. In my opinion they made the wrong choice because they thought Michael Douglas would be in *Cutthroat Island*, but he backed off, and instead of rotating around [to *Crusade*], they continued along that track, and got Matthew Modine." When *Cutthroat Island* flopped, Carolco went into bankruptcy, still owing Schwarzenegger his full salary for *Crusade*. "I think there was some anger over it," says Goldman. "In any case, they couldn't or didn't pay him, but they'd had a long relationship, and to pay someone twelve or fifteen million dollars for a film they don't make... well, it's a lot of money." Eventually, Schwarzenegger reached a decision with the producers that was mutually agreeable: the actor would take over all rights to the screenplay of *Crusade*, without any of the negative costs accrued against it, in return for forfeiting his payday.

Schwarzenegger was soon developing it through his company, Oak Productions, hoping that Verhoeven would remain on board as he tried to set it up at Sony-owned Columbia Pictures. The actor made *Last Action Hero* for Columbia, but rather than being the biggest hit of the year as expected, the film grossed just $50 million in the US — a fraction of the usual performance of an Arnie movie. Columbia passed on the chance of co-producing *Crusade*. Although *True Lies* recovered some of Schwarzenegger's box office clout, it was followed by a string of under-performers, including *Junior*, *Eraser* (written by Walon Green), *Batman & Robin* and *End of Days*, effectively arresting the rise of the Schwarzenegger machine. Meanwhile, Verhoeven was busy making one of the costliest flops in history, *Showgirls* (another nail in Carolco's coffin), followed by *Starship Troopers*, neither of which repeated the success of his earlier Hollywood films. As Goldman explains, "All of a sudden neither of them were that 'hot' — and it just isn't possible to make a movie of that size with people who aren't hot, because it wasn't an obviously commercial idea anyway."

Another factor working against the film was the fact that, at the time, the historical epic was a moribund genre; rather than reviving it, *Braveheart* (1995) was seen as the exception which proved the rule. Nevertheless, in February 1999, *Variety* announced that Schwarzenegger was in "serious talks" to revive *Crusade* with producer-financier Arnon Milchan – the man behind such hits as *Pretty Woman*, *Under*

*Siege*, *Falling Down*, *LA Confidential* and some fifty other films – under his company's deal with 20th Century Fox. "Long considered one of the best unproduced scripts of recent years," *Variety* noted, "the Walon Green-penned *Crusade* has a fascinating history that ended up with Schwarzenegger himself owning the project. Schwarzenegger long has been expected to play the hero, Hagen, a reluctant warrior who begins the film as a prisoner set to die... It's unclear who Schwarzenegger and Milchan would choose to direct," the report went on, "though Paul Verhoeven is interested, five years after he nearly directed Schwarzenegger when the film was to be financed by Carolco." A year later, during publicity duties for *The 6th Day*, Schwarzenegger confirmed that *Crusade* was still in active development, and that he hoped Verhoeven — then busy making *Hollow Man* — might shoot it sometime in 2001.

Then came the events of September 11: an attack by Islamic fundamentalists against a Judeo-Christian economic stronghold, to which the US government reacted by targeting two Islamic nations with spurious links to the attacks, Afghanistan and Iraq. As Verhoeven pointed out to *DVD Monthly*, "Even the *word* 'crusade', which was used by [George W.] Bush in the beginning... when he said 'This is a crusade against terrorism.' He had to take the word 'crusade' out of the speeches, because [the Arabs remembered it] and the slaughterhouse that the Crusades were. Of course," he adds, "Bush, not knowing what happened in the year 1100, thought the Crusades were something great, and that's why he used it at the beginning of his campaign. But somebody in the government, to my great astonishment, knew a little bit more and decided that it wasn't the greatest way to approach the Arab world." Nevertheless, in November 2001, the staunchly Republican Schwarzenegger told *Cinescape*'s Beth Laski that he was still pursuing the project: "We have to bring it up to date, which means rewriting and then finding the right studio, someone who believes in it. We're negotiating with Disney and Jerry Bruckheimer and we're very well on our way."

In some ways, it is both the best of times and the worst of times to make *Crusade*. On the one hand, with the world's largest Christian nation (America) waging war on some of the smaller Islamic countries (Afghanistan, Iraq), warnings of insensitivity may be valid. On the other hand, what better time for a film-maker to bring to an audience the idea that there is a millennium-old precedent for the current strife in the Middle East, and that then, as now, there are political and economical reasons behind the slaughter, rather than fundamental religious ones?

In a February 2002 story entitled 'Now Showing: The Flag' and subtitled 'Hollywood is Storming Out of its 9-11 Foxhole with a Barrage of Patriotic Flicks', *The Washington Post* reported that studio head-turned-independent producer Mike Medavoy — who produced Schwarzenegger's *The 6th Day* — had optioned the rights to *Warriors of God*, James Reston Jr's book about the Third Crusade, in which the principal characters are the Christian warrior-king Richard the Lion-Hearted and his noble Muslim nemesis, Saladin. "At its core, it harkens to what's going on today," Medavoy commented. Reading the book, he said, "it's like the light bulb goes off and you go, 'Wow, here's an interesting approach to what's going on in the world, but at a different time.' How similar things are. And it's about humanity, about how human beings can help each other." The same article noted that even *Crusade* might be revived as a direct result of the current climate. "In the end, you see the stupidity of the Crusades," said original *Crusade* screenwriter Walon Green. "The theme is about the danger and amorality of war anytime you attach a holy aspect to it." Thus, he added, "It's absolutely the right subject for now." Verhoeven agreed. "The story of the Crusades is the murderous attack of the Christians on the Arabs and the Jews," he said in early 2002. "Do you think that's a politically interesting situation?" Adds Goldman, "Ten years ago, the word 'crusade' was a dead word — it had no connotations. It was a historical period that had no relevance. Now the Crusades are incredibly relevant."

Certainly, 20th Century Fox seemed to think the Crusades were relevant. A month after *The Washington Post*'s story, Variety announced that director Ridley Scott — who had single-handedly revived the historical epic with the DreamWorks/Universal co-production *Gladiator* — would join forces with Fox on a film about the Crusades scripted by William Monahan (who wrote another historical epic, *Tripoli*, for Scott). "The Crusades, which began in the 11th century, will provide a highly visual canvas for a drama featuring armour-clad warriors who bore red crosses on their breastplates and battled with spears, swords and shields," the report stated. "It's a movie I've been thinking about for twenty years," Scott told *The San Bernadino County Sun*. "It's going to take place in the middle of the Crusades, around 1130, 1136, and feature Saladin, a Muslim, who was the wisest of all the knights, a trustworthy man of his word... I don't want the movie to be about knights in armour and chaps charging around with red crosses and waving swords and hacking off heads. It really should be a fundamental discussion between the two religions and not only that, but the actual misrepresentation of the Holy Roman Empire by the Catholic church, which was in those times seriously corrupt. When they got down there, the people the church regarded as infidels had a faith that was as strong, if not stronger, than the fundamental rules of Christianity." Speaking at a press conference for *Matchstick Men*, he added: "The subject has to be dealt with in such a delicate fashion. It's one giant misunderstanding." Although he admitted that the budget would be "high", very little of it would be spent above the line. "We are trying to get no star, we're trying to go that route," he explained.

The fact that Scott planned to begin shooting his Crusades film (entitled *Kingdom of Heaven* and produced by *Gladiator* producer Branko Lustig) in early 2004 seemed to be another reason why Arnold Schwarzenegger's *Crusade* might never reach the screen, despite widespread rumours that Arnie had managed to coax his old friend and collaborator James Cameron — with whom the actor made three of his biggest hits, namely *The Terminator*, *Terminator 2: Judgment Day* and *True Lies* — into helming the historical epic.

With *Terminator 3: Rise of the Machines* having put Schwarzenegger back on the box office map in 2003, and a slew of high-priced historical movies in production — including *Troy* (starring Brad Pitt), *Alexander* (starring Colin Farrell), *The Last Samurai* (starring Tom Cruise) and *Master and Commander* (starring Russell Crowe) — Schwarzenegger may yet see his decade-old dream come true (political aspirations notwithstanding).

"Arnold's never given up on the project," says Goldman. "I think he's a little old for the part — Hagen is a rogue, and you don't have fifty year-old rogues, you have young rogues — though it could be rewritten to fit an older Arnold." Would Verhoeven still be interested in directing it? "The answer is yes," he says emphatically. "I think it's a great script. I don't know if Arnold wants to do it, or if he still wants to do the same part. I've heard rumours that he might want to change the script a little bit, because of course he's older than that now. He might have to adapt it a little bit so he doesn't have to play a thirty year-old. But I think that it can be adapted, and I fully agree it's one of the greatest scripts ever written. But on the other hand the cost of a movie like that would ultimately be higher in my opinion than *Terminator 3*, which must be close to the $200 million mark."

Even with the digital multiplication used in films like *Gladiator*, Verhoeven doubts that the film is fiscally feasible. "Don't forget that *Gladiator* was a limited situation of gladiators in an arena," he points out, "and here you might need a couple of thousand people to shoot it and then multiply it by ten, so that you get the twenty thousand people that there were — at least to get the feeling for the audience, because it was an enormous army. Even with digital multiplication and digital people in the background, you are still looking at a couple of hundred horses that are very difficult to digitally paint, because they're too complex, so you have to shoot them. Even the digital shots would still be in the order of a hundred, hundred and fifty thousand dollars for a couple of seconds." Besides, he says, "I'm not so sure that anybody can shoot in the Arab world at the moment. It might be dangerous."

Equally problematic could be finding a way to tailor the story so that the parallels with the present political climate would not be drawn, as Goldman explains. "People would now naturally try to re-interpret the present time as another Crusade, which is how Muslims see it. So it would come across as an anti-Zionist piece. That would be very problematic now, unless it was rewritten to take that point of view out. But there's a slaughter at the end which really happened, and to make a movie now about Christians going into the Middle East and slaughtering Muslims..." In other words, Goldman concludes, "I don't expect that movie to get made for the foreseeable future."

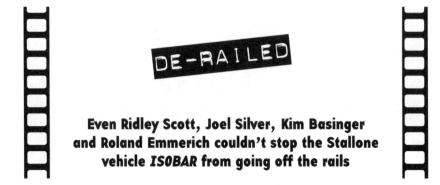

# DE-RAILED

**Even Ridley Scott, Joel Silver, Kim Basinger
and Roland Emmerich couldn't stop the Stallone
vehicle *ISOBAR* from going off the rails**

"We were... a week away from construction when they
cancelled the movie because Carolco got in such financial trouble.
And [that] was a shock to me, because everything that
I'd worked on always got made."
*— screenwriter Steven de Souza*

Sometime around 1987, emergent independent production
company Carolco Pictures purchased a script for a futuristic
science fiction/horror hybrid described as "*Alien* on a train".
The script, entitled *Dead Reckoning*, was written 'on spec' by future *Fight
Club* screenwriter Jim Uhls. "It was a sci-fi action thriller," he says, "set
in the future, in which an altered form of life gets loose on a high-speed
runaway underground train. The creature was a humanoid with a
genetically-altered brain that was intended to be used as the 'hard
drive' in an artificial intelligence project." The setting was near-future
Los Angeles, which Uhls describes as "a traffic-infested dystopia, with
wide shots of freeways and streets — even residential streets — completely jammed with non-moving, honking cars. And billboards that
admonished, 'Did you allow yourself three hours to get there?' There
was reference to a new law, just passed, outlawing horns on vehicles in
LA County. The super-subway was the only viable means of transportation. The script was bought by Carolco, with Joel Silver as producer,"
Uhls adds, referring to the producer of the *Lethal Weapon* and *Predator*
blockbuster series, and the first two *Die Hard* films.

At the time of its purchase, Carolco had yet to score big with the
science fiction milestones *RoboCop*, *Total Recall* and *Terminator 2:*

*Judgment Day*. Nevertheless, they saw *Dead Reckoning* as their answer to Ridley Scott's 1979 masterpiece *Alien*, and immediately set about wooing Scott as director. Scott had sworn off science fiction following the dismal critical reception and commercial performance of *Blade Runner* in 1982, but his most recent films — the fantasy flop *Legend* and the neo-noir thriller *Someone to Watch Over Me* — had nudged him from Hollywood's A-list, and he perhaps saw *Dead Reckoning* as a way to recapture his former glory. Says Uhls, "Ridley Scott came aboard as director, with the purpose of developing it with me. He started Norris Spencer [who would later work on Scott's *Black Rain*, *Thelma & Louise*, *1492: Conquest of Paradise* and *Hannibal*] on some production design."

No sooner had Scott coupled himself to the project than he contacted H. R. Giger, the Swiss artist with whom the director had collaborated on an aborted adaptation of Frank Herbert's epic science fiction novel *Dune* and, more successfully, *Alien* — for which Giger had won a special Academy Award. "Sometime in 1988, Ridley Scott telephoned me and asked me if I would like to make a science fiction movie with him," the artist wrote in his book *Giger's Film Designs*. "For me, there is nothing greater than this. I was enthusiastic about it and immediately accepted, because a remarkable movie always originates from a director like Ridley Scott." Scott seemed equally enthusiastic at the prospect of working with Giger again. "I have come close to working with Giger on a number of projects since we did *Alien*," he commented later, "and it is my strong hope that we can work together again in bringing something special to the screen."

At this early stage, Giger noted, there was no agreement between Scott and Carolco: "he told me to just think about the project and to capture my ideas in sketches. He would negotiate a contract with Carolco in the meantime." Giger set to work with his customary enthusiasm, without discussing the project further with Scott or signing a contract with Carolco, producing many colour and black-and-white sketches for the project, under the new working title *The Train*. "If somebody is telling me something I am always so enthusiastic that I don't wait until the contracts are done, otherwise I will lose interest," he explains. "I have to do it when I have the spark." Giger worked for almost nine months, between the summer of 1988 and the spring of

1989, working up numerous bizarre designs for trains, stations, passenger compartments — even a radical new kind of emergency exit in which passengers are ejected into a spontaneous ejaculation of soft foam.

During this time, Giger was frustrated by his inability to reach Scott by telephone, and unaware that the director had already moved on to direct *Thelma & Louise* for MGM. "Shortly thereafter he telephoned me late in the evening," Giger recalled, "and disclosed to me that he had already gotten out of the project, three weeks before, because he would have been given too little artistic freedom." Says Uhls, "Ridley Scott left the project, seemingly out of some disagreement with Joel Silver." Giger continued, "He promised me that he would still negotiate with 20th Century Fox," referring to the film's proposed distributors, "and that if he would be able to deal with them, he would of course take me on." As a result, he says, when the project derailed, "I never got engaged and I never got paid." Nevertheless, Giger was able to exploit some of his unused designs for *The Train* when he was engaged to work on designs for 'Sil', the beautiful but deadly alien at the centre of the science fiction horror movie *Species*. "I had an idea about Sil dreaming about a ghost train," he explains, "a train which comes and picks up people who are waiting in the station, [and who] she eats to get power. I worked on this train, and I put a lot of my own money into it," he adds. Giger went as far as building a three-dimensional model of the train, which he filmed in action in the back garden of his home just outside Zurich. In the event, *Species*' director Roger Donaldson did use the train as part of Sil's dream, giving science fiction fans their only chance to see what might have been if Scott had decided to board *The Train*.

Following the departure of Scott and Giger, Joel Silver set about reworking the script in earnest, beginning with the title page. Silver's preferred title was *Isobar*, defined in *The Oxford Modern English Dictionary* as "a line on a map connecting positions having the same atmospheric pressure at a given time, or on average over a given period." One problem was that *Isobar* happened to be the title of a script which another screenwriter, Jere Cunningham, had written for Silver and fellow producers Lawrence Gordon and John Davis around 1986-1987, described by Cunningham as the story of "a mutant professional fighter in a future world, on a quest to discover the truth of his origins."

According to the writer, Arnold Schwarzenegger was interested in playing the role, but his asking price — $5 million — was too rich for 20th Century Fox, and he signed to star in *Total Recall* instead. "A year or two later," Cunningham reveals, "Joel Silver called and said he wanted to use my title for another project because he loved the word 'isobar'. I said, 'Whatever, Joel, it's cool.'" Explains Uhls, "He wanted the name, so it had to be made to work." Uhls dutifully came up with an explanation for the title with an acronym — Intercontinental Subterranean Oscillo-magnetic Ballistic Aerodynamic Railway. "It was basically a magnetic levitation train underground that was a subway connecting the entire world," he explains, "travelling as fast as a commercial jet plane — in a vacuum." (The scientific principle was reasonably sound: a vacuum-propelled locomotive developed by Isambard Kingdom Brunel was in use for some time, until the amount of sealant required to constantly re-seal the vacuum tubes running along the centre rail began to reach impractical levels, and the whole system was scrapped.)

Rewriting continued from the title page onwards. "The new version of the script was set in a more distant future, with the surface of the earth uninhabitable," Uhls explains. "The creature was changed to be an evolutionary leap — a super-adaptive humanoid that was caught thriving outside, in the environment that's hostile to humans. It is put onto the train to be transported to a special lab. It breaks free, then must adapt faster and more dramatically to stay alive inside the train. It requires massive doses of adrenaline to do this, so it kills people to get it." Uhls says that he continued to work with Silver until German-born director Roland Emmerich came on board. Emmerich's interest in science fiction was evident from his résumé, which then included *Moon 44*, *Universal Soldier* and *Stargate* (he would later add *Independence Day*, *Godzilla* and *The Day After Tomorrow*). "Roland Emmerich began to work with me on changes," says Uhls. "Then, Joel set up a meeting with Roland, myself and Sylvester Stallone."

Stallone was interested in taking the main role: the leader of the group in charge of bringing the alien in. But first, he wanted extensive rewrites by his new favourite screenwriter, Steven de Souza, writer of *48HRS*, *The Running Man* and *Die Hard*, who had recently worked briefly with Stallone on another science fiction film, *Demolition Man*. "They wanted a total reinvention of the script," says de Souza. "The original script was one of these usual dystopic, post-apocalyptic futures, and the movie was a complete rip-off of *Aliens*. It was sort of like *Aliens* combined with *Alien*, with a squad of guys assigned to catch this monster and bring it in for study by 'The Company' — a shameless rip-off — but then they had to get the train to its final destination, which made no sense at all." After all, de Souza reasoned, if The Company wants to keep the existence of the monster secret, and has reason to believe that it may be dangerous, it would be more prudent to land the creature closer to its final destination. "Plus, if they're going to take it to some military facility where they're going to study it, wouldn't they have an airstrip there? So from page one it made no sense. The script was just embarrassing."

De Souza was equally nonplussed by the script's description of the monster itself, which he describes as "a guy in a suit kind of creature. It lived off adrenaline," he adds, "sucking adrenaline out of your body with these big nails, like a vampire. It reminded me way too much of a picture called *It! The Terror from Beyond Space*, which was itself a rip-off of A. E. van Vogt's short stories called 'Black Destroyer' and 'Discord in Scarlet', from *The Voyage of the Space Beagle*. When they made *Alien*, van Vogt showed up with a letter and they paid him off, because the things from those stories that were not in *It! The Terror from Beyond Space* were in *Alien* — you know, that the creature is indestructible because of the density of his body, that its blood is acid, that it catches people and puts eggs in them. So with [*ISOBAR*] you have a rip-off of a rip-off. It was too much like *Alien*, the monster wasn't fresh enough and there was no explanation of why the world was this way — it was one of these science fiction movies where it's supposed to be the near-future, but it's a completely implausible near-future without any kind of explanation."

De Souza had recently encountered a similar problem on *Demolition Man*, in which a cop, played by Sylvester Stallone, is frozen in the twentieth century, then thawed out years later, and finds the world a very different place. "I was going to do *Demolition Man* but I didn't do it — I was unavailable — although I did write one scene for Sly in the movie," he says. "I was telling him all along he had to [set the film] further in the future, or it's preposterous. It's supposed to be twenty-five years from now, and the girl says, 'What is a kiss in your world, Earthman?' And yet she has movie posters in her office, so they still have Blockbuster. I said, 'It's like if somebody says to me, "That's the cat's meow" and I go, "What does that mean, Earthman?" I mean, I can handle slang from the 1950s!'" De Souza says that the producers of *Demolition Man* refused to make the changes because of a subplot involving Stallone's character finding his grown-up daughter, "But by the time they cut the movie down and tightened it up, the whole subplot about finding his daughter was out of the movie, so he could have woken up in the year 2500AD. The reason he woke up twenty-five years later was so he could be reunited with his infant child, which got cut out of the movie entirely."

Stallone was by now firmly attached to *ISOBAR*. "At this time, Sly wanted to do something different to break the mould. I think he'd recently done *Stop! Or My Mom Will Shoot*," de Souza recalls, referring to Stallone's comedy flop. "He still wanted to stretch, but he was wobbling. So I said, 'The biggest problem you have here is Sly doesn't want to be 'sci-fi Rambo', and even if he's not sci-fi Rambo, you want to make him a scientist, which makes him culpable because he brought the thing onto a civilian train, and as soon as he let his superiors convince him that it's a good idea to bring a dangerous creature onto a civilian train, he's poisoned [as a hero].'" In other words, audiences are unlikely to respect a character who makes the wrong moral choices, unless the consequences are dealt with in the course of the film — as in the case of, say, *Dances With Wolves*. "So I said, 'If Sly's trying to do something different, and if everybody keeps saying he wants to do something like *Die Hard*, let him be just an ordinary guy on the train,'" De Souza continues. "I mean, [in *Die Hard*] Bruce Willis was a cop, but he was so over matched, he was like an ordinary guy — they didn't make him a Green Beret or Special Forces; he was just a cop and he had nine cartridges in his pistol, and that was it. So I said, 'Let's do something like that with Sly.' And they said, 'Well, what about a security guard?' and I said, 'No, let's just have him be a guy on the train.' I kept coming up against walls, because they said, 'That's not special enough.'" A compromise would be to make the train's passengers (and the audience) *assume* Stallone's character was a hero type: "Let's make the audience *think* he's something special, so people [on the train] go to him and say, 'Oh, you must be the hero because of your strange behaviour.' But he says, 'Well, actually, I'm...' — not that this would be it — 'researching a role for a movie,' or something, so that the audience is misled, and it turns out Sly is just an ordinary guy." It was Mario Kassar who finally found the solution, recalling a British Airways Concorde flight in which the passenger sitting next to him had made the cabin crew's journey as difficult as possible. "Mario said that this guy kept ringing the stewardess for all kinds of stuff, like he doesn't like his pillow — and then at the end of the flight, he called over the stewardess and said, 'I work for British Airways. That's why I was being difficult, and you were really great.' I said, 'That's great, Mario, let's make Sly that guy.' So once the Sly character identifies himself to the stewardess or the purser, and tells her why he's been such a pain in the ass, they sort of have to be in charge because they're at least minor company officials."

The next challenge de Souza faced in rewriting Uhls' script was to explain why, if this is the far future, trains are the preferred form of transport. De Souza's solution was to suggest that the ozone layer had become so damaged that jet-powered air travel was no longer viable — a theoretical possibility, since airliners are one of the largest contributors to ozone layer erosion. "You would still have prop planes," he says, "but they're so slow that the magnetic levitation train would be faster." Added to that, "people were wearing masks, cities were burrowing deeper, there were air alerts and large portions of the country had deadly pollution." Now that de Souza had made the trains ubiquitous, he decided that the one on which the monster gets loose should be a special one. "Let's make it the inaugural transatlantic train," he suggested. "Let's say they've built a bridge between Greenland and Iceland, and it's actually the first train from New York to London; the first transcontinental trip of a magnetic levitation train, so there's all kinds of hoopla." Suddenly, *ISOBAR* began to look less like a traditional Sylvester Stallone vehicle and more like an ensemble piece. "Now it becomes like *Murder on the Orient Express* or *Grand Hotel*, with all these wonderful characters," de Souza points out. Jim Uhls comments, "I never read his version. I heard that it changed everything to be more of a large-cast Irwin Allen-type of disaster movie."

One by one, cast members began to board the project. Future Academy Award-winner Kim Basinger, who had recently appeared as

Vicki Vale in *Batman*, was Stallone's leading lady. Character actor Michael Jeter (a supporting player in Stallone's *Tango & Cash*) signed on as a con artist who had tricked his way onto the train. A part was written specially for Italian screen legend Sophia Loren. James Belushi (*Red Heat*, *K-9*) was cast as a boorish entrepreneur who had made his fortune selling eggs and sperm over the equivalent of the Internet. "I could see this coming," says de Souza, of the inspiration behind Belushi's character. "He had a thing called 'Babies R Us' and he did his own commercial like a car salesman. You saw his ad in the movie, and it was like, 'Are your sperm slow swimmers? Have your eggs been out of the fridge too long? Call us now — only US, grade A choice farm girls provide our eggs.' It was comical, but it could be real." Naturally, de Souza says, the other first class passengers looked down on this *nouveau riche* figure. "He was like that character in *Dinner at Eight*, the rich guy who'd made his money in pork rinds. There was also a rich lady travelling with her granddaughter, who's being taken to an arranged marriage, and a poor boy who's like a nomad kid, a stowaway. So there was a teenage romance, an older romance between Sly and Kim Basinger, and a couple of great older characters, [one of whom was] like a Walter Matthau character — because we wanted to get Walter Matthau."

Perhaps the most important character of all, however, was the creature. Here, de Souza was inspired by the 1957 film *20 Million Miles to Earth*, in which the Ymir, an alien creature brought back from Venus, grows to enormous size and threatens the Italian city of Rome. "It starts out very harmless, so you actually feel sorry for it. And then because people are mean to it and a dog attacks it, it ends up becoming violent, and as it gets bigger and bigger it's a menace, and they kill it on the Colosseum. So we wanted to have some sympathy for this monster until it moults and changes a little bit." De Souza also suggested making the creature plant-based: "I said, 'Since we're stealing from the best, let's do Howard Hawks' *The Thing From Another World*,' and we decided that it was not a [flesh and blood] creature, but a plant. Because the whole ecology was screwed up, this company had tried to genetically engineer this hybrid plant that would clean up the air. They'd done all kinds of illegal gene-splicing, and they'd created this fast-growing hybrid plant that would manufacture oxygen at a tremendous rate. It was their industrial secret. But they were having problems with it — the previous ones had died, and they had to get this one to London because this time they'd figured out what was wrong. And the thing had this tremendous thirst for water, so once it broke out, it sucked all the water out of its victims, so they'd find somebody and they'd be like a mummy and they'd crumble to dust."

The creature was designed by multiple Academy Award-winner Rick Baker, whose credits ranged from *An American Werewolf in London* to *Gorillas in the Mist.* "I actually have a video tape of a monster test Rick Baker did," de Souza reveals. "He also made the first victim — a very real-looking guy, who had one arm that could move. And when the creature got bigger it had tentacles that wrapped round you and sucked all the water out. It really was amazing." Despite its influences, he says, "We made a really fresh monster. I liked the monster a lot."

One of the things de Souza wanted to do was to subvert the audience's expectations by having the creature kill a character they didn't expect — a trick as old as Alfred Hitchcock's *Psycho.* "We wrote a part for a guy like Clint Eastwood," he says, "a big star who would come into the movie and say 'I'm the hero, I'm in charge,' give everybody a big stirring speech — and then get killed. That happened in *Deep Blue Sea*," he adds, "where Samuel L. Jackson comes in and then gets killed." Up to this point, Stallone's character had reluctantly assumed the role of hero: "He says, 'Until we get to the next train station, when we can sort this out, we have to do things.' They've barricaded the back cars, and they know there's some kind of creature on the train that's killing people and they need help. So they go to the next stop, and this guy gets on the train — and we immediately kill him! It was pretty cool."

The tension is further ratcheted up by the failure of the communication system, meaning that no one on board the train is able to contact the outside world. "Of course, they don't know that the reason for the failure of the communication system is that the people who brought the thing on the train have sabotaged it, because they don't want the story getting out — they have to do damage control now," de Souza explains. "Their plan is to get the creature back under control, get off the train at some point on the line, and kill anybody who knows the truth." By now, however, the train is out of control, and everyone, good and bad, is forced to work together in order to save the day: "At this point they were probably all in the same cage — they need to keep the creature from coming into this car. So the bad guys and good guys are working together, but you know at a certain point their agendas will diverge."

De Souza's draft, which bore little resemblance to the one which Carolco had purchased, was the one which Roland Emmerich signed on to direct, at which point pre-production began in earnest. Production designer Dante Ferretti, a regular collaborator with Federico Fellini and, later, Martin Scorsese, began designing sets, while Academy Award-winning costume designer Marilyn Vance (*48HRS*, *Predator*, *Die Hard*) created "some very prescient costume designs [describing a] very retro future," de Souza says. So far advanced was the project that set construction was due to begin within a week, when Carolco collapsed under the strain of a string of flops, filing for Chapter 11 bankruptcy. Mario Kassar and Andy Vajna went their separate ways, with Vajna going on to form Cinergi, where he would draft in de Souza to rewrite another Sylvester Stallone vehicle, *Judge Dredd*. It was almost a decade before Kassar and Vajna reunited to form C-2 Productions, whose first film was *Terminator 3: Rise of the Machines*, a belated sequel to their biggest hit, *Terminator 2*.

Ironically, Carolco's bankruptcy almost gave *ISOBAR* a second chance, several years after the film and the company collapsed. At the bankruptcy hearing for the company, Kassar and Vajna, its two founders and former chiefs, showed up to bid for several of the properties their dissolved company had owned, despite the fact that Carolco's collapse had left millions of dollars worth of debts unpaid. "You'd think the judge would say, 'Wait a second — you guys ran the previous company,'" says de Souza, who was also in attendance. By now, de Souza was fast becoming one of the most successful screenwriters in Hollywood, with almost one billion dollars' worth of box office receipts from films bearing either his name, or his imprint. He attended the hearing hoping to buy back the *ISOBAR* script, which he felt was among his best work. "I think they showed maybe five or seven million dollars 'negative'," he recalls, referring to the cumulative amount of money Carolco had spent on the script, set designs, Rick Baker's creature tests and the director's customary 'pay or play' deal. Although the bailiffs initially set a price of fifty cents on the dollar, meaning that the project could be bought for half of the costs accrued against it, it was too rich for de Souza's blood. "There was no way I could go there," he says. However, by the time Carolco's corpse had been picked clean, the bailiffs were willing to take ten cents on the dollar for *ISOBAR*, and Jim Uhls believes that the script was acquired by Sony for Roland Emmerich.

At least one person appeared to believe that de Souza had made a successful bid for the project. Sylvester Stallone's career had suffered a slump in the decade following 1993's *Cliffhanger*. Although he had been lauded for his acting performance in *Cop Land*, the box office performances of films like *Judge Dredd*, *Get Carter*, *Driven* and *D-Tox* were indicative of a general downturn in his popularity. He needed a sure-fire comeback film like Schwarzenegger's *Terminator 3*, but he also wanted to stretch — just as he had when *Dead Reckoning/ISOBAR* was being tailored for him. "Sometime in late 2002 or early 2003 I went to a dinner party, and Sly was there, with his manager," de Souza recalls. "I started to think that the reason I was invited to this dinner party was because they thought I controlled the rights to the [*ISOBAR*] script. The conversation turned in a very clumsy fashion to [that project], you know: 'We should make that now. I'm ready to do that now.'"

Even if Stallone was able to buy the rights to the derailed project himself, or get another studio or independent production company interested in financing the film, de Souza feels that *ISOBAR* might enter another phase of Development Hell. "Movies get made not because the script is great," he points out, "but because somebody likes the script *at that point*. Today, somebody may say, 'No, the hero needs to be more heroic,' or 'The hero needs to be more superpowered, like *X-Men*,' or more like whatever else just opened that week." Today de Souza looks back on *ISOBAR* as "a great script" which should have been filmed, and the collapse of which surprised him more than most. "It was a shock to me, because everything that I'd worked on always got made," he says, marking himself out as one of a very small minority of writers in Hollywood. "It's a good thing I didn't buy that Rolls-Royce."

# WHO WANTS TO BE A BILLIONAIRE?

**Before Scorsese's *The Aviator* took off,
Brian De Palma, Milos Forman and
the aptly-named Hughes brothers had their own
pet Howard Hughes projects**

"I had lots of people calling me up to say it's one of the best
scripts they ever read, but of course they wouldn't
be making it. People say that to you all the time,
even about dreck, but this time I kind of believed them."
*— screenwriter David Koepp on his unproduced script* Mr Hughes

onsidering that the name Howard Hughes is as synonymous with Hollywood as it is with wealth, eccentricity and aviation — and crackpot schemes combining all three — it is surprising that more films have not been made about the famously reclusive billionaire. Not that Hollywood hasn't tried, however: in the decades between Jonathan Demme's *Melvin and Howard* and Martin Scorsese's *The Aviator*, at least half a dozen directors of equal prominence — many of them with a more commercial track record than Scorsese — saw their own diverse Howard Hughes projects wither on the vine. Nevertheless, the fact that so many tried, and failed, to bring to the screen their own vision, or version, of Hughes' multi-faceted life is testament to Hollywood's fascination with a man who, at one time, produced a plethora of films, bedded a string of starlets, and even ran a studio of his own. As *Variety* columnist, author and former studio head Peter Bart said recently, "Who else could have taken on the censors, the Mafia, the studio power elite and virtually every nubile star and starlet and still survive?" Well, almost.

Between his careers as aviator, inventor and corporate mogul, Howard Hughes somehow found time to foster such films as *Hell's Angels*, *Bringing Up Baby*, *The Philadelphia Story* and *The Outlaw*, with advertisements for the latter implying that star Jane Russell's ample bosom was "two great reasons" to see the film. It was later followed by a 3-D Russell vehicle, *The French Line*, which, the ads promised, would "knock both your eyes out!" But while Hughes was gaudy even by Hollywood standards, his heart seemed to be in the right place: when chief censor Will Hays, the driving force behind the Hays Code which hobbled Hollywood from the 1930s onwards, tried to alter the ending of *Scarface* and subtitle the film *The Shame of the Nation*, Hughes objected vociferously — though the changes were forced through in the end. Earlier, at the age of twenty-four, he orchestrated a lavish première for *Hell's Angels*, described by Charlie Chaplin as "the greatest night in show business." Fifteen thousand people jammed Hollywood Boulevard, resulting in the biggest traffic jam in the history of Los Angeles (no matter what the ads for *The Italian Job* remake might claim). Once, he let it be known that he was simultaneously negotiating to buy Fox, Paramount, Universal and Warner Bros, though in the end he settled for RKO Pictures, which — despite his apparent moral stance on censorship — he almost shut down when he discovered one alleged Communist among the staff. Along the way, he kept gossip columnists up at night with his frenzied pursuit of such starlets as Jean Harlow, Ava Gardner and Katharine Hepburn, despite biographers' claims of impotence, homosexuality, or both.

Away from Hollywood, Hughes' lifestyle was as eclectic as it was eccentric: having inherited the family business at the age of sixteen, he led the Hughes Tool Co from strength to strength, founded Trans World Airlines and the Hughes Aircraft Company, and amassed a personal fortune large enough to make him America's first billionaire — even though he blew millions on such crackpot inventions as the Spruce Goose, a gigantic seaplane. Despite his enormous wealth, success, popularity and matinée idol looks, following a near-fatal plane crash which left him dependent on painkillers, his last years were spent as a total recluse, living in a Las Vegas hotel in mortal fear of germs and nuclear fallout, growing his hair and fingernails long, wearing tissue boxes on his feet, and suffering a codeine dependence which made him alternately paranoid and incoherent. (By the time he died in 1976, one biography revealed, his arms were spotted with broken pieces of hypodermic needles embedded in his skin.)

Despite his association with Hollywood, there were no stars at his funeral, and his long estrangement from his family meant that few of his own flesh and blood were at the graveside either. *Mighty Joe Young* star Terry Moore, Hughes' legal widow, is one of the few who really knew him who remembers him fondly: "He had seen me in *The Return of October*, where I played an orphan girl," she says. "He was an orphan himself, and had a very close-knit family and grew up very naïve. He met me through doing *Mighty Joe Young* and we became friends. He taught me to fly, and I became the third woman in the world to fly a jet. Howard and I had so much in common in astrology: our sun and our moon and rising signs were exactly the same — a horoscope that only one couple in ten million have. And we had the same interests: we loved flying and motion pictures. He was the first love of my life — someone you don't forget — and raised me almost as much as my parents. I loved him then, I love him now and I will always love him."

Since the early 1970s, actor-producer-director Warren Beatty — who most physically resembles Hughes in his later years — had talked of making a Howard Hughes biography, which he planned to write with Bo Goldman (*One Flew Over the Cuckoo's Nest*) when a proposed collaboration with Paul Schrader (*Taxi Driver*) failed to coalesce. In the event, Goldman wrote his own script, *Melvin and Howard*, for which he won the Academy Award for Best Original Screenplay in 1981, with Jason Robards earning a Best Actor nomination for his take on Hughes. Although Hughes appeared as an incidental character in several films — played by Dean Stockwell in George Lucas' *Tucker: The Man and His Dream* and Terry O'Quinn in *The Rocketeer* — and was channelled by Treat Williams for his villainous turn in *The Phantom*, the first of the new wave of proposed Hughes biopics did not begin until the 1990s. The declassification of 2,500 FBI and CIA documents shed light on the last years of Las Vegas' most famous recluse, and sparked a new wave of biographies, including the critically-acclaimed bestseller *Howard Hughes: The Untold Story* by Pat Broeske and Peter Harry Brown, and Donald L. Barlett and James B. Steele's *Empire: The Life, Legend and Madness of Howard Hughes*.

Barlett and Steele's book became the first firm subject of a proposed film when, in March 1998, Johnny Depp signed on to star in an adaptation, to be directed by the aptly named Armenian-American film-makers Allen and Albert Hughes (*Dead Presidents*) from a screenplay by Terry Hayes (*Dead Calm*). Though the project ultimately went nowhere, Depp, Hayes and the Hughes brothers later collaborated on the Jack the Ripper saga *From Hell*.

In the meantime, Mutual Film Company had announced plans to produce its own film based on *The Hoax*, Clifford Irving's 1981 book about a fake Howard Hughes autobiography he sold to publisher McGraw-Hill, and the prison term he served when Hughes alerted the publisher to the fact that he hadn't written a word of it. (Irving, of course, claimed that Hughes had read the book and changed his mind about publishing it. He has since revised and released the book exclusively on the Internet.) "I was caught up in a rushing stream from which I could not free myself, even though it was self-destructive and crazy," Irving told 'Mr Showbiz', "because everyone else was just as crazy as I was in accepting the legitimacy of it. I couldn't get off the speeding bus." Appropriate, then, that one of the producers of *The Hoax* was Mark Gordon, producer of *Speed*.

Then, in August 1998, *Variety* announced that three key figures behind that summer's thriller *Snake Eyes* were collaborating on a unique and intriguing take on the Hughes legend: versatile actor Nicolas Cage, an Oscar-winner for *Leaving Las Vegas*, and star of the action thrillers *Face/Off*, *Con Air* and *The Rock*; director Brian De Palma, who had helmed a remake of the Hughes-produced *Scarface*; and screenwriter David Koepp, who had written De Palma's *Mission: Impossible* and *Carlito's Way* in addition to such blockbusters as the first two *Jurassic Park* films. As Koepp recalls, "I was working on *Snake Eyes* and Nic Cage mentioned to De Palma that he'd always been interested in playing Hughes. So Brian and I bought a bunch of books and started digging into it." Koepp had initially suspected that they had taken on an impossible mission: "The impossible part about telling anyone's life story is it never plays out in three acts; lives aren't inherently dramatic, structurally speaking. Aristotle would not approve of the way your average human life is laid out. But then Brian hit on the idea of telling the story of Howard Hughes from the point of view of

Clifford Irving, and that seemed to me to be genius, because Irving's hoax had a perfect dramatic structure for the spine of the film — conception (of the hoax idea and of Hughes as a young man), execution (of the hoax itself and Hughes as an adult running his empire and his love life), and collapse (hoax revealed and Hughes' descent into mental illness)."

"That's a vast project," De Palma told *Entertainment Tonight Online*, "because his life has so many aspects to it. To convey it into a compelling dramatic story is a great challenge." Nevertheless, Koepp says that this approach, "influenced by half a dozen books, not least by Irving's own boastings about his scheme, in various public record articles and books," gave him a unique advantage over the other Hughes projects, since he was not limited to the facts of Hughes' life, but Irving's portrait of him. "Since we were telling the story via his lying Boswell," he explains, referring to Dr Samuel Johnson's biographer, "we had access to the whole of his life. We encapsulated his childhood in a speech or two, then focused on three eras, which roughly paralleled the three chapters of the Irving story: conception, execution, collapse." There were many aspects of Hughes' life — or, at least, Irving's interpretation of it — that interested Koepp. Above all, though, "it was the fingernails. I just remember being a kid and watching the CBS news during the Irving hoax, and they had all those reporters crowded around a speaker box in Los Angeles interviewing Hughes over the phone line, and he was denying all the eccentricities of his lifestyle that Irving had posited, and it just had the opposite effect of what he intended — because you couldn't see him, your mind drew a truly insane portrait of the guy on the other end of the line."

One equally bizarre aspect of the De Palma/Koepp project, entitled *Mr Hughes*, was the fact that Nicolas Cage planned to play dual roles in the film: not only Hughes himself, but Irving as well. "That was Brian's idea, but I never agreed with it," Koepp admits. "I felt they were both such strong roles that we had a great chance to get two terrific actors. I also felt the stunt would be distracting, and didn't contribute much." Nevertheless, the conceit of having Oscar-winner and $20 million man Cage play the subject and architect of the fraudulent autobiography arguably gave the project an advantage over the Hughes brothers' proposed film, and Mutual Film Company's own take on *The Hoax*.

Nevertheless, says Koepp, "There have been Howard Hughes projects floating around for decades. We tried not to worry about them. We knew [ours] was probably doomed, but we figured since we had a director and a star we probably had a leg up."

Echoing the last years of Hughes himself, Koepp holed up in a hotel room in New York, writing the script in "a crazy burst in May and June 1998. The first draft was dated July 4th, which I liked," he recalls. "I was very happy with it. Brian loved it. I still think it's the best thing I've ever written. Off it went to the studio, which immediately put it in turnaround, and after that we were deader than a doornail." Unfortunately, in the interim, *Snake Eyes* had failed to match its box office and critical expectations — as Koepp puts it, "just not big enough — didn't lose money, but didn't make any either" — as a result of which no studio was willing to roll the dice on *Mr Hughes*, despite Disney having spent a reported $1.75 million on the script. "Nobody wanted Brian and Nic back on another movie, especially a (very) expensive biography. It was sad, I had lots of people calling me up to say it's one of the best scripts they ever read, but of course they wouldn't be making it. People say that to you all the time, even about dreck, but this time I kind of believed them. Foolishly, probably. I don't know, I loved it. Still do.

"I made a brief run at directing it myself for a much smaller budget than Brian felt he needed," Koepp adds. "[I] had dinner with Nic to talk about it and he seemed very enthusiastic, but then I never heard back. By that point he'd lost his nerve, I think." By that time, Cage had arguably satisfied his desire to play dual roles in a single film with his Oscar-nominated turn in Spike Jonze's *Adaptation*, in which, ironically, he plays screenwriting twins trying to crack an adaptation of an eccentric man's biography. Would Koepp, who has since directed Kevin Bacon in *Stir of Echoes* and an adaptation of Stephen King's novella *Secret Window, Secret Garden*, consider anyone else for the role of Howard Hughes? "Johnny Depp," he says. "Why is simple — he's one of our greatest actors. Fearless and inventive. I'm biased," he adds, referring to his collaboration with Depp on *Secret Window, Secret Garden*, "but I know I'm hardly alone in this opinion. Unfortunately, Nic [Cage] is also one of the producers [of *Mr Hughes*] and won't let the thing go, either. So it's stuck in limbo. Maybe someday I'll try to pry it out of his fingers."

In June 1999, *Variety* announced that director Michael Mann (*Heat*, *The Insider*) had set up a Howard Hughes project under his deal with Disney, with Leonardo DiCaprio on board to portray Hughes as the dashing, womanising aviator of the 1930s, from a script by *Gladiator* co-screenwriter John Logan, whose diverse output includes *RKO 281*, *The Time Machine*, *Star Trek: Nemesis* and *Any Given Sunday*. "Leo's been phenomenal to work with," Logan later enthused to BBCi Films. "He is such an intelligent and polite and responsive young artist. When I first met him, I didn't know what to expect. I thought, 'Is he just going to be a movie star?' But he was so polite and so completely committed and involved and going through it page by page, discussing and tweaking things, I couldn't be more impressed." Charles Higham, author of *Howard Hughes: The Secret Life* — which documented Hughes' alleged homosexual affair with Cary Grant, and his arrest for molesting a young man in Santa Monica — was among those to comment on DiCaprio's casting. "Hughes was childlike in many ways, pampered and spoiled, and he was very self-centered and self-absorbed," he told the *New York Post*. "There is something in DiCaprio's personality which is very singular and concentrated, and I think [he'd] do well at conveying a self-obsessed, self-concerned personality." Added Mann, "Leonardo has all of those qualities of the young Hughes — he's high flying, has lots of sexuality and is iconoclastic."

After the commercial failure of Mann's critically lauded *The Insider* and the lacklustre performance of *The Beach*, DiCaprio's first starring role in the wake of *Titanic*, Disney appeared to have second thoughts about what would inevitably be another big-budget production, and soon put the project in turnaround. While Mann went on to direct another biopic, this one starring Will Smith as Muhammad Ali, New Line picked up his still-untitled Howard Hughes film in February 2000, with studio president Michael De Luca describing the film as "Hughes' formative years while he was setting air-speed records and charging through Hollywood," and Mann as "the quintessential actor's director who has proven time and again that his gift for dramatic storytelling is rivalled by none." The fact that Logan's take on the Hughes story ended with the triumphant test flight of the Spruce Goose on 2 November 1947, long before the dashing womaniser became a reclusive paranoiac, suggested that it would be easier to secure financing for the film, since *Titanic* star DiCaprio would not be required to cover his matinée idol features with heavy make-up to play the older Hughes. Nevertheless, when De Luca left New Line — after backing the smash hit *Lord of the Rings* trilogy — the untitled project was put in turnaround again, although Mann and DiCaprio remained committed to it.

In March 2000, Alan Ladd Jr entered the fray with a project closely linked to actress Terry Moore (*neé* Helen Koford), who was married to Hughes between 1949 and 1956, and won the right to call herself Hughes' widow after a protracted legal battle. "I never got a divorce from Howard," she explains. "I left him because I thought he was cheating on me, and married Stewart Cramer." A staunch defender of Hughes and naturally antipathetic to many of the published biographies, Moore met Ladd through a mutual friend and urged him to tell her version of events in a film project to counterbalance productions focussing on the more bizarre, and possibly baseless, stories surrounding the troubled tycoon.

"Much of what has been written about him was just false," Ladd told *Variety*. "He never had those huge fingernails and toenails, that was just not true." Nevertheless, he added, "There are some wonderful anecdotes. He was deaf in one ear, which caused his shyness, and his mother had a major clean fetish. In fact, when he came over, he would have to wash his hands in lye — all kinds of awful stuff." More shocking were Moore's claims that her ex-husband's death was caused by a group of former employees who kept him isolated from the world. "He was kept a drugged, virtual prisoner," said Ladd. "It's just a horrible story." The basis of the film would be two books which Ladd had optioned, *The Passions of Howard Hughes* and *The Beauty and the Billionaire*, as well as Moore's 'life rights'. "What I want to tell is the story of his true genius," he stated. "I'm not interested in his sleeping with Rita Hayworth, Ava Gardner, Katharine Hepburn. This would approach the genius of a man, while exposing the myths and truths, not the sexploitations." Whether this was the version of events likely to appeal to Hollywood, however, was open to question. Although no actor was connected with the Ladd project, Moore herself reveals a number of candidates whom she would find suitable. "Jeremy Irons, Pierce Brosnan, Nicolas Cage would be very interesting," she says. "You could go with Tom Hanks — he's got the same kind of qualities that

Howard had: he's tall and lanky and has that kind of sweetness about him, and great charisma." Moore claims that licensed pilot John Travolta had bought one of Hughes' old aircraft to endear himself to her, and that Nicolas Cage took flying lessons in a bid to win the role. "So when you come down to it, there's really a lot of people."

There were more Hughes movie projects yet to emerge... It transpired that New Regency, which was once lined up to partner Disney in the Mann-DiCaprio production, had fomented plans to make a film of its own, pairing Edward Norton — who had won his breakthrough role in *Primal Fear* after DiCaprio backed out — with veteran director Milos Forman. The untitled film had been scripted by Scott Alexander and Larry Karaszewski, who had co-written two other biopics directed by Forman, *The People Vs. Larry Flynt* and *Man on the Moon*, which starred Jim Carrey as comedian Andy Kaufman. "Ten years ago, we would have said, 'How can you go up against Warren Beatty?' and now it's 'How can you go up against Michael Mann and Leonardo?'" Alexander told *Variety*. Karaszewski, meanwhile, admitted that fierce competition from fellow film-makers made the project a dicey prospect. "As writers, the problem is we'd have to spend the year working hard before finding out the project across the street had gotten a green light and we've wasted our time," he said. "With both Andy Kaufman and Larry Flynt, we knew we were the only ones."

Events took a turn for the weird in February 2001, when Inside.com reported that Charles Evans Jr, nephew of one-time studio head and film producer Robert Evans, was suing New Line Cinema, Michael Mann and Artists Management Group (AMG), claiming that the Howard Hughes project he had nurtured for years had been taken away from him. "No one has worked harder to bring the story of Howard Hughes to the screen in contemporary Hollywood than Evans," Pat Broeske, co-author of *Howard Hughes: The Untold Story*, asserted. "It is a passion of Charlie Evans." In his lawsuit, Evans claimed to have conceived the idea for a film about Hughes' tempestuous youth in 1993, and spent several years poring over the details of his life, before securing the rights to adapt *The Untold Story* for a film. Through his company Accapella Films, Evans hired actor Kevin Spacey to direct the film, securing financing from New Regency, which hired Jack Fincher to write a screenplay. Meanwhile, Evans learned that

DiCaprio was interested in playing Hughes, and entered into negotiations with DiCaprio's manager at AMG, Rick Yorn. "As a result of these discussions," the suit stated, "Yorn, acting on behalf of DiCaprio, informed Evans that DiCaprio would never join the project as long as any director (ie Spacey) not selected by DiCaprio, was attached." After what he described as "many sleepless nights", Evans picked DiCaprio over Spacey, and when DiCaprio settled on Michael Mann as his favoured director and made a studio production pact, Evans found himself cut out of the deal. The suit was eventually settled, with Evans winning the right to a credit as producer, along with Mann and his partner Sandy Climan, DiCaprio, and co-financer Graham King, president of Initial Entertainment Group (IEG).

Yet another Howard Hughes project emerged when *Variety* announced in September 2001 that William Friedkin (*The Exorcist, The French Connection*) would produce and direct a "feature film or telefilm or miniseries" based on *Hughes: The Private Diaries, Memos and Letters: The Definitive Biography of the First American Billionaire*, written by Richard Hack and based on archive material supplied by Hughes associate Robert Mahue (who would serve as a consultant on the film). "I've been fascinated by Hughes ever since I came to Hollywood in the sixties," said Friedkin, then preparing to direct Tommy Lee Jones (who had coincidentally portrayed the title character in the 1977 TV movie *The Amazing Howard Hughes*) in *The Hunted.* "He is a kind of King Lear — without the daughters. There are so many stories — his genius as a visionary, the weird Hollywood saga, how he transformed Vegas, how he revised the airline industry and, of course, the sex." Friedkin went on to reveal that he intended to begin the epic biopic — which he admitted could run to three hours — with Hughes as a sixteen year-old schoolboy who, upon his father's death, inherits the family business, the Hughes Tool Co. Asked about casting, Friedkin listed the usual suspects: Leonardo DiCaprio, Johnny Depp, Edward Norton — all of whom were already attached to, or hovering around, other Hughes projects. At the time, Friedkin was embroiled in a court battle over profits for Warner Bros' *The Exorcist*, and the fact that the rights to Hack's book had been purchased by Warner Bros subsidiary Castle Rock suggested that the film might find a home there.

Within a few months, however, Friedkin had ceded the director's chair to writer-director Christopher Nolan, who had followed his mind-bending *Memento* with a star-studded remake of Scandinavian thriller *Insomnia*. "It was the extreme nature of his story [that attracted me]," Nolan told *SF Chronicle*. "Here was someone who had everything and nothing at the same time." Speaking to christophernolan.com, he added, "It's about the extremes to which one man can live — the glamour, the wealth, then the claustrophobic unhappiness."

Nolan set to work on the script after *Insomnia* wrapped, with comic actor Jim Carrey, whose gift for mimicry was obvious from his portrayal of cracked genius Andy Kaufman in *Man on the Moon*, in mind for the title role. "It is the sort of great unmade Hollywood movie — and if you ask me why, I don't know and I don't want to find out," Nolan stated. "But I think casting is a large part of it, and I think Jim Carrey is just perfect for the role. He'll be able to pull off something I don't think many performers could." Speaking to *The Calgary Sun*, he added, "Jim was born to play Hughes. He has this amazing gift to channel real people. I'm convinced his Howard Hughes will be every bit as astonishing as his Andy Kaufman was in *Man on the Moon*." As Carrey himself told *Entertainment Weekly*, "In certain ways, I probably am him. I want to find out what personal chasm needed to be filled — his 'Rosebud'," he added, a reference to the obsessive subject of Orson Welles' *Citizen Kane*. "Hughes is like everyone else, trying to find that thing you're missing, but it's in the fire and you have to let it go, you don't go on and you don't grow up."

When Carrey became attached to the Christopher Nolan project, Michael Mann decided to step aside as director of the John Logan-scripted Howard Hughes film, to which Leonardo DiCaprio had remained attached since Mann had brought it to New Line from Disney two years earlier. Mann's decision allowed director Martin Scorsese — then busy directing DiCaprio in *Gangs of New York* — to take over as pilot of the Hughes project, newly titled *The Aviator*. As *Variety* reported it, "Mann apparently agreed to step aside as director because the Carrey-Nolan project looked ready to go, and he didn't want to hold up the DiCaprio pic; when their first choice, Scorsese, said yes, his decision was made easier." "I was never, like so many others, obsessed with Howard Hughes," Scorsese later told *Variety*, revealing that it was

DiCaprio who brought the script to his attention during the shooting of *Gangs*, "but by page three of the screenplay I knew this was a film I had to do."

By January 2002, the race between the various competing Hughes projects was hotting up, with *The Aviator* having emerged as the front-runner, thanks to a financing deal struck between Miramax, Warner Bros and IEG (which also co-financed *Ali* and *Gangs of New York*) to back the $100 million-plus picture, scheduled for release in late 2004. Nevertheless, the scope of Hughes' life, and the diverse ways in which his story might be approached is reflected in the fact that the star-heavy Scorsese movie — which boasts Cate Blanchett, Kate Beckinsale, Willem Dafoe, Ian Holm, Alec Baldwin, John C. Reilly, Alan Alda and even pop star Gwen Stefani (as Jean Harlow) among its supporting players — has not seemed to stall the Nolan-Carrey project covering Hughes' declining years. After all, as Nolan told *The Z Review*, "There's no sense of any kind of race simply because it's too difficult a subject. And I think that's why these projects have tended not to happen in the past, so I don't think there's any point in worrying about what other people are doing... Any time you go into making a film there are other factors around and you just have to believe in the project you are doing, that it will find it's way to get made." Even David Koepp, who has described his own project, *Mr Hughes*, as "deader than a doornail", suggests that there might still be room for his own film to be made, *The Aviator* notwithstanding. "Stranger things have happened," he points out, "many of which are documented in *Mr Hughes.*"

# PERCHANCE TO DREAM

**The title character of Neil Gaiman's critically acclaimed comic book *The Sandman* went to Hell. Unlike the film version, however, he made it back**

"The *Sandman* movie has nothing to do with me. It's in Development Hell and may it rot there forever."

*— Neil Gaiman*

In September 1987, DC Comics editor (and British liaison) Karen Berger called Neil Gaiman, one of the UK's most promising comic talents, and asked if he would be interested in writing a monthly title for the publisher. Berger had already been editor on Gaiman's *Black Orchid*, a lavish comic book miniseries illustrated by Gaiman's friend and collaborator Dave McKean; now she proposed reviving a long-forgotten DC character, 'the Sandman', and taking him in a radical new direction.

After a few false starts, Gaiman finally arrived at the premise and characters which would, over the course of the series' seventy-five-issue lifetime (not counting a few additional stories in prose and sequential form published outside of the ongoing monthly title), become familiar to millions of fans worldwide: the Sandman — also known as Morpheus, the Lord of Dreams, the Dream-King, or sometimes simply Dream — is the personification of the dream world where we spend a third of our lives; older and more powerful than the gods, he is also one of the seven 'Endless': the others being his brothers Destiny and Destruction, and sisters Death, Desire, Delirium and Despair. Early collaborators, including artists Sam Kieth and Mike Dringenberg, colourist Robbie Busch, letterer and logo designer Todd Klein and cover artist Dave McKean, helped shape the many and varied worlds of *The Sandman*, while many others — including Malcolm

Jones III, Chris Bachalo, Steve Parkhouse, Kelley Jones, Charles Vess, Jill Thompson, Vince Locke and Daniel Vozzo — would help to carry the series through its seven-year life cycle.

The first issue of *The Sandman* appeared in comic stores in December 1988, signalling the arrival not only of one of the most important, critically acclaimed and commercially successful titles of the era, but also, in Gaiman, of a significant new talent. (Gaiman was immediately bracketed with a group of British writers who would finally earn comic books — a medium barely a half century old, and still in its infancy as an art form — the right to be taken seriously in literary terms.) "Looking back, the process of coming up with the Lord of Dreams seems less like an act of creation than one of sculpture," Gaiman wrote in the afterword to the first collection of tales from *The Sandman*, entitled *Preludes & Nocturnes*. "[It was] as if he were already waiting, grave and patient, inside a block of white marble, and all I needed to do was chip away everything that wasn't him."

In its lifetime, *The Sandman* won a great many awards, not the least of which were the two most prestigious in comics: the Eisner Award and the Harvey. Issue nineteen, a self-contained story entitled 'A Midsummer Night's Dream' (and inspired by the play) won the 1991 World Fantasy Award for Best Short Story, making it the first ongoing comic ever to win a literary award. The title also won acclaim from a wide variety of other sources — Mikal Gilmore wrote in *Rolling Stone* that "to read *The Sandman* is to read something more than an imaginative comic: it is to read a powerful new literature fresh with the resonance of timeless myths" — and won such diverse fans as Clive Barker, Stephen King, Harlan Ellison, Norman Mailer and singer-songwriter Tori Amos (the lyrics of her song 'These Precious Things' refer to "me and Neil" and "the Dream-King").

With Tim Burton's *Batman* heralding a new wave of films based on comic books, and the takeover of DC Comics by Time Warner (the parent company of Warner Bros), there seemed to be little doubt that *The Sandman*'s own destiny lay on the big screen, despite Gaiman's heartfelt belief that, "To make it film-shaped [is] like taking a baby and cutting off both of its arms and one of its legs and nose and trying to cram it in this little box, and filling the rest of the box up with meat."

One of the first screenplay adaptations was undertaken by Ted

Elliott and Terry Rossio, whose previous credits included *The Mask of Zorro*. In May 1998, the website Coming Attractions quoted Rossio's summary of his and Elliott's involvement in the project over the previous few years: "After turning in a draft that we felt was pretty good, very true to the book (Neil Gaiman liked it — good enough for me), we were told the script was so bad, the studio considered it undeliverable." This meant that Warner Bros felt it was within its rights to refuse delivery of the script, withholding the delivery tranche of Elliott and Rossio's fee until they had reworked it to the studio's satisfaction — a response almost unheard of among A-list writers. "I probably should mention [that] between the time we took the assignment and turned it in, Jon Peters got himself attached as producer. Like a parasite. That makes the host sick, and kills it... As of this writing," he concluded, "our version of *Sandman* is dead, dead, dead..."

Elliott subsequently wrote a more detailed analysis of his and Rossio's involvement with the *Sandman* project for their own website, Word Play. "Since its inception, Terry and I had been fans of *The Sandman* comic book," said Elliott. "We had told our agent that if anyone ever became interested in an adaptation, we had better be the first writers they meet. And so we were... We met with Lorenzo Di Bonaventura, the exec on the project, and with the producers, Orin Coolis, Alan Riche and Tony Ludwig. They liked our approach, they commenced us, and so we went to work. We were happy. We were working on a dream project (literally); everyone seemed to want to adhere as closely as possible to the comics; we were certain that we could convey the mood, intelligence, sensibilities and brilliance of Neil's work. And then darkness fell...

"Producer Jon Peters got himself attached to the project. We took a meeting with him. We were unimpressed with his story sense (it took twenty minutes just to get across this idea: Sandman, the King of Dreams, is captured. Twenty minutes). But we didn't let it bother us; we knew we were on the right track, and the script would carry the day. We must all have our pleasant fictions... After we turned in our first draft, our agent received a call from an extremely junior-level exec, and was told that the script was so bad, [Warner Bros] considered it to be 'undeliverable'. They didn't want to pay us our completion money; they didn't want to pay off the rest of our contract; they even maintained that to do so would probably mean the project would be so prohibitively expensive it could never get made." (Elliott mentioned in passing that, the same day, Steven Spielberg had phoned to say how much he had enjoyed working with the pair on *Men in Black*, and how much he was enjoying their *Mask of Zorro* script, which would soon be fast-tracked for production.) As Elliott saw it, the principle problem with their first draft was that it had included Gaiman's single-issue story 'A Dream of a Thousand Cats' — in which an ordinary house cat learns that human subjugation of felines began when a thousand humans dreamed of such a world, and that the reverse could happen if enough cats dream of taking it back — as a means of having the Sandman explain the dangers of the villainous Corinthian's meddling with the dream realm. "While it was ambitious, it really didn't work," Elliott admitted, adding that he and Rossio knew it would be the first thing to go on any subsequent rewrite. (For the record, this notion of including a 'sacrificial lamb' in a screenplay is not uncommon, because screenwriters know that studio personnel who write 'coverage' of scripts for their executive bosses always like to have things they can single out which they feel don't work in a script, much as surveyors like to draw attention to minor flaws in a building to show they've done their jobs properly.)

Elliott — whose online publication of his and Rossio's screenplay, it might be noted, bravely (or foolishly) may have violated the terms of their contract — went on to speculate that the studio might have termed the script 'undeliverable' for a number of reasons: one, the studio wanted a free rewrite, which Elliott said they would have been happy to undertake; two, Peters Productions wanted Rossio and Elliott to leave the project because, in Elliott's words, "we didn't incorporate his single, off-the-cuff and incredibly lame suggestion that a bunch of teenagers at a slumber party holding a séance are the ones that capture Dream"; or both. "Things looked bad," he admitted. At least until writer-director Roger Avary (*Killing Zoe*) asked the studio to send him the script, read it, and loved it. Given that Avary had won an Oscar co-writing *Pulp Fiction* with Quentin Tarantino, Warner Bros wisely figured that he ought to know a good script when he read one. According to Elliott, "He went back to Warners and told them they were (in his words) 'throwing out a diamond', and insisted that this was the movie he wanted to make. Suddenly, not only was our script 'deliverable', it was also now on the fast-track with a director attached."

Avary subsequently confirmed this version of events on his own website, Avary.com. "[Elliott and Rossio] had been paid a king's ransom and had delivered what was widely considered, by the WB studio folks, to be a bad script. But I felt that while it wasn't a hundred per cent there, it was at least written by someone who loved Gaiman's work and had done him the honour of attempting to stay faithful to his original material. I eagerly told Lorenzo [Di Bonaventura, head of production] that I felt this script simply needed some tailoring and the application of a director's vision. I also told him that I would be delighted to work with the writers to execute another rewrite of this draft. I subsequently spent the next year overseeing Ted and Terry, and reworking the writing to accommodate my directorial vision. They had already distilled the entire series of comics down to 120 pages (a near impossible task) and they just needed some continued focus to score a goal."

Drawing largely from the first two *Sandman* storylines, *Preludes & Nocturnes* and *The Doll's House*, and with the meeting of The Endless borrowed from the fourth *Sandman* story arc, *Season of Mists*, the Elliott/Rossio/Avary draft opens in the 1930s as Roderick Burgess — the self-styled "wickedest man alive" — sets out to capture Death, but ensnares instead her younger brother, Dream. Years pass; Roderick grows old, leaving Dream in the care of his son, Alex. When Death comes to claim Roderick, she sees her brother for the first time in fifty years, but is powerless to help him. Finally, the circle is broken and Morpheus escapes. He returns to the dream realm to find his palace in ruins. His older brother, Destiny, summons Dream and his siblings Death, Delirium and Desire (forming a Hecateae-like triptych), who persuade Dream to restore his kingdom. To do this, he must retrieve his three powerful symbols of office: a pouch of sand, a helm and a ruby.

Retrieving the pouch is easy enough: it remains in the care of a woman named Rachel — here, ingeniously, a former girlfriend of Roderick Burgess (rather than fellow DC-owned character John Constantine, whose own feature film destiny lay elsewhere) — the mother of a young insomniac named Rose Walker. Next, the Sandman goes to Hell to retrieve his helm (almost exactly as in the comics, except that he meets Roderick there, suffering for his sins). Finally, he must collect his ruby, which is in the hands of the Corinthian, a nightmare personified, with teeth where his eyes should be, who has been terrorising the real world since escaping the dream realm two decades earlier, when a Vortex created a disturbance. The Vortex turns out to be Rose, who is herself half dream, because Rachel had, while in possession of the pouch of sand, conjured a father for her child. The Sandman knows he must kill Rose to protect the dream realm, but before he can do so, the Corinthian turns up with the ruby, which harbours enough of the Sandman's power to ensure the Corinthian's victory. He kidnaps Rose, taking her to a convention of serial killers with the intention of sacrificing her, but when he destroys the ruby, the Sandman's stored power is released, allowing him to destroy the Corinthian. The Sandman is still forced to kill Rose to protect the dream realm, but before Death claims her, he grants her a final dream, in which she sits by the Sandman's side as the Dream-King's queen.

'Widgett', a senior scooper and script commentator for Coming Attractions, described the script as "one of the best I've read in quite some time, due to its ability to adapt a very complicated storyline for the screen and yet not lose anything crucial in the process. Unbelievably, they managed to add things as well, and do so in a way that did not seem 'tacked on' or forced." Although one might question the validity of one such creation, a love interest for Rose (albeit a Platonic one) in the shape of a tormented artist named Paul, Widgett singled out another which spoke volumes about Rossio and Elliott's ability to capture Gaiman's style: "When Sandman looks in a mirror [after Rose's death] he catches a glimpse of Despair who promptly says, 'I don't want you in here.' They *are* additions," Widgett noted, "but done correctly so that if you haven't read the comic books lately, you think, 'Wait? Was that in the original?'" Similarly, Gaiman, when asked by the website Cold Print what he thought of the scripts he had read, said, "It's very hard to dislike them because there'll be these 110-page-long scripts and I wrote ninety-five of those pages in one form or another at one time or another. [Although] not necessarily in that order."

Following Rossio and Elliott's departure — they went on to write *Shrek* and *Pirates of the Caribbean* — Avary wrote his own draft of the *Sandman* script, which, he said, "kept the basic structure that they had created, but refined some of their more 'Hollywood-ish' ideas. Ted and Terry are incredibly gifted writers," he added, "but what the script really needed was a director's vision. I tinkered with almost every scene to reflect exactly what the film would look like." Aside from relocating the action to San Francisco, placing Alex Burgess in Madonna's former home in the Hollywood Hills, and making the Corinthian Rose's father, Avary's draft wisely removed Rose's love interest, Paul, but added a first person voiceover from Morpheus which fans may have found unappealing. Avary also throws in a dialogue line suggesting that the dominance of the dream realm had been sublimated in the Sandman's absence by "a thing called Hollywood [which] has grown to consume the dream hungry Earthworld. People now look to a box called television to fill the broken void."

"He made some interesting changes," Elliott said of Avary's version. "We don't agree with all of them, but it's a very viable, very solid draft." Nevertheless, in January 1997, it was widely reported that Avary had pulled out of the *Sandman* project due to what the website Coming Attractions described as "creative differences with the Peters Company — apparently they wanted a Sandman in tights and a cape punching out The Corinthian." Avary, writing on his own website, offered his own explanation: "I incorporated a concept that would ultimately result in my leaving the project over creative issues with Jon Peters." The concept was the rendering of several dream sequences in the rough film-making style of Czechoslovakian animator Jan Svankmajer, described in the script as "a strange nightmare that's a lucid cross between the visions of [*Sandman* cover artist] Dave McKean and Jan Svankmajer." Despite the fact that Avary had shown a "very enthusiastic" Lorenzo Di Bonaventura his references — Svankmajer's *Alice* and [Roman] Polanski's *Rosemary's Baby* — "everyone at the studio feigned ignorance when Jon Peters nixed my vision. It was like I had crawled out on this creative limb and when I looked around all of my supporters were gone and Jon-fucking-Peters was sawing the branch off."

Avary further noted that, as producer of *Batman*, Peters had famously fought with director Tim Burton against the darker tone Burton preferred, and which had not prevented the film from grossing a record-breaking $400 million worldwide. Peters, Avary suggested, "views *Sandman* as his next *Batman* meal ticket, and while *Sandman* has its dark elements, it's not *Batman* — at least not with me at the helm. With me, *Sandman* would have had its own distinct look and feel. But look and feel wasn't the worrisome issue with me, it was that Jon Peters wanted the Sandman in tights beating the life out of the Corinthian (on page 1). When I brought up the fact that the Sandman would never raise his fists like a brute and cold-cock someone, I was asked if I wanted to make the movie or not." Avary's response? Not. "So a year of my life vanished like dreams into the air (did I mention that I made nothing for my writing services? Multiple drafts, all for free. So much for idealism). I wish them all well and hope that they make the movie they want to make. Just don't look for me in line on opening day — I can't stand to see Neil's baby, who I consider my godchild, barbecued."

Following Avary's departure, a new writer was brought aboard to start over: William Farmer, whose sole produced script remains *Bullethead*, but who had impressed the *Sandman* producers with his (as yet unproduced) script adaptation of another comic book, *Jonah Hex*. Although a fan of *Jonah Hex*, Farmer admits he wasn't at all familiar with *The Sandman*. "I read the graphic novel called *Preludes & Nocturnes*, and some of the comics," he says. "I found them to be very imaginative but undisciplined, as comics often are. I don't mean that to be condescending. What I mean by that is, comics are generally free to take flights of fancy without the cumbersome weight of a three-act structure, since the story can presumably just go on and on and on. There's nothing wrong with that; it's what the medium calls for. But it's not a movie. I was working for Jon Peters' company," he adds, "though I only met the man in passing. I'm sure he had no idea what was going on with the story and didn't care. The producers were Alam Riche and Tony Ludwig, who went on to do *Mouse Hunt* and *Deep Blue Sea*. But they weren't really involved in the story development; they were basically just standing by listening to story conferences, trying to decide how much the thing was going to cost, where to shoot it — practical production concerns. The actual story executives I was working with on a day-to-day basis I won't name. They know who they are. They're parts in a machine, and I'm sure they've all gone on to take different slots in other machines by now.

"Basically, it was clear from the start that the goal of the project was to take the *Sandman* name and use it as a franchise, while making the actual story something more 'for the masses'. So I was essentially brought in to do a whole new story that would simply be called *Sandman*." Farmer read the most recent draft, by Roger Avary, which he found "interesting, but in the studio's opinion — and I must admit, in mine as well — absolutely unfilmable. [A] very twisted and surreal kind of thing you might have been able to do in the 70s, not the 90s. No studio would have touched that version. I had some ideas that were very loyal to the source material," he explains, "yet would tweak things here and there to make it more of an audience picture. But there were things the producers wanted done with it that took it in a different direction, and as I was a fledgling screenwriter, I figured you take the suggestions of the ones writing the cheques. Big mistake, for the project as well as the writer. Things were forced into it that really didn't belong there. The producers were adamant that the coming Millennium must play a big role. Every film in development at that time had some damn thing to do with the Millennium. Of course this was folly, as the Millennium turned out to be no big deal, in the real world *or* in film — nobody really gave a shit. So it was a case of trying to bring my 'vision' to the project, but the range of that vision was squeezed into an increasingly narrow field by things the producers insisted must be in there. For example, one executive producer insisted, for reasons I'll never understand, that there be a scene of Morpheus in a rave club. Don't ask me why. There was no place for it and I can say with a tiny amount of pride that I at least refused to write *that* one."

At one point, Farmer recalls positing the idea of meeting with Neil Gaiman to discuss things. "The reply was basically, 'Nah, we don't need to get him involved.'" (Besides, as Gaiman told Ain't It Cool News in 1998, "Where *The Sandman* movie is concerned, I'd rather not get involved. No one should be made to barbecue their own baby.") Farmer says that he wrote several drafts between 1997 and 1998. "When all was said and done, and we had the definite draft of my involvement, they were ecstatic. They were talking about a big franchise, this thing would be huge, blah blah blah... Of course everyone knew the source material had been massacred, but nobody really cared. It wasn't about that, it was about a product name." While Farmer's approach found favour with the producers and the studio, *Sandman* fans felt their worst nightmares were coming true when a review of his script appeared on Ain't

It Cool News, written by 'Moriarty'. "Mistake number one: the whole thing is tied to the Millennium," he wrote. "That's rapidly becoming one of the most heinous, preposterous clichés in film. Stop it. By the time you get this thing finished and in theaters, even if you started right now, the year 1999 will essentially be over... The best quality of Gaiman's work is its timelessness. Don't make the mistake of grafting some momentary gimmick onto what's already so good. Mistake number two: did you actually read any issues of the book, Mr Farmer, or were you doing the evil bidding of Jon Peters himself? And if the answer is the latter, then tell me, does Mr Peters in fact have horns and cloven hooves? The soft skull's a given, but I'm trying to figure out if he has any real malice in his heart. After all, he's currently working overtime to destroy one of America's finest icons, Superman, and now he's actively mauling one of the few examples of true graphic literature. This is one of those cases where changes are made for the sake of making changes, as a matter of ego, and not for any sort of sound dramatic reasons."

Moriarty went on to summarise Farmer's story outline: "Rose Kendall is the daughter of wealthy industrialist and all around Really Famous Wacko Harlan Kendall. When she was very young, her father used her in some nutty experiment in which he killed her, opened the Dream Gate, captured Dream, then brought her back to life. In doing so, he also managed to take the ruby, the bag of sand, and the helmet. So far — well, it's at least vaguely recognizable. The Kendalls are new, but at least we've got Morpheus imprisoned and the icons of his office being scattered. Rose is afflicted with lifelong nightmares in which the man from her dreams asks to be released. Finally, just a few days before the Millennium, Rose is attacked by someone yelling about the Nightmare Man. She's taken to a hospital where she has an encounter with someone vaguely like Gaiman's Death (although with far more 'zany' wisecracks) and an 'Angel' appears, coming through from another world when Rose dies briefly on the table. Nice how she keeps doing that, eh? He takes away her nightmares and disappears. Back at the building her father built, there's some sort of construction going on and the secret magic chamber where Kendall stuck Morpheus is found and blown up, releasing Morpheus. And here's where things really go wrong, since the character that is released is a fairly indiscriminate killer with no real power of any kind. He beats some people up, jumps off something, gets hurt, and gets taken to the hospital. Morpheus. Lord of Dreams. Gets taken to a hospital after yelling tripe like, 'As though your puny weapons could harm Morpheus! The lord of sleep! The Sandman!'" (Farmer subsequently contacted the website Comics 2 Film to deny the claim: "The horrible line... has NEVER been typed by the fingers of yours truly," and declare that "this was not at all the tone of my script for Warners.")

"Well, of course the hospital that Morpheus is brought to just happens to be the same one Rose is in," Moriarty continued, "and suddenly we're in lame *Terminator 2* rip-off country, with Morpheus going to look for Rose, and the Angel appearing again to save her. The twist here is that Morpheus is trying to kill Rose to save the world, while the Angel is actually The Corinthian, Morpheus' brother, who has bet Lucifer, their other brother, that he can find the icons of Dream's office first. Whoever gets them before the year 2000 wins. If neither does, then Lucifer takes over the earth for torture, misery, sorrow, yadda, yadda, yadda. Really. That's really the story. And the rest of the film's just a dumb action film with these two fighting over and over, and with them beating up people to get the various items. The ruby's in a safe in a pawn shop. The sand's in the study of Rose's house. And the helmet? Well... giggle, giggle... dare I say it? It's hidden inside Rose!"

Perhaps understandably, Moriarty took umbrage at what he saw as the wholesale reinterpretation — or, at best, misunderstanding — of Gaiman's *magnum opus*. The Corinthian and Lucifer as Morpheus' brothers? A character called Love as his sister? And an ending in which it was all just a dream? "Gaiman never, never cheated us like that. Even if something happened in a dream, it mattered. It counted. That's the whole point. Our dream lives and our waking lives are one and the same. One affects the other. Gaiman made the point over and over, and Farmer has ignored it utterly." Although Farmer had created a 'nightmare plague' loosely based on the '24 Hours' issue of *Preludes & Nocturnes*, Moriarty dismissed the idea as "nothing but a bunch of pointless atrocities without moral heft or payoff." Overall, he added, "[Farmer] misses everything that makes the original work so unique, so special, so brilliant."

Gaiman agreed, describing Farmer's script as "the worst one yet. It was just sort of nonsensical, poorly written trash," he told the *Philadelphia City Paper.* "These are not people who particularly care about *Sandman,*" he added. "They want it to be the new *Batman and Robin,* which is a little like deciding you want to make *David Copperfield* the new *Batman and Robin.*" To Andy Mangels, Gaiman claimed that the script was "not only the worst *Sandman* script so far, but quite easily the worst script I've ever read. That was sad, especially when it's something like *Sandman* which you love and you've been close to all these years and then you read this nonsense." Farmer responded by contacting the website Coming Attractions with an appeal to *Sandman* fans: "If any of you are waiting for Mr Gaiman's esoteric 'opus' to arrive on screen intact, forget it," he wrote. "A hardcore gaggle of fans would no doubt attend, but hardly enough to support the $100 mil budget that would doubtless be required. The best that can be hoped for is a reworking of the source material which retains the concepts, but makes them more accessible to a mainstream audience. I feel that my script was success-ful in this endeavour; it's unfortunate Mr Gaiman doesn't agree." Suggesting that Gaiman was unlikely to be satisfied with *any* screenplay which the studio might consider produceable, he added: "I did my best, only to join five or six others in the growing ranks of the 'Screenwriters of *Sandman*' club. It'll be interesting to see whether or not this troubled project ever gets off the ground. And just to set the record straight," he concluded, "my version of *Sandman* didn't have one fistfight in it."

Farmer now says that he has "mixed feelings" about the Internet trashing of his script: "I couldn't blame *Sandman* fans for being upset; of course this was how they would react. But the personal nature of the attacks was a little un-called for, in my opinion. Gaiman used the word 'idiot' in one interview I read, and said that the script was not only the worst *Sandman* [script], but the worst screenplay of any kind he had ever read. I can of course understand the former statement, but the lat-ter was a little harsh. Taken on its own, the script was intelligent and well written, if I do say so myself. Of course it mangled *Sandman;* I would never argue that." Farmer says that he would probably have been hurt more by the attacks if he had believed in the script himself; as it was, "I never really considered it 'my script'. It was a big monster written by committee, and I just happened to be the schmuck being paid to make the whole thing read like a script and sign my name to it. So while I did not exactly like being called names, I couldn't very well get on the Internet and say, 'Hey, you guys are wrong! This thing is great and we didn't mangle *Sandman!*' Because of course, we did. The only time I countered anything was when I read an angry review of the script on a popular film-gossip site that I won't honour by naming. The reviewer ranted on and on about how stupid it was, and how stupid I was for having created it. Then, to demonstrate how bad it was, he included the first page. And guess what? I had never seen that page before. It was obviously a script written by a fan-boy or something, that had been circulated on the Internet as the 'official' Warner Bros script. So I tried to set the record straight, but by the time I stumbled across this site the controversy had already died down, anyway."

Following the Internet backlash, little was heard from the producers. "I think right now they're licking their wounds," Gaiman told Andy Mangels. "They got laughed at rather more heartily than they expected for their last idiot script." As Farmer recalls, "A few weeks went by with the buzz that it was about to go into pre-production, then I got a call saying they were going to look for another writer, with no explanation why. Later I realized it was probably due to the Internet reaction — which is a silly attitude if you think about it. They're perfectly willing to destroy the source material and piss off the fans, but if the fans find out about it *ahead* of time, they pull the plug. There was also some talk about an option on the DC source material coming up, so the idea was in the air that Gaiman had pulled it somehow. But I never found out if that was indeed the case." (Gaiman, for the record, denied this possibility. "Warners own Sandman outright; always have done," he told Ain't It Cool News. "DC Comics owned all rights back in the days when I signed the original contract with them. Obviously Roger [Avary] couldn't have taken the rights away to shop around. Nor could I.")

For Farmer, in addition to earning him a great deal of money and — for a time, at least — kudos from the producers who had hired him *and* the studio which paid him, his involvement with the *Sandman* project also taught him a valuable lesson. "If someone hires you to write something, then presumably they think you can write better than they can; otherwise they'd just do it themselves," he points out. "So, rather than do what you're told, you're far better off doing what you believe is best. Had I done that with *Sandman*, I might still have created a version that didn't get produced, but at least I would have kept my personal dignity intact. Because at the end of the day, the only one who'll get the blame for the script is the writer. *Sandman* was a project that no studio should have tried to do," he adds. "It was doomed to fail. Now, after all is said and done, everyone involved in that failure can simply say, 'It was Farmer's fault.' In hindsight, it's clear that this was the sole purpose for which I was hired." In other words, he says, "Live and learn."

Following the Farmer *débâcle*, two years passed before anything of substance emerged regarding the *Sandman* project, although for a time the Internet was rife with casting speculation, mostly from fans. "They always have ideas for casting," Gaiman told the website Cold Print. "It's one of the immutable laws of the universe now — if you get two *Sandman* fans together in an enclosed space for more than fifteen minutes, one starts saying, 'So, if you were doing a Sandman movie, who would you have play him?' and the other would say, 'Oh, Daniel Day-Lewis.' And the first one says, 'Well, I don't know,' and they go off from there. The world is currently split into those factions who believe Winona Ryder should play Death," he added, "and those who believe that Natalie Portman should play Death." Gaiman had already written to Ain't It Cool News dismissing as "silliness" the rumours that *Stand by Me* star Wil Wheaton (*Star Trek: The Next Generation*'s Wesley Crusher) had been cast as Morpheus, and noted that when he had last been consulted on the project — during the period of Roger Avary's attachment — he did not recall the director having named a favourite actor for the role, "although he mentioned a number of people, including Daniel Day-Lewis, David Thewlis and Rufus Sewell as people he'd be interested in. All English actors." As ever, Gaiman refused to be drawn on his own dream casting, preferring to speculate instead about his own proposed directorial début, an adaptation of his *Sandman* spin-off comic book miniseries *Death: The High Cost of Living*. (Suffice to say that the names Winona Ryder and Natalie Portman came up again.) Nevertheless, in November 1998, actress Fairuza Balk (*Things to do in Denver When You're Dead*, *The Craft*, *The Island of Dr Moreau*) revealed on her official website, www.fairuzasfansite.com, that she had "been in contact with Neil Gaiman who wrote and created *The Sandman* comics... I'm a huge fan of them, but he asked me if I would play Death and I replied that I would be very honoured, so who knows?" In July

1999, she added: "In regards to the Neil Gaiman *Death* movie, it's on the backburner for now but hopefully will happen someday."

As for the *Sandman* movie, it was not until June 2000 that a new screenwriter became attached, but it was somebody who seemed like a good fit for the project. David J. Schow was one of the revolutionary horror writers who had emerged around the same time as Clive Barker; along with John Skipp, Craig Spector, Ray Garton and others, Schow was part of the 'splatterpunk' movement which tore away the last taboos in horror, writing the kind of works that made James Herbert look like Barbara Cartland. When he turned to screenwriting in the early 1990s, one of his first assignments was adapting J. M. O'Barr's tragic comic book *The Crow* for director Alex Proyas. It was Schow's draft which got the film a green light, and if it worked for *The Crow*, it might work for *The Sandman* — the two tales, it might be said, had more than superficial similarities. Says Schow, "I was approached by Brian Manis of Peters Entertainment in June of 2000. He had several script drafts and a whole raft of treatments, all in pursuit of what the studio wanted, which was 'a more commercial approach' [to the material]. What that means, who can really say? I immediately contacted Neil Gaiman to get his pre-approval, or at least his sanction, for any damage I might wreak on his creation, and Neil basically said, 'You're free to try anything you want.' He insisted that I read the Avary-Elliott-Rossio draft and made sure I received 'the whole of *The Sandman*' — ten books. That was my first exposure to the material."

Schow received no notes from the producers prior to commencing work on his 'pitch'. "I was left pretty much to free-range," he says. "In retrospect, [I realise] this was because they had a number of writers working on a number of approaches simultaneously, which isn't uncommon." As well as getting up to speed on ten volumes of *The Sandman* comics, Schow undertook what he calls a "breakdown read" of an undated draft of an earlier *Sandman* script credited solely to Elliott and Rossio. The draft was not bad, he felt, "just diffuse — it tried to cram in too many characters and incidents from the source book. It seemed arcane, mannered, and discursive, with no actual characters until about halfway in." In addition, he felt that the script suffered from a problem endemic to comic book adaptations: a pressing desire to tell the 'origin' story. "Ever since *Superman* and *Batman* established the 'template' for [comic book] adaptations," he observes, "studios have become obsessed with 'origin' stories they hope to parlay into series franchises. Well, in most endeavours, the origin buries the story. Story becomes secondary and, *voilà*, no franchise. This has happened more times than I can count. So if *The Sandman* was to follow the origin-story route, I felt the origin had to be secondary, or better yet, left for another movie. If the first movie is confusing, or no good, there won't be a franchise. I think the emphasis on the Sandman's origin is what jumped the script off the rails in the first place."

Schow's approach was to tell a more focused story. "Face it, the source material ran to nearly a thousand pages," he says. "So I reduced the players, basically, to four: Sandman, Death, Corinthian, and a normal human character I invented, named Grace, who suffers from every sleep disorder known to science. Grace's mother was essentially Rachel from the comic, and her link to Sandman. She's also blood-linked to Corinthian, hence, all kinds of conflict. Once Grace and Sandman are paired up, we experience the horrible *wrongness* of Corinthian, we quest for the recovery of the Sandman's power objects, we visit Hell, we meet The Endless, and Sandman battles Corinthian in the dream realm, then the fight slops over into the real world." For Schow, equally important to doing justice to the story, and Gaiman's writing, was to capture the tone of the comic book. "The triumph of the comic is its melancholy tone, its atmospherics, its emotional resonance," he explains, "not the chapter-and-verse on who came from where. I wrote for this tone. Corinthian is turning all the world's dreams into nightmares, and needs to drive Grace to suicide to accomplish his programme. Sandman must regain his lost tools and reinstate himself as one of The Endless. He's even forced to sleep like a normal human, in order to gain access to the dream realm, and this moment of frailty, of course, undoes him. Grace has to find Sandman in the dream realm, basically, without a map. But the rules of The Endless have only caused Sandman suffering and grief. Grace tells him, 'Don't save the world. Save me.' And, wham — third act. It was very bleak, but uplifting in the way of a single candle flame in darkness. I could tell you more," he adds with glee, "but you would be driven totally insane."

Schow worked on his treatment for a month, between June and July 2000. "I didn't write a script," he says. "I wrote two fleshed-out and fair-

ly detailed treatments. Then, game over. And I was never paid a dime."
After that, he says, "It descended back into the dream realm-type limbo
where it remains to this day, because there is no Sandman — at least,
not one powerful enough to rescue all of us from studio executives."
Despite the lack of a screenplay commission, Schow looks back fondly
on his month in the dream realm. "I loved twisting and turning Neil's
clay," he says, "and still think it would make a great movie. And I hope
Neil does, too."

Gaiman, as ever, is not so sure. "I couldn't quite see why they got
him to do what they did, having seen his outline," he says. "The powers that be had already thrown out the Jon Peters/William Farmer script
and plot approach and decided (at the time) to go back to the Avary
draft, so I suspected that Dave Schow was just an attempt by the Jon
Peters people to prove that their approach really would work."

A year after Schow's brief sojourn with the project, the website
Universo HQ quoted Gaiman as saying that he had received another
outline "for another [version of the] movie a lot like the really bad one.
It's always the same. They want a love interest now, for the Sandman.
They want the Corinthian to be the big bad guy. He's like the Sandman
only more powerful. And they want them to fight, and for the
Corinthian to menace to kidnap his girlfriend. It's just stupid." Little
has been heard of the stalled *Sandman* project since what Gaiman has
described as "the strange, sad, Development Hell morass that Jon
Peters has thrown it into... With any luck it will remain there forever. I
would much rather that a Sandman movie were never made, than that
a bad Sandman movie was."

There is hope, however. Even as the dream project died,
Gaiman's proposed adaptation of *Death: The High Cost of Living* began
to show signs of life. Pandora Films — which, since its acquisition by
Warner Bros and subsequent transfer from the Left Bank of Paris to
Burbank, California, has produced such diverse films as *Welcome to
Collinwood*, *White Oleander* and *Cypher* — approved not only Gaiman's
screenplay, but also his choice of director: himself. Gaiman then
moved one step closer to realising his ambitions as a feature director in the summer of 2002, when he directed a short film inspired by
the work of artist John Bolton, Gaiman's collaborator on *The Books of
Magic* (another comic collection in development as a film, as indeed

are most books Gaiman has written).

If *Sandman* is ever granted a reprieve from Development Hell, Gaiman has said, "I just desperately hope that it's a good movie. I don't have any control over it, so I'd much rather keep it at a distance and keep my fingers crossed. I hope that I get one of the good movies from comics, rather than *Howard the Duck*." Perhaps, he has suggested, Sandman's destiny lies on the small screen. "I would love *Sandman* as a television series. I think it would be a wonderful television series. But I don't think that it will ever happen. They have been doing these drafts of the script and they have been getting worse and worse and they have fired anybody who did have a clue. The last draft of the script [I read] had the Sandman stripped of his powers by giant electro-magnets underneath New York, all by the machinations of his good-looking brother, the Corinthian, because he is the Lord of Good Dreams."

"My own hope," Gaiman concludes, "is that some time in my lifetime you'll get a director who loved *Sandman* and wants to make it, in the same way that Sam Raimi made *Spider-Man* or Peter Jackson made *The Lord of the Rings*."

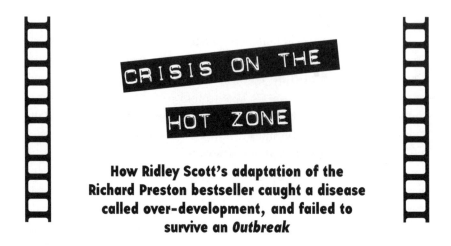

# CRISIS ON THE HOT ZONE

**How Ridley Scott's adaptation of the Richard Preston bestseller caught a disease called over-development, and failed to survive an *Outbreak***

"We had Redford, Ridley Scott and a script in progress. That's a lot to have. But instead of making it better, that just made everyone push to do a Hollywood number instead of an intelligent, thoughtful and honest film."

— The Hot Zone *screenwriter Richard Friedenberg*

I n 1992, journalist Richard Preston was researching article ideas for *The New Yorker* magazine when he stumbled across what was to become one of the biggest stories of the decade. His original intention had been to write about viruses, but while the AIDS epidemic seemed the logical choice, a lot had already been written on the subject; instead, he asked Professor Joshua Lederberg at New York's Rockerfeller University if he knew of any other 'interesting' viruses. "He mentioned Ebola," Preston recalled, referring to the lethal and incurable filovirus which kills nine out of ten of those infected — liquefying their internal organs and causing them to haemorrhage through every orifice. "He said there'd been a frightening outbreak of Ebola near Washington a few years earlier, which had been dealt with by the US Army — by soldiers wearing space suits, killing monkeys. He added, 'Well, you probably know about it.' I said, 'God, no! How do I learn more?'" Lederberg suggested that Preston call the Army, which he did. "Eventually I got permission to interview the Army officers who'd led the Ebola mission. Among them were Colonels Jerry and Nancy Jaax, husband and wife."

The result, published in October 1992, was an article entitled 'Crisis in the Hot Zone', detailing the seemingly superhuman efforts of the two USAMRIID (US Army Medical Research Institute of Infectious Diseases) virologists to contain an outbreak of the virus, which had not only travelled from the African rainforest to the eastern seaboard of the United States, but also jumped species from monkeys to humans. If it was not contained, it threatened to become a worldwide pandemic, a so-called 'slate wiper' for the human race. Since the tiniest tear in the Jaax's biohazard suits could have resulted in a swift and horrible demise, they lived and worked in a state of constant paranoia, and put their lives at risk throughout the entire endeavour. "In [my] very first interview with Nancy Jaax, she told me the story of how she'd gotten a leak in her space suit," Preston said later, "and her glove had filled up with Ebola blood, while she'd had a cut on her hand. It was a gripping story." The fact that the pair were married — and that Nancy had, at the time, outranked her husband — only made the story more thrilling. That it was also *true*... well, that was almost too good to be true. No sooner had the article been published in *The New Yorker* than Hollywood was on the phone.

In fact, it was on 18 January 1993 that Preston told the teenager babysitting his two children that he was going to work in his garage office and did not wish to be disturbed. Moments later, Hollywood heavyweight Arnold Kopelson — producer of such hits as *Platoon*, *The Fugitive* and, most recently, *Falling Down* — was on the line, prefacing the conversation with the to-the-point question: "Do you know who I am?" As Kopelson explained to *Entertainment Weekly*, "I want people to know I'm a serious film-maker; I'm an Academy Award-winner." Preston recalled, "I don't know if he had a cigar in his mouth, but I think he did. You could almost hear the faint sucking sound in the background. He said, 'First of all, call me Arnold. How are you, any-way?' and I said, 'I'm fine,' and he said, without missing a beat, 'I'm terrific,' and I thought, sitting there in my garage, 'Oh my God, I'm in Hollywood.'" Kopelson went on to say that he wanted the rights to 'Crisis in the Hot Zone'. He told Preston he wanted to make an important movie that would effect social change. He was passionate to make the movie. He wanted to spend money on it — indeed, he claimed never to make a film for less than $50 million. "By the way," Kopelson added, somewhat ominously, "we have the lawyers' opinion that we can make this movie without you."

Unbeknown to Preston, Kopelson had already been working with screenwriters Laurence Dworet and Robert Roy Pool on a screen version of events similar to those detailed in Preston's article. This was possible because facts are generally considered to be in the 'public domain', and since no one can own them, anyone can exploit them for dramatic effect, as long as the names of real life people are not involved, or if they are, their 'life rights' are purchased. Dworet and Pool's first stab at the screenplay was, Kopelson said later, "totally unsatisfactory". Warner Bros, with which Kopelson had a production output deal, wanted a grittier thriller, and hired Academy Award-winner Ted Tally (*The Silence of the Lambs*) to tackle the next draft. Kopelson says that his initial plan had been to hire Preston as a consultant on a film that would be based only loosely on the article, but use it as the backdrop to a more dramatic, fictionalised account of an outbreak. "[The article] wasn't a movie, it was merely background," the producer explained. "It was about 100 monkeys, and all of them end up getting killed. First of all, I would have the animal rights activists all over me. Secondly, it did not have a beginning, a middle and an end." According to Preston, however, the rights to the article were auctioned off, with producer Lynda Obst (*The Fisher King*) emerging the victor, paying $100,000, with a proviso that a further $350,000 be payable on the first day of production.

"Fox and I had won the initial skirmish by convincing Preston of our sympathetic intentions," Obst later wrote in her memoir, *Hello, He Lied*. "He had elected to interview all the interested producers and choose from among them." As a former reporter, Obst was attracted to the true story; as a working mother, she was attracted to Nancy Jaax's heroism. "We did not want to make an exploitative horror film. Credible argument. We won the auction. Credible victory. That was the last moment any of it made any sense." Kopelson maintains that no such auction took place. "On my life, the lives of my children, my wife, and everything that is dear to me, there was no auction," he insisted, stating that Preston merely rejected his offer — a suggestion which Preston dismissed as "baloney".

The fact remained, however: Obst had beaten Kopelson to the rights. "To our astonishment," said Obst, "the losing producer from Warner Bros decided to proceed regardless of the fact that he had lost the auction. His idea was to make his own knock-off version of the Preston article." As Kopelson explained, "I'm from Brooklyn and I don't like to lose." Thus, while Obst set *The Hot Zone* up at 20th Century Fox, Kopelson continued to develop his rival version — originally titled *Pandora*, a reference to the Greek myth about a box containing all the evils of the world. So closely related were the two projects that when Obst and Preston travelled to Fort Detrick, Maryland, to meet Jerry and Nancy Jaax, they were astonished to discover that Kopelson and one of his screenwriters, Laurence Dworet, had just left. According to Preston, Nancy Jaax had greeted Kopelson with the following: "Number one, get your goddamn limo out of my parking space. And another thing, if there's a female colonel who looks like me in [your] movie, there's going to be a major lawsuit." While Kopelson continued working on his version, now retitled *Outbreak*, Obst was expected to hire screenwriting/producing partners Rick Jaffa and Amanda Silver (*The Hand That Rocks the Cradle*), who had originally brought the article to the attention of Fox senior vice president of production, Michael London. When they were not available, Obst called in screenwriter James V. Hart (*Hook, Bram Stoker's Dracula*) — with whom she had been working for some time on an adaptation of Carl Sagan's *Contact* — to write the first draft.

"I had just finished *Contact* for Lynda Obst at Warner Bros," Hart recalls, "which had been a two-and-a-half-year process with Carl Sagan and his wife. I was fired immediately off the project when I turned the script in [because] the head of the studio hated it. So although there was no reason to bring it to me, having just been fired from *Contact* and my draft genuinely being hated by the head of the studio, Lynda to her credit came to me [with *The Hot Zone*]. I think she knew that the science problems were not frightening to me, that I actually enjoy that challenge." His mission, he says, was simple: "'Go tell this story, but find great characters.'" Hart began by meeting everyone he could who had been involved with the incidents detailed in Preston's article. "I spent time with all of them," he says. "And as soon as you meet Nancy, you just go straight to her. Even though in reality her husband was the leader of the team that led the investigation and also went into the monkey house in Reston, Virginia, Nancy emerges as the most interesting character: she's a housewife, she raises all kinds of animals, they have a daughter who is a spectacular gymnast. Once you take her outside the spacesuit and put her in a car driving home, she's a commuting housewife, yet every day she went in and dealt with the deadliest diseases known to man. We had not seen that before. You put a military guy in a spacesuit, that's easy. The hard thing was making Nancy Jaax the centre of the story, and for me that was the most fun about this: finding a way to make this great female character work."

Hart recalls only three mandates from the studio. The first was that the good guys must win in the end. "Of course," says Hart, "every virologist you talk to will say, 'You don't win — you just manage to put the genie back in the bottle until the next one pops out.'" The second was to "scare the shit out of people," he says. "Tom Jacobson, who was running Fox at the time, said, 'Make the virus as scary as the shark in *Jaws*.' So we were able to do that, because [these people] had enormous reverence for the viruses, and when they talk about them it's like they're talking about a great work of art; what incredible, soulless, beautiful creations they are, and how powerful the microbe is against all society, against all our technology, everything we can create as Mankind — this one microbe doesn't give a shit." The third mandate would be the toughest of all: "Tom Jacobson said, 'You've got to deliver a script *fast* because we're in a race, there's another project called *Outbreak*.' At that point I thought there was some protection — I still think they did — because they had bought a copyrighted article and paid a lot of money for it, and Richard had done all this work. So I had ten weeks to do the research, do the outline, and write the script. *Ten weeks*. Tom Jacobson said, 'That's all I can give you, and you've got to hit it out of the park on the first draft. We've got to know there's a movie there — we don't have time to guess.'"

Hart began his research in April 1993. In June, he sent his wife and two young children away for the summer, moved into a converted barn in upstate New York, and set to work on the script, conferring with Lynda Obst and her associates Lynn Harris and Dean Georgaris (with whom, years later, Hart would share credit on the script for *Lara Croft Tomb Raider — The Cradle of Life*). At the time, Preston had yet to turn his article into the 'non-fiction novel', *The Hot Zone*, which would become one of the hottest bestsellers of 1994. "There was no book at that time," says Hart, "all there was was the article in *The New Yorker*, which was a fantastic article. Richard Preston was writing the book as I was writing the screenplay, so I was on the phone every day to Richard, and to Nancy Jaax and her husband. It was amazing — it was like having your own lab at your fingertips. They were all encouraging me to fictionalise the story to make the point. The problem was, [the story] had no third act, and the big climax was killing monkeys, and there were no bad guys. Who are the bad guys in that scenario? You don't make the monkey handlers the bad guys. They were doing their job — they didn't intentionally bring Ebola into this country, like a terrorist act. The CDC [Center for Disease Control and Prevention] and USAMRIID are not the bad guys — they have bureaucracy, but they're out there trying to save the world, not destroy it." The solution was simple yet brilliant: "It was the virus. The bad guy was the virus itself."

An equally tough challenge was finding the drama in the story of an outbreak of a deadly virus in which not a single person died. "The lethal Ebola virus that came to this country did not kill one human being," Hart states. "In my research, I went to USAMRIID, I spent a very intense week with Nancy Jaax and her husband, and everybody who worked at USAMRIID, and *to a person*, the biggest problem — and I want to make sure this is said right — the biggest problem they had with the Ebola outbreak at the monkey house was the fact that no human being died. If *one* human being had died, it would have moved their cause for prevention and preparation for these kinds of outbreaks forward in the government's mind — that it was a real threat and needed to be addressed. Because it was only monkeys, nobody in the government took it seriously enough to increase funding, to advance listening posts, check-points for fruits coming in to this country. They spend more time quarantining an animal coming into the United States, and you can go to Dallas airport or Kennedy, and people just walk right through, right off the plane, as we've seen with SARS. They all said you can infect half this planet in about seventy-two hours by international air traffic.

"So what they wished had happened — and it's a horrible thing to say — was that a person had died of Ebola brought over here by monkeys, so it would give them the strength and the 'go juice' to go get government funding to begin work on a vaccine, on anti-serums, on controls about people coming in to this country with infectious diseases. That was the hope of people co-operating with the project," Hart explains. "All they wanted to do was scare the shit out of the public, so they'd have some more juice to go back to Congress and get more funding for virology research, for virology protocols, for infectious diseases — how they're diagnosed — for immigration controls, checks at airports, all of which came into focus during the SARS outbreak. And every one of those virologists I worked with said, 'We are not ready, we are not doing anything to get ready,' and, 'It's not a case of *if*, it's a case of *when*.'" It was for this reason, Hart says, the real-life protagonists gave him dramatic licence to fictionalise the third act, "to dramatically show what would have happened had this outbreak been virulent to humans, and how quickly it could spread and how unprepared we were."

They also gave Hart licence to bring one of the world's most famous virologists, Karl Johnson, into the script, because although he played no part in the Reston outbreak, and did not interact with the Jaaxes in real life, everyone agreed he should be part of the story. Says Hart, "I was able to fictionalise a professional relationship [between Nancy and Karl] based on their real credentials, [as if] Karl had been involved in the outbreak at Reston. Nancy had actually studied Karl's work in real life, so all of the strings we pulled together had roots in reality, we just fictionalised them." At one point, Hart flew to Montana and spent time with Johnson and his wife: "He sat me down and played me audio tapes that he still had from the 1976 Ebola outbreak in Zaire, where they stood in the middle of a village not believing what they were seeing, and trying to set down for voice record a tape to send back to London, so they would know how serious this outbreak was. So I got to go back and do Zaire [in the script] the way nobody had ever seen it, what really happened on the ground when they went into these missions and these villages, and the whole primitive approach to disease control, and how these native tribes dealt with it."

Although elements of the story would be fictionalised for dramatic reasons, both Hart and Preston were adamant that the pathology and histology of the virus itself must remain absolutely true to life. "I was writing a work based on non-fiction that was going to be fiction," Hart explains, "but every element of it had to be true. We couldn't invent a cure. We couldn't say, 'Okay we're gonna do this because this is how the virus behaves, or we're gonna make this happen.' Everything in those early drafts absolutely comes from the pathology of virus research and what the pathogens actually do and how they're tracked and what they do to the human body." Hart's numerous consultations and conversations with Preston yielded other nuggets of fact he was able to use in his script, including a so-called 'magic bullet' — a nun who had been infected with Ebola during the 1976 outbreak, but whose antibodies had somehow fought off the disease, and could perhaps be used to generate a serum. "The nun is real," Hart says. "Karl Johnson told me about [her]. They actually still had her blood samples recorded at USAMRIID or CDC. Now ultimately she died, but she lasted a long time, and there were two or three other people who survived it, and all of their blood samples were sent back to this country in 1976. Tiny, the worker at the monkey house, was real, but nobody had ever told those stories, so we just amped up the story of Tiny — that if he was a carrier but also immune, he might hold the 'magic bullet', his might be the magic blood antibodies that could save people if they could throw off an antiserum. Karl even explained to me how to spin a blood sample in a helicopter with a coat hanger when they were in the field: because they didn't have the lab equipment where you throw off the red and white blood cells, they would get a coat hanger and spin it as fast as they could to try to spin off the blood cells. So these guys knew what they were doing, and nobody understood how serious the outbreak was in the monkey house, and how widespread the Ebola virus could be — the only evidence we had of how virulent it was was 1976."

Hart wrote intensively throughout the summer of 1993, finally delivering his first draft on 9 October that year. The script opens in the Ebola River region of Zaire in 1976, as Center for Disease Control virologist Karl Johnson visits ground zero during the first outbreak of the Ebola filovirus among humans. Ten pages later, the equivalent of ten minutes of screen time, the story leaps forward to 1989, as Nancy Jaax and her ex-Army husband, now a veterinary surgeon, learn of a disease which is wiping out imported monkeys at a biological research laboratory located next to a day care centre in Reston, Virginia — just twenty-five miles from Washington, DC. It is another thirty pages before Jaax contacts Johnson to ask for his help, from which point on the pair work together to contain the spread of the virus by culling the infected monkeys. Within days, however, one of the monkeys' handlers, Tiny, shows symptoms of the disease, indicating that the virus can jump species and is airborne. In one particularly gripping sequence, Tiny, unaware that he is carrying the virus, walks into a crowded cinema — a scene which would certainly bring home to a cinema audience the risks involved with such a virulent contagion.

Hart says his script was greeted with great enthusiasm by all concerned. "The studio were real happy, the real-life people were happy, Lynda was happy, and I was thrilled because I'd redeemed myself for getting slaughtered on *Contact*. The studio wanted me to do one more draft," he adds, "[and] there was a lot of anticipation about it from actors, directors — everyone was sort of in line to see what we were up to. I did a bunch of drafts, but the next 'official' one was in December of 1993, and that's the draft that Jodie Foster signed on to." With Nancy Jaax very much the heroine of the film, it was perhaps unsurprising that finding an A-list actress proved relatively simple. Nevertheless, signing two-time Academy Award-winner Foster was a major coup. "Jodie loved the character of Nancy Jaax," says Hart, "and I was thrilled when she signed on. She was the first piece of talent to attach herself."

Behind the camera, *Das Boot* director Wolfgang Petersen — then riding high on the success of *In the Line of Fire* — topped the wish-lists of the producers of both *The Hot Zone* and *Outbreak*. "I got the scripts on my desk the same day," Petersen told *Entertainment Weekly*. "I decided to do *Outbreak*. Sometimes you can tell a better story with fiction." When Petersen passed on *The Hot Zone*, Fox began negotiating with director Ridley Scott, on whose behalf Paramount had unsuccessfully bid for the rights to the article, and whose own production company, Scott Free, was ready to bring half of the financing to the table. Says Hart, "It turned into a very complicated negotiation, and we were losing time against *Outbreak*, [because] they had a script they were somewhat happy with." Preston clearly did not agree, describing Neal Jimenez's *Outbreak* shooting script as "*Curious George Gets the Andromeda Strain*".

Scott finally signed on to direct the film in February 1994, at which point Hart suddenly found himself off the project, another victim of

Hollywood's fondness for developing a great script into a mediocre one by throwing too many writers and too few ideas at it. Thus, he says, "After all this excitement about the script, I found out one day that Michael London, who was the executive on the project, had called other agencies looking for new writers. I was not happy," Hart continues, "because the one thing I said to Lynda Obst after *Contact* was, 'If I deliver for you, don't replace me. Let me stay in the trenches with you — I'll have done the research, these people will trust me.' Richard Preston and I had been in constant contact, and every one of the real people was thrilled with how they had been portrayed in the script, with how the science worked, how the histology of the disease worked. To his credit, Tom Jacobson called and said, 'Look, Jim, you've done the heavy lifting here, you've gotten us this far — this was a decision that was made in order to develop this further, because of this time crunch we're up against,' blah blah blah. And I said, 'Okay, Tom, you make your own decision.' I took my family, and went to Florida on vacation, and said, 'You know where to find me.'"

In the meantime, Scott brought in screenwriter Tom Topor (*The Accused*) for what he describes as "an eleventh-hour, page-one rewrite" of the script, which Topor says Scott saw as "a science-fact thriller". Although Topor describes Preston's story as "brilliant", he notes that it was basically about how everybody dodged a bullet, "and you can't really make a movie about that. So Ridley's picture was going to have to *invent*. It wasn't exactly *fantasy*," he adds, "because the research starts with the Ebola virus. But the script went way beyond the science." Before Topor could begin work, however, Robert Redford had entered into negotiations for the role of Karl Johnson. The resulting disagreements over the direction the script should take sparked an internal power struggle between Robert Redford — who had signed on for $8 million and script approval — and Ridley Scott, with Topor caught in the middle. "I had a long talk with Ridley and Lynda Obst," Topor recalls, "and the next thing I know, Lynda told me that Bob [Redford] wanted a writer he'd worked with before." Redford's choice was Richard Friedenberg, who had scripted Redford's most recent film as director, *A River Runs Through It*.

"I can't remember how I got on the project, although I'm sure Bob [Redford] had something to do with it. I read and worked from Jim

Hart's script," Friedenberg recalls, adding that he was guided by 'notes' — Hollywood jargon for advice on how the script should be developed — from Obst, Scott, Scott's producing partner Mimi Polk and others. "Everybody gives writers notes," he points out, "[even] the garbage man. And the notes always conflict." Friedenberg says that Redford was not involved in the day-to-day development, yet his prime directive was to expand the role of Karl Johnson into one more suitable for an actor of Redford's stature. "I met the author, Richard Preston, a wonderful guy," says Friedenberg. "We had a good time. Talked a lot. I did research in Maryland at the centre that was in the book. Met a lot of very interesting people, learned a lot. That's the best thing about what I do."

Although unable to recall specific problems which he was called upon to solve, or issues his rewrite was to address, Friedenberg says that he was trying to create something "real and tough, without the usual Hollywood crap. That was the big battle — no dying daughter, or dying girlfriend, etc. How do you dramatise the situation realistically? How could it actually spread? How could you stop it? And how could you make it appeal to the studio mentality without adding in a lot of stupid, improbable rubbish? I worked out a story [outline] that I thought was quite good," he says. "Lynda agreed. We presented it in a meeting with a lot of people. Everyone liked it except Ridley's partner," he adds, referring to Mimi Polk. "She said, 'It's crap,' as I recall, and suddenly everyone agreed. I remember Lynda excused herself at that point and went into the lobby of the office and lay down for a while. That was the beginning of the end." After working on the project for several more weeks, Friedenberg says he hated it so much that he begged to be fired. "I spoke to the Fox executive after a particularly egregious notes meeting and gave him all the reasons he should fire me. He took pity and let me off the hook."

Jim Hart was still in Florida when he received a call from Tom Jacobson, begging him to come back to work on *The Hot Zone*. "He called me and said, 'We're under pressure from the Warner Bros project, [and] I've got a week to land a new outline for Redford.' I said, 'What happened?' And he said, 'It's moving away from what we all like.'" Hart learned that Richard Friedenberg's outline had expanded Karl Johnson's character, since that was the one Redford was going to play, and moved it away from Nancy as the hero of the piece. "Richard and I spoke," Hart remembers, "and he said, 'Use any of my work you can find in there, if you can do it. Read it, use it, good luck — I'm so glad to be off this.'" Hart agreed to come back to work on the film as soon as his vacation was over, and was ultimately able to salvage several ideas from Friedenberg's outline, including a major plot point about a worker in the monkey house who would emerge as a carrier, and drive the third act as Jaax and Johnson hunt him down.

At this point, more cracks were beginning to show in the relationship between Ridley Scott and Lynda Obst. Says Hart, "The politics started getting real strange, because you had Redford's influence creeping in, Ridley's entire gang of talent that came to the table, and you had Lynda, who really had been the driving force behind this, and is one of the most creative producers that we have in the business — she is a writer, she works well with writers, and she's very tenacious and knows storytelling. But Ridley brought his whole company, and he was bringing half the financing to the table, so it was going to be a Ridley Scott movie, and suddenly Lynda Obst is moved outside the inner circle. And Ridley was not necessarily the friend of movie stars, and I don't think there was any love lost between Ridley and Redford, and Ridley and Jodie."

On top of which, Hart says, "the project had suddenly become more important than any element involved. It was now a cause: the race between this project and *Outbreak*." It was a race that Fox wanted to win, he adds, "but at the Warner Bros studio, they had one of the longest running managements at any studio at that time, they knew what they were doing. They'd played this game before, and they knew how to win." As Obst put it in *Hello, He Lied*, "Getting any picture mounted is a Sisyphean task, but this one was complicated by a closely observed struggle between studios and rival producers... The press and each side's self-interest had turned [the production] into a frenzied competition between studios and rival producers that soon escalated into a pitched battle... It was the most unstable project I'd ever worked on."

"I thought I had seen the extent of the joys and disappointments that Hollywood had to offer," Obst added. "But none of it had prepared me for the highs and lows and lower lows of *The Hot Zone*... Every Friday, after I'd spent a full week keeping the package — the director, the script, and stars — together, it would fall apart again." Every weekend, Obst had to hustle to put it back together. Every Monday the press would call to ask (for example), 'Is it true that Ridley Scott is dropping out?' 'Of course not,' she would reply, relieved not to be lying (at least for the moment). Then the package would threaten to fall apart again, Obst would put it back together, and another Monday would come... "This is the greatest crisis for a producer: the threat of watching your baby die. I had to keep it alive, hour by hour, day by day." Ultimately, says Hart, "*The Hot Zone* began to founder because there were — and rightfully so — all of these very successful egos to-ing and fro-ing over this project. I remember being on the phone to Richard Preston and he would say, 'What's happening?' And I'd say, 'This is what's gonna happen, this is why it's gonna happen. Just watch — this is why it's gonna unravel.'"

For Obst, keeping each party from fatally losing faith in the face of such adversity was all part of her role as producer: "Like Atlas, I felt like I was balancing all the issues of the movie on my shoulders: the director's fear of the studio, the studio's fear of the director, all of our fears of the potent movie stars — Robert Redford and Jodie Foster — who could make us or break us at any juncture. But all of these opposing forces could have been tamed with the proper amount of time. In the context of a race to production — everyone believed that there was a place for only one such movie in the marketplace, but no one was folding — time was a luxury we didn't have. All of us — director, studio, stars, me — were deeply concerned about how the race would compromise the movie." Meanwhile, the press was eating up the story, until the coverage of the race began affecting the basic process of putting the movie together, a situation she described as "a kind of media Heisenberg uncertainty principle."

"I felt that Ridley was going to make a great film," says Hart, "but I began to see how all the work you do in the beginning starts to get unravelled as other film-makers come on board and — rightfully so — bring their vision to it. It was fascinating to work with Ridley because my job became, 'How do I take this idea Ridley has for a brilliant shot or a brilliant sequence and make it work in the movie?'" For instance, Scott had an idea about Tiny's character getting on an aircraft, trying to get home to his mother, and being sick. "This actually comes from a scene out of Richard Preston's book that really happened. Ridley wanted this guy coughing up his guts into a [air sickness] bag, and then when the military ground the plane and surround it and want him to come out, he goes into the men's room and tries to flush the bag down the vacuum toilet, and it explodes and sends blood out under the door and up into the air conditioning system... This is all Ridley's idea, and I'm going 'Wow!' So this was in the best draft, the last draft I wrote, this whole sequence where Karl Johnson and Nancy Jaax go into the plane to get Tiny out, and it is a scary sequence, when the blood bag explodes. That's what Ridley brought to the table: his extraordinary visual facility, which is at his fingertips. It didn't always fit into the narrative, and didn't always take the narrative into consideration — there were several things in Topor's shooting script that Ridley wanted to do that I still don't get — but it was exciting. So I had been brought back to try to help here. They were under enormous pressure from Warner Bros, and I was also told that Jodie wasn't happy with the shift away from her character and the move toward Redford's character."

It was at this point that Obst received a call from Redford's agent at Creative Artists Agency (CAA), whom she described as "a close ally and friend", informing her that the director and screenwriter of *Outbreak* were flying out to meet with Redford, ready to offer him the lead in *their* film. "You just start laughing at what you're up against," says Hart. "They're just feeding off of each other — 'take my arm and his leg and this guy's heart...'" Somehow, *Variety* reporter Mike Fleming got a whiff of the rumour. "Now I'm really screwed," thought Obst. "If it's reported, it could unravel Jodie. Two actors gone, no movie... Bosnian Muslims were under genocidal siege, Hutus were slaughtering Tutsis, the prospect of national health care was falling to pieces while O.J. ran, and I wish I could tell you that I was aware of any of it. But this kind of pseudodrama shrinks perspective, rendering us (or at least me) myopic to the rest of the world. All news becomes the trades' industry news, and you are it." In the event, Redford declined the rival offer. Says Hart, "To his credit he said, 'No I'm gonna do *The Hot Zone*' — one, because he'd committed to it first, and two, because it was a more true to life project, and if he was going to be involved, he wanted to be involved in the one that was trying to break new ground, as opposed to just an action-adventure movie."

Next, Hart flew out for a meeting with Redford, whom he had known through the writers' workshops at the Sundance Institute, where Hart had previously worked with fellow *Hot Zone* writer Richard Friedenberg. "I *begged* him to *please* play the character that I was writing," says Hart. "I wrote a living legend in Karl Johnson — literally, a living legend. I gave Karl Johnson a role he never got to play in real life, and it was a great character: a romantic character who didn't have to have a romance, [who] every female in the audience would gravitate to and every male in the audience would want to be like. It was like having a hero out of *King Solomon's Mines* or Denys Finch Hatton," he adds, referring to a real-life figure Redford's character in *Out of Africa* had been based on. "A guy that was *of the world*, who brought enormous experience to the table and who was a renegade and a rogue and an outsider and who struck fear into bureaucracy!" Hart is not sure if Redford was confusing the size of the role with its stature, but "all I know is, I lost."

Redford brought in another of his favourite writers, Paul Attanasio, who would earn an Oscar nomination for his script for Redford's next film as director, *Quiz Show*. "Attanasio is a fantastic writer," says Hart, "but nobody had done the research, and nobody had been in the soup with these people, except me and Richard Preston. And the speed, the pressure, the race all began to take its toll on where the project had been a year earlier. Jodie Foster was plenty a movie star, Redford would have been brilliant in the [Karl Johnson] role, but I think that the romance that crept into the Attanasio script, that did it for Jodie. I think there was actually a kiss between Karl Johnson and Nancy Jaax in the 'hot zone' lab, and this movie was not about a romance — it was about heroic people in an extraordinary situation; people that you see driving a station wagon full of kids to school who are also saving the world. It wasn't about a romance between people that were working in close quarters with each other. But, I will say this, *The Hot Zone* was a perfect situation for a male-female romance to emerge if that was where you were going with the movie. This movie did not have to hang on a romance or the attraction of two people to each other to make it interesting, yet it was the perfect set-up for that kind of relationship to evolve." Hart was among the first to hear that Foster had quit the project. "Someone had seen Jodie at a party in New York and she said that she was pulling out because the character I had written was no longer the character in the script. The focus had changed, and she was going. I remember calling Lynda Obst from New York — I woke her up — and I felt terrible because I thought Lynda knew. She was very upset and very angry." Nevertheless, Foster "jumped species" onto another Obst production, *Contact*, which she had read more than a year earlier (when she was sent it as a sample of Hart's writing), and in which, after several more years in Development Hell, she would play the lead role.

Even with Foster gone, Hart agreed to come back in for the third and last time. "I took Richard's outline and folded his great ideas about 'patient zero' — the carrier — into the draft," he says. "I met with Jerry and Nancy Jaax and explained to them that if I was going to make this work dramatically, I would have to take licence with their relationship, and that I was gonna make one of them sick, and I was gonna invade their family — and in the script it's their daughter who gets sick. [The Jaaxes' colleague] Peter Jarling told me their wives would always say 'Don't bring your work home from the office,' because the worst thing that could happen is that you walk out of the lab and take something home in your system that's gonna infect your family. And when they told me that, I just went, 'Okay, the daughter's gonna get infected.'" Hart also attempted to address some of the romantic elements which Attanasio had brought into the script, apparently at Redford's request, but which Hart felt threatened the reality of the relationship between Nancy and Jerry. His solution was simple: "I put Jerry in Desert Storm, in an outbreak where they were hunting for biological weapons, believe it or not. And he was gonna be brought home for Thanksgiving, but he was leading a biohazard team to turn up weapons of mass destruction in Iraq! So he is reintroduced into the story at a time when Nancy and Karl have been spending a lot of time together, so there is a natural tension in his return. But there is never any doubt that Nancy is madly in love with her husband, and has a successful relationship and a successful family.

"The May '94 draft brought together Richard Friedenberg's work, Paul Attanasio's work, the work Ridley had brought to the table, [and] Redford's desires — yet still maintained the integrity of Nancy and Jerry Jaax. The end of that draft is still talked about," Hart adds. "Karl Johnson is saying goodbye to Nancy after the monkey house is over and they've successfully spun off the serum and begun to deal with the outbreak, and Karl gets on the plane and you see from the point of view of the virus up in the air system, moving to the little nozzles, and suddenly it stops over Karl Johnson, and just as it rushes down towards him, he reaches up and turns off the nozzle, and the screen goes black. It is the way the movie should end, and I still get calls about it from people who read the script. That unproduced screenplay has gotten me more work than *Hook* and *Dracula* put together. It was my swansong," he says. "I turned that draft in — it's 154 pages long — and I said, 'Here — I'm going.'"

"After Jodie went, we went to Meryl Streep," said Obst, relishing the opportunity to re-team the multiple Oscar-winner with Redford, her co-star in *Out of Africa*. "Her agents thought we had a great shot." With *The Hot Zone* now a mere eighteen days from the date principal photography was due to begin, Tom Topor received a call from one of Scott's associates, asking him if he was available for "an instantaneous production rewrite" which they could use to entice Streep aboard. "They sent me all of the scripts," Topor recalls, "and then Ridley and I got on the phone, and I said, 'Look, you email me a list of all of the big set-pieces that you absolutely want to keep, because I'm going to treat this as though I'm doing a musical on Broadway — you tell me the songs you want to keep, and I'll write around your songs.' I said, 'I will give you all your set-pieces, but you've got to give me a lot of manoeuvring room for the rest of it.'"

Scott agreed, but requested that Topor talk with Redford, and with Streep, who was considering whether to replace Foster on *The Hot Zone* or join Clint Eastwood for *The Bridges of Madison County*. Says Topor, "I got on the telephone with Bob, and we had sort of a 'meet and greet' conversation, and then I talked to Meryl, and she gave me a lot of ideas about her character. But then she said, 'When do you think it'll be done?'" Topor was forced to admit that, despite the approaching start date, he was still taking notes from Scott and Redford, and had yet to begin work on his screenplay. "I could tell that the moment she heard I had nothing on paper, she was going to take the offer from Eastwood. *The River Wild* [an action-packed thriller toplining Streep] was about to be released, and everybody thought that was going to be a huge hit. So she bowed out."

The next time Topor spoke with Redford, he suggested that Redford and Scott needed to have further discussions about the direction the script was taking: "I said, 'The way Ridley sees this is essentially a duet, and the way you're talking, it doesn't sound like that. So I will do anything you want, but I have to have a consensus between you and the director.' And not long after that, Bob disappeared, too." Redford officially quit on 12 August. "It was like a train wreck in extended slow motion," Preston told *Time*'s Richard Corliss. "It begins with a smell of smoke; then one wheel hops the track; then a freight car goes off; then it turns sideways and the whole train begins to telescope. That's when it goes off the rails and into the canyon. By Hollywood standards, this project took a long time to come apart," he added. "Usually they explode immediately."

While *The Hot Zone* was haemorrhaging stars, *Outbreak*'s cast list was beginning to read like a 'who's who' of Hollywood: two-time Oscar-winner Dustin Hoffman and *In the Line of Fire*'s Rene Russo would headline as virologist Colonel Sam Daniels and his colleague and ex-wife Robby Keough; Kevin Spacey and Cuba Gooding Jr would play USAMRI-ID personnel; and Morgan Freeman would play a Brigadier-General. Then, when Joe Don Baker (*Edge of Darkness*) was dismissed several weeks into production, a bigger star, Donald Sutherland, took his place. Yet *Outbreak* was having script problems of its own: after Dworet and Pool's initial drafts, a succession of screenwriters, including Jeb Stuart (*The Fugitive*) and Carrie Fisher (*Postcards From the Edge*), worked on the script, the latter at a reported cost of $100,000 per week. Petersen later brought in *The Waterdance* screenwriter Neal Jimenez to "improve the pacing and structure", while Hoffman, unhappy with his lines in one scene, brought in prize-winning poet and novelist Maya Angelou to sharpen the dialogue. The script was still far from finished when, on 13 July 1994, Kopelson sent Petersen and his crew to shoot exteriors in Eureka, California, effectively announcing the commencement of principal photography, and throwing *The Hot Zone* into further crisis. "They shot second-unit monkey footage for weeks on end," said Obst, "as they were raced into production without a script, too."

The other difficulty for *The Hot Zone*, Topor explains, was trying to cast the film barely two weeks before production was due to begin. "There were very few [actors] available at such short notice," he says, "and by this time there had been so much bad publicity in the papers, that even for people who might have wanted to work for him [Scott], it looked like they were coming into a troubled movie that was similar to a movie that was already in production." "When the Fox project exploded, they didn't want to talk about it," said Preston. "They were resolutely insisting that all was hunky-dory, and ten minutes later someone would be weeping [to me] about how the Fox project was like a shipwreck." The fact that Scott was unable to set it up elsewhere — even at Paramount, which had originally bid for the story on Scott's behalf — did not surprise Tom Topor. "I can understand why other studios didn't pick it up," he says. "It was a very expensive picture — $40 or $50 million — and *Outbreak* was already in the works. As [Paramount president] Sherry Lansing said to Ridley, 'I like what you've got better, but it's not *that* much different.'"

"There was a sense of outrage that the producers of [*Outbreak*] had violated a kind of unspoken code: that if you spend a lot of dough and get the rights to a project — in this case an article — then you have in effect protected yourself from being ripped off. It's yours to do and no one else's," says Friedenberg. "The *Outbreak* people lost the battle for the rights to 'Crisis in the Hot Zone', and instead of going away as everyone else does, they just went ahead, claiming their right to use material in the public domain, like newspaper reports, etc. There was talk of suing and so forth, but they just ploughed ahead and won." Adds Hart, "I was so angry because I thought Fox had a copyright infringement suit against Warners. They claim they didn't, but Richard [Preston] and I both know that there were things in that screenplay that did not exist in any article, that had not been previously published, but that came out of the research [for *The Hot Zone* script], and the producers [of *Outbreak*] freely admitted they read every draft we turned in. The scene of the aerosol in the monkey house going up in the vents and coming down in the next room, the scene in the movie theatre, [and] people coughing and having it backlit in the air from a movie projector — stuff that's in my script that didn't exist in any book. But Fox business affairs did not feel they had a successful case against Warners. Warners out-managed and out-produced Fox. It was a big learning curve for everybody." Worst of all, says Friedenberg, was that "it looked like a 'go' movie. We had Redford, Ridley Scott and a script in progress. That's a lot to have. But instead of making it better, that just made everyone push to do a Hollywood number instead of an intelligent, thoughtful and honest film. I'd just worked with Bob on *A River Runs Through It*, a totally uncompromised project, and I naïvely thought that this could be the same. What an idiot."

Finally, in August 1994, Fox pulled the plug on *The Hot Zone*. Warner Bros took the opportunity to shut down *Outbreak*, which was having problems of its own. According to Robert Roy Pool, the script for *Outbreak* had become a battleground, with both he and Laurence Dworet engaging in "extreme creative conflicts" with one of the Warner Bros executives, apparently over the writers' desire to keep the story as realistic as possible. After working on the script for a year, they left by mutual agreement. Nevertheless, Pool maintained his link with the production, making frequent visits to the set, and remaining friendly with Petersen, producers Kopelson and Gail Katz, and the incoming screenwriter Neal Jimenez, "an old poker buddy" of Pool's. Pool also claimed to have read "every draft by every writer", and was therefore in a position to state that although as many as fifteen screenwriters had contributed dialogue to the final script, "ninety-five per cent of the dialogue changes were simple enhancements of ideas we had already introduced in our final screenplay of December 1993."

According to Pool, the story, characters, structure and scenes in *Outbreak* were his and Dworet's creations: "Ted Tally contributed exactly one scene in the movie, and it's a very good one — Dustin Hoffman looks up at an air vent, the camera dollies through the vent, and Hoffman says, 'It's airborne.'" Pool noted that after Tally departed, Jeb Stuart was hired, but soon left through the door marked 'creative differences'. Once Fox's competing project fell apart, the *Outbreak* crew took a week's hiatus, and Neal Jimenez was hired to rework the dialogue to Dustin Hoffman's satisfaction. Nevertheless, Pool suggested, "the phrase 'Dustin Hoffman's satisfaction' is an oxymoron. Neal began to realize that Dustin would never be happy — not in this lifetime, anyway — and once the picture started rolling again, Neal showed up on the set less and less often. He felt insulted and ignored when the actors refused to speak the lines he'd written and substituted their own phrases." On the final day of shooting, Jimenez told his old poker buddy that he might not have signed on for the job if he'd known what lay ahead.

*Outbreak* opened in the US on 10 March 1995, grossing $13.4 million in its opening weekend, and a total of $187 million worldwide. "On opening day, [Fox chairman] Peter Chernin and I were talking on the cellphone," Hart recalls, "and he said to me, 'We shut down for the wrong movie!', meaning we never should have folded our tent. They could have opened both of those movies on the same day and *The Hot Zone* would have been the one that people went back to see a second time." Preston was among those who paid to see *Outbreak*. "I'm just sitting here laughing," he told *Entertainment Weekly* afterwards. "It just wasn't scary. You have scabs that look like Gummi Bears. The blood was put on with an eyedropper. In a real [Ebola attack], the men bleed out of their nipples. I would have liked to see Hoffman bleed out of his nipples." Robert Roy Pool, one of only two credited screenwriters on the finished film (Dworet was the other), had had enough. In a letter to *Entertainment Weekly* published in full on 21 April 1995, he strove finally to set the record straight about the origins of the movie, stating that he and Dworet had not "ripped off" Preston's story — but that the author had gained a great deal of publicity from claiming otherwise. On the contrary, Pool went on, he and Dworet had written the entire screenplay for *Outbreak*, notwithstanding embellishments by three subsequent writers, the cast and Wolfgang Petersen.

According to Pool, Warner Bros had been trying to persuade him and Dworet — a qualified medical doctor — to write an action-suspense film for them for more than two years, but had not found the right project until November 1992, when a senior executive asked them if they would be interested in writing a screenplay based on 'Crisis in the Hot Zone'. At the time, they declined, believing that the story had several fundamental problems. "First, nothing very dramatic happens — it just threatens to happen," Pool explained. "Second, the climactic action of the story is the euthanization of hundreds of monkeys — an extraordinarily grim finale for a major studio feature." The writers believed that a movie was unlikely to emerge from Preston's story — and even if it did, would struggle to find an audience.

Instead, Pool and Dworet drew the studio's attention to an idea they had been working on for more than a decade, following Dworet's research into another haemorrhagic illness, Lassa Fever, at medical school in 1975, which seemed to presage the end of the world. The pair worked up a story idea in February 1982 which Pool described as follows: "an emergency room doctor leads a battle against a bizarre African virus spreading in a small Idaho town. This battle eventually assumes a military dimension when the National Guard has to be called in to enforce the quarantine and protect the world from a devastating plague." Pool and Dworet were fascinated by the social and moral implications of the story. What would really happen if such a virus broke out? Tough decisions would almost certainly follow. Would they isolate — or even annihilate — an entire town in order to prevent the spread of a contagious and incurable disease? A decade later, in 1992, Pool and Dworet sold the pitch to Warner Bros, at which point Arnold Kopelson suggested optioning Preston's magazine story. "We told him that we had no intention of using Preston's story," Pool said, "and that Preston didn't own the underlying subject matter — no one could." Although Kopelson's lawyers agreed, the producer decided to bid for the story regardless, feeling that Preston's research might prove useful to the project. When he was outbid, he went back to working on the Pool-Dworet story while Fox fast-tracked its adaptation of 'Crisis in the Hot Zone'. And so the race was on.

In spite of the chaos surrounding the picture, however, Pool felt that Wolfgang Petersen had ultimately managed to make one of the most exciting movies he had ever seen, and that while *Outbreak* stretches credibility, "it's never boring." As for Richard Preston, "[he] is very talented... but he has amazing arrogance to think that, by writing one story for *The New Yorker*, he somehow owns an entire scientific subject." On the contrary, Pool said, many other writers have addressed the subject of deadly plagues, from Daniel Defoe's *A Journal of the Plague Year* in 1722 to John Fuller's *Fever!*, published 250 years later, detailing Nigeria's Lassa Fever mini-epidemic of 1969. "Laurence and I read scores of articles about haemorrhagic fevers in medical journals and found hundreds more we didn't have time to retrieve. We won the competition fair and square," he concluded. "Richard Preston should stop whining and start writing his next book."

Yet, like the virus it described, it appears that *The Hot Zone* cannot easily be subdued, and may yet return in mutated form. "Because I lost the race on *Hot Zone* doesn't mean it won't be made," Obst wrote in 1996, by which time Preston's book had been on the bestseller list for almost two years. "Maybe I just lost the race to mediocrity; so every time I meet a new director who could be right or read a new writer who could save the script, *Hot Zone* moves to the front burner, ready to start cooking." Sure enough, on 2 July 2002, *Variety* reported that Fox was reviving the film, with Scott McGehee and David Siegel (*Suture*, *The Deep End*) set to direct a new draft by Emmy-winning writer Erik Jendreson (*Band of Brothers*, *The 300 Spartans*). "It's a great script," said McGehee, "very similar to the original story." Hart remembers being contacted by Lynda Obst when Jendreson was first brought in, around the same time that a small outbreak of the Ebola virus occurred as thousands of refugees were streaming across the border to escape the genocide in Somalia. "Lynda called me — I think it was after *Contact*, so it must have been 1998 or 1999 — and said they were bringing in [Jendreson,] who had just won an Emmy for *E.R.*. She wanted to know if I would be willing to work as an executive producer on the project, and work with this writer in a supervisory capacity. I was flattered," he says, "but I also was not stupid — I had been through this a number of times before.

"We spitballed what the take would be, how we evolved what we did in *The Hot Zone* to now, and it was gonna be a global outbreak like SARS, as opposed to just being contained in Reston," Hart continues. "That was almost going to be a main title sequence, and we were gonna do a global outbreak using the airline scenario. The problem was that if I was gonna get involved as an executive producer, it was going to have to be *very* clear what the credit situation was going to be." After suffering through a tumultuous credit arbitration process — "a horrible situation which pitches writers against each other" — on *Contact*, he had worked on two films where the writers had agreed among themselves what the credits should be: an all too rare process, which the Writers Guild of America encourages in its governing agreements. "I said to Lynda, 'I can't do this unless we agree up front on how credits are gonna be shared. I'm happy to take second position or third position, but I should be in there for screen story credit because I had pioneered the first draft,'" Hart recalls, "and she was not willing to let me have that conversation with Eric." She did, however, subsequently let Hart know that the draft had not worked, and that the project had been abandoned once again. "I later ran across this script," Hart says, "and again it just misses the characters of Nancy and Jerry Jaax and Karl

Johnson and all the people that I was lucky enough to meet. I don't care how many writers they put on it, if they could get something they were happy with and just do it, if it was closer to Richard Preston's book, or even what I did with Richard Preston at the beginning with Lynda Obst... Karl Johnson has now written his own non-fiction novel about his experiences with outbreaks, and asked me if I'd be interested in adapting the screenplay — and I can't wait to read it. He is a guy who has been at the epicentre longer than anybody else in virology, and I hope his story, which he's going to try and get published, is as exciting and terrifying as anything that happened in *The Hot Zone*."

Richard Preston, who has since published further bestsellers, the movie rights to which were sold for millions of dollars, has described his first encounter with Hollywood as akin to "watching people break and enter cars in broad daylight — it just happens and everyone shrugs," yet insists he hasn't come out empty-handed. "I've had so much fun telling the 'Call-me-Arnold' story," he said, of his memorable first phone call with Kopelson, "it's almost worth it." He also hopes that *The Hot Zone* may yet be revived by Hollywood: "I don't know that the story is completely dead. In Hollywood, it always depends on if you believe in reincarnation."

Indeed, despite the problems which have plagued the film for more than a decade, *The Hot Zone* remains in 'active development' at 20th Century Fox. "I think they want to go back to Richard Preston's book and try to make it work," says Hart. "The most recent rumour was that Julianne Moore was going to come in and do it, and that they were going back to my script, but I hear that's been put on the back burner." Richard Friedenberg is among the casualties of *The Hot Zone* who remains optimistic that the film will eventually be made, declaring, "It's a worthy project and a terrific book." Nevertheless, Friedenberg does not expect to see his name on the credits of any eventual adaptation. "My paltry input has been swept away long ago, and will not be reflected in any way in some future film," he says. Nor is the crisis that was *The Hot Zone* an experience on which he wishes to reflect: "It was a very bad time for me. For some reason it was more disillusioning than most of my experiences, and I took it hard." Ridley Scott also found the film's eleventh hour collapse frustrating. "I would have loved to work with Jodie [Foster]," the director told biographer Paul M. Sammon, shortly before the actress bowed out of another Scott-directed project, *Hannibal*. "I also thought [*The Hot Zone*] was one of those rare projects, like *Thelma & Louise*, that was actually about something."

Since the collapse of *The Hot Zone*, Hart has managed to use elements of his research in at least two scripts: *Lara Croft Tomb Raider — The Cradle of Life*, which has a brief reference to the Ebola virus and is largely concerned with the potentially lethal effects of a deadly disease contained within Pandora's Box (echoes of *Outbreak*'s original title, *Pandora*), and a major science fiction project for MGM in which a plague spreads across the globe in days, a precursor to an invasion by aliens. Yet *The Hot Zone* was not science fiction. "It was a new kind of thriller," he says. "It was like *Invasion of the Body Snatchers*, a brilliant film about paranoia which Philip Kaufman did, based on the original directed by Don Siegel — but this wasn't science fiction, it was real."

With diseases back in the media following outbreaks of everything from SARS to anthrax to West Nile virus, and — perhaps more importantly in Hollywood terms — Danny Boyle's fictional yet grippingly real *28 Days Later* scoring big for 20th Century Fox in the summer of 2003, *The Hot Zone* may yet survive, mutate and flourish. After all, as Preston has pointed out, "It's not like *Alien*, where people could shrug it off as science fiction. Now they'd be seeing someone come apart before their eyes and realising that the virus could be sitting next to them in the theatre. It could be anywhere."

# THE DARK KNIGHT STRIKES OUT

### Did George Clooney's Batman kill the most successful franchise of the 90s?

"I told them I'd cast Clint Eastwood as the Dark Knight, and shoot it in Tokyo, doubling for Gotham City. That got their attention."

— *proposed* Batman 5 *director Darren Aronofsky*

**F**ew heroes have inspired so many stories as the costumed crime fighter known to almost every man, woman and child on Earth as Batman. The creation of cartoonist Bob Kane and his (mostly uncredited) partner Bill Finger, Batman made his first appearance in *Detective Comics* #27, published in May 1939 — a year after Superman's début, and a full fifty before Tim Burton's *Batman* reached the big screen. Lacking Superman's superpowers, Batman was forced to rely on his physical prowess, and the enormous wealth of his *alter ego*, the millionaire playboy Bruce Wayne, who provided his costumed counterpart with a house (the Batcave), a car (the Batmobile), an aircraft (the Batplane) and a utility belt full of gadgets. Kane credited numerous influences for his creation, including Zorro, The Shadow and a 1930 film entitled *The Bat Whispers*, which featured a caped criminal who shines his bat insignia on the wall just prior to killing his victims. "I remember when I was twelve or thirteen... I came across a book about Leonardo da Vinci," Kane added. "This had a picture of a flying machine with huge bat wings... It looked like a bat man to me."

Batman first reached the silver screen as early as the 1940s, with the first of two fifteen-chapter Columbia serials: *Batman* (1943), starring Lewis Wilson as the Caped Crusader, and *Batman and Robin* (1949), with Robert Lowery. Almost two decades later, on 12 January 1966, the ABC television series starring Adam West and Burt Ward brought the characters to an entirely new generation, running for twenty-six months and earning a quickie big-screen spin-off within the first year. Although Kane's earliest stories had a *noir*-ish sensibility, over time the characters developed the wisecracking personae that were magnificently captured by the camp capers of the TV series. "Batman and Robin were always punning and wisecracking and so were the villains," Kane said in 1965. "It was camp way ahead of its time." In the 1970s, Batman continued to appear in an animated series, *Superfriends*, but the legacy of the 1960s TV series meant that it was not until Frank Miller reinvented the character for the darkly gothic comic strip series *The Dark Knight Returns* and *Batman: Year One* in the mid-1980s that the world was ready to take Batman seriously again.

Just as Batman had made his first appearance in comic strips a year after Superman, the development of the *Batman* movie — the first since the 1966 caper with Adam West — began a year after the blockbuster success of *Superman: The Movie* in 1978. Former Batman comic book writer Michael E. Uslan, together with his producing partner Benjamin Melniker, secured the film rights from DC Comics, announcing a 1981 release for the film, then budgeted at $15 million. Uslan and Melniker hired *Superman*'s (uncredited) screenwriter Tom Mankiewicz to script the story, which was set in the near future, and closely followed the *Superman* model: an extended origin story, followed by the genesis of his superhero *alter ego*, and his eventual confrontation with The Joker. It ended with the introduction of Robin. It was Uslan's wish to make "a definitive Batman movie totally removed from the TV show, totally removed from camp; a version that went back to the original Bob Kane/Bill Finger strips."

By 1983, the project was still languishing in Development Hell, as potential directors including Ivan Reitman (*Ghostbusters*) and Joe Dante (*Gremlins*) came and went. It was following the surprise success of Tim Burton's slapstick comedy *Pee-Wee's Big Adventure* that Warner Bros — whose stewardship of the project resulted from a deal with Peter Guber's Casablanca Film Works, with whom Melniker had a development deal — offered the project to lifelong Bat-fan Tim Burton, who was busy making *Beetlejuice* for the studio. "The first treatment of *Batman*, the Mankiewicz script, was basically *Superman*, only the names had been changed," Burton told Mark Salisbury. "It had the same jokey tone, as the story followed Bruce Wayne from childhood through to his beginnings as a crime fighter. They didn't acknowledge any of the freakish nature of it... The Mankiewicz script made it more obvious to me that you couldn't treat *Batman* like *Superman*, or treat it like the TV series, because it's a guy dressing up as a bat and no matter what anyone says, that's weird." Although Burton had fond memories of the series, which he would run home from school to watch, he had no wish to duplicate its campy tone. Yet it would take the comic book boom of the late 1980s — notably the success of the collected edition of *The Dark Knight Returns* — to convince Warner Bros that Burton's approach might connect with audiences. "The success of the graphic novel made our ideas far more acceptable," he observed.

With Warner Bros' blessing, Burton began working on a new draft with emerging screenwriting talent and fellow Bat-fan Sam Hamm, whose comedy script *Pulitzer Prize* had sparked a bidding war and landed him a two-year contract with Warner Bros. Hamm felt that the *Superman* model was wrong; that rather than dwell on Batman's origins, the character should be presented as a *fait accompli*, with his background and motivations emerging as the story progressed, so that the unlocking of the mystery becomes part of the plot. "I tried to take the premise which had this emotionally scarred millionaire whose way of dealing with his traumas was by putting on the suit," Hamm said. "If you look at it from this aspect, that there is no world of superheroes, no DC Universe and no real genre conventions to fall back on, you can start taking the character seriously. You can ask, 'What if this guy actually does exist?' And in turn, it'll generate a lot of plot for you." Burton liked the approach: "I'd just meet Sam on weekends to discuss the early writing stages. We knocked it into good shape while I directed *Beetlejuice*, but as a 'go' project it was only green-lighted by Warners when the opening figures for *Beetlejuice* surprised everybody — including myself!"

Mel Gibson, Alec Baldwin, Bill Murray, Charlie Sheen and Pierce Brosnan were all rumoured to be on Warner Bros' shortlist for the title role, although Jack Nicholson's casting as The Joker meant that the studio could afford to go with an unknown — after all, it had worked with Christopher Reeve for *Superman*. Burton had his doubts. "In my mind I kept reading reviews that said, 'Jack's terrific, but the unknown as Batman is nothing special,'" he told Mark Salisbury. Neither did he want to cast an obvious action hero — "Why would this big, macho, Arnold Schwarzenegger-type person dress up as a bat for God's sake?" Finally, it came down to only one choice: Michael Keaton, whom he had just directed in *Beetlejuice*. "*That* guy you could see putting on a bat-suit; he does it because he *needs* to, because he's not this gigantic, strapping macho man. It's all about transformation..." observed Burton. "Taking Michael and making him Batman just underscored the whole split personality thing which is really what I think the movie's all about."

By this time, Hamm's involvement had been sidelined by the writers' strike, so Burton brought in *Beetlejuice* writer Warren Skaaren and Charles McKeown (*The Adventures of Baron Munchausen*). Their principal job was to lighten the tone — not because of Keaton's casting, but because of studio fears that a troubled and disturbed Batman, full of self-doubt and unresolved psychological issues, might turn off audiences. "I see what they're doing," Hamm conceded, "in that they don't want to have a larger-than-life, heroic character who is plagued by doubts about the validity of what he's doing, but it's stuff that I miss."

Principal photography began under tight security in October 1988. Although Sean Young's riding accident threw the schedule out at an early stage, it could have spelled disaster for the production had it occurred later in the shoot; as it was, none of her scenes had to be re-shot when Kim Basinger stepped into Vicki Vale's shoes. In spite of this early setback, the sheer scale of the production, the complexity of the special effects, the extensive night shoots, the large number of interior and exterior locations, and the restrictive nature of Jack Nicholson's contract — which, despite his enormous fee, meant that he could only be called for a specified number of hours per day, including time spent in the makeup chair — Burton delivered the film on schedule, and only a fraction over budget. The anticipation for *Batman* was running at fever pitch by the time the film finally hit US cinemas on 21 June 1989, swooping to a record-breaking $42.7 million opening weekend, becoming the first film to hit $100 million after just ten days on release, and grossing $413 million worldwide. 'Bat-mania' swept the planet, with the film becoming not only the biggest film of 1989, but perhaps more significantly the most successful in Warner Bros' history. Thus, it came as no surprise when the studio invited Burton back up to bat for the sequel. No one was more surprised than the director, however, when he said yes.

Although Warner Bros left the Gotham City set standing at Pinewood Studios (at a cost of $20,000 per day) in the hopes that the success of *Batman* would warrant a sequel, *Batman Returns* was ultimately shot in Los Angeles, with Burton again at the helm, and Michael Keaton back in the Batsuit. This time, Burton's dark sensibilities were given a freer reign, with The Penguin (Danny DeVito) and Catwoman (Michelle Pfeiffer) as the villains. Sam Hamm's script (which also featured Catwoman) was rejected in favour of one by *Heathers* scribe Daniel Waters, which was subsequently doctored by Wesley Strick (*Cape Fear*). "When I was hired to write *Batman Returns* ([called] *Batman II* at the time), I was asked to focus on one (big) problem with the current script: Penguin's lack of a 'master plan'," Strick recalls. "To be honest, this didn't especially bother me; in fact I found it refreshing — in comic book stories, there's nothing hoarier or (usually) hokier than an archvillain's 'master plan'. But the lack of one in *Batman II* was obsessing the Warner brass." Strick says that he was presented with "the usual boring ideas to do with warming the city, or freezing the city, that kind of stuff." (Warner executives evidently continued to have similar ideas as the years passed: a frozen Gotham ended up as a key plot device in *Batman & Robin*.) Strick pitched an alternative approach — inspired by the 'Moses' parallels of Water's prologue, in which Baby Penguin is bundled in a basket and thrown in the river where he floats, helpless, till he's saved (and subsequently raised) by Gotham's sewer denizens — in which Penguin's 'master plan' is to kill the firstborn sons of Gotham City. Warner Bros loved it, and so did Burton. However, as Strick admits, "It turned out to be a controversial addition. The toy manufacturers were not alone in disliking it — it also did substantially less business than the first [*Batman*]." Indeed, although *Batman Returns* scored a bigger opening weekend ($45.6 million) than its predecessor, its worldwide gross was $282.8 million, barely two thirds of *Batman*'s score.

Joel Schumacher's *Batman Forever* (1995) — featuring Val Kilmer as Batman, Jim Carrey as The Riddler, Nicole Kidman as love interest Dr Chase Meridian, Chris O'Donnell as Robin, and (despite the casting of

Billy Dee Williams as Harvey Dent in *Batman*) Tommy Lee Jones as Harvey Dent/Two-Face — bounced back, with a $52.7 million opening weekend and a worldwide gross of $333 million. Yet the $42.87 million opening weekend and mere $237 million worldwide gross of the same director's *Batman & Robin* (1997) — with George Clooney and Chris O'Donnell as the titular dynamic duo, Arnold Schwarzenegger as Mr Freeze, Uma Thurman as Poison Ivy and Alicia Silverstone as Batgirl — effectively put the franchise on hiatus, despite a reported $125 million in additional revenue from tie-in toys, merchandise, clothing and ancillary items.

Despite the fact that, as far as Warner Bros was concerned, the future of the franchise remained in doubt, a plethora of rumours, lies and/or wishful thinking circulated about a fifth Batman film. Madonna had been cast as The Joker's twisted love interest, Harley Quinn. The adversary in *Batman 5* was to be The Sacrecrow — a second rank villain first introduced in the comics in 1940 — played by John Travolta, Howard Stern or Jeff Goldblum (depending on which source you believed). Jack Nicholson was returning as The Joker, possibly in flashback or as hallucinations invoked by The Scarecrow. "The Joker is coming, and it's no laughing matter," Nicholson himself reportedly teased journalists when asked about upcoming projects at a press conference for *As Good As It Gets*. In fact such was the level of scuttlebutt in the months following the release of *Batman & Robin* that several of the most prominent Internet rumour-mills — including Dark Horizons and Coming Attractions — took the unusual step of placing a moratorium on *Batman 5* rumours. Yet from all this sound and fury a few tales of the Bat did emerge which appeared to have an element of truth. One was that Mark Protosevich — who scripted *The Cell* and Ridley Scott's unproduced adaptation of *I Am Legend* for Warner Bros — had written a script, entitled either *Batman Triumphant* or *DarkKnight*, which featured Arkham Asylum, The Scarecrow and Harley Quinn, as well as numerous nightmarish hallucinations of Batman's past.

One of the biggest rumours centred on the casting of Batman himself. Despite the fact that George Clooney was contracted to make at least one more film in the series, Kurt Russell — then starring for Warner Bros in Paul Anderson's ill-fated *Soldier* — was widely reported to be in line for the role, although producer Jon Peters was dismissive.

"He's not Batman," he told *Cinescape*. "Forget it. How could he be Batman? He's my age. He could be Batman's father, but not Batman." The studio, apparently hoping to break the 'revolving door' casting of the Batman role, publicly stood by Clooney, who appeared willing to fulfil his contract. "If there is another, I'd do it," he told *E! News* in September 1997. "I have a contract to do it. It'd be interesting to get another crack at it to make it different or better. I'll take a look at [*Batman & Robin*] again in a couple of months," he added. "I got the sense that it fell short, so I need to go back and look at it, see what I could have done better."

Although Clooney believed he had "killed the franchise", it was director Joel Schumacher, who had wrenched the series almost all the way back to the campy style of the sixties TV show, who bore the brunt of the blame for the relatively poor performance of *Batman & Robin*. "I felt I had disappointed a lot of older fans by being too conscious of the family aspect," he told *Variety* in early 1998. "I'd gotten tens of thousands of letters from parents asking for a film their children could go to. Now, I owe the hardcore fans the Batman movie they would love me to give them." The implication was that he would be asked to make another *Batman*, and on 1 July 1998 he went further, telling *E! Online* that he had talked with Warner Bros production chief Lorenzo di Bonaventura about the possibility of doing another one. "I would only do it on a much smaller scale, with less villains and truer in nature to the comic books," he said.

Schumacher's chief inspiration was Frank Miller's *Batman: Year One*, illustrated by Miller's *Daredevil: Born Again* collaborator David Mazzucchelli, using a heavily-inked, high-contrast style which recalled newspaper strips like *Dick Tracy*, and coloured with earthy tones by Richmond Lewis. In just four twenty-four-page issues, Miller rewrote the first year of Batman mythology from the point of view of James Gordon, a young police lieutenant still years away from his promotion to the more familiar rank of Commissioner. As Miller wrote in his introduction to the collected edition, "If your only memory of Batman is that of Adam West and Burt Ward exchanging camped-out quips while clobbering slumming guest stars Vincent Price and Cesar Romero, I hope this book will come as a surprise."

*Year One* begins as Gordon arrives in Gotham with his pregnant wife Ann, just as Bruce Wayne returns to the city where his parents were shot dead before his eyes eighteen years earlier. After twelve years of self-imposed exile, Wayne begins training himself for the double life he is soon to lead: layabout playboy by day, masked vigilante by night. However, while Bruce is discovering the difficulties inherent in trying to clean up streets that want to stay dirty, Lieutenant Gordon is finding that the corruption he encounters among street cops is endemic, and goes all the way to the top. Although Gordon initially endangers himself by exercising zero tolerance towards his corrupt colleagues, he also earns a reputation for heroics, making him as untouchable as he is incorruptible — until he slips into an affair with a beautiful colleague, Detective Essen, forcing him to admit his infidelity rather than give in to blackmail. Meanwhile, just as a freak encounter with a bat has inspired Bruce Wayne to adopt an *alter ego* to strike fear into the dark hearts of the Gotham underworld — not to mention the same corrupt cops Gordon is fighting from the inside — so the 'Batman' inspires a cat-loving prostitute named Selina to switch careers, leaving the 'cathouse' (brothel) to become a costumed cat burglar. Finally, Batman narrowly escapes after being cornered in a tenement building and fire-bombed by Gordon's superiors — just in time to save Gordon's newborn baby from thugs, and thereby create an unofficial alliance between the two idealistic crime fighters, one in plain clothes, one in costume.

Despite Schumacher's interest in using *Year One* as the basis for a darker, grittier adaptation, in the summer of 1999 Warner Bros asked New York film-maker Darren Aronofsky, fresh from his breakthrough feature, *Pi*, how he might approach the Batman franchise. "I told them I'd cast Clint Eastwood as the Dark Knight, and shoot it in Tokyo, doubling for Gotham City," he says, only half-joking. "That got their attention." Whether inspired or undeterred, the studio was brave enough to open a dialogue with the avowed Bat-fan, who became interested in the idea of an adaptation of *Year One*. "The Batman franchise had just gone more and more back towards the TV show, so it became tongue-in-cheek, a grand farce, camp," says Aronofsky. "I pitched the complete opposite, which was totally bring-it-back-to-the-streets raw, trying to set it in a kind of real reality — no stages, no sets, shooting it all in inner cities across America, creating a very real feeling. My pitch was

*Death Wish* or *The French Connection* meets *Batman*. In *Year One,* Gordon was kind of like Serpico, and Batman was kind of like Travis Bickle," he adds, referring to police corruption whistle-blower Frank Serpico, played by Al Pacino in the eponymous 1973 film, and Robert De Niro's vigilante in Martin Scorsese's *Taxi Driver*. Aronofsky had already noted how Frank Miller's acclaimed *Sin City* series had influenced his first film, *Pi*; in addition, the director already had a good working relationship with the writer/artist, since they had collaborated on an unproduced feature adaptation of Miller's earlier graphic novel, *Ronin*. "Our take was to infuse the [Batman] movie franchise with a dose of reality," Aronofsky says. "We tried to ask that eternal question: 'What does it take for a real man to put on tights and fight crime?'"

The studio was intrigued enough to commission a screenplay, in which Aronofsky and Miller took a great many liberties, not only with the *Year One* comic book, but with Batman mythology in general. For a start, the script strips Bruce Wayne of his status as heir apparent to the Wayne Industries billions, proposing instead that the young Bruce is found in the street after his parents' murder, and taken in by 'Big Al', who runs an auto repair shop with his son, 'Little Al'. Driven by a desire for vengeance towards a manifest destiny of which he is only dimly aware, young Bruce (of deliberately indeterminate age) toils day and night in the shop, watching the comings and goings of hookers, johns, pimps and corrupt cops at a sleazy East End cathouse across the street, while chain-smoking detective James Gordon struggles with the corruption he finds endemic among Gotham City police officers of all ranks.

Bruce's first act as a vigilante is to confront a dirty cop named Campbell as he accosts 'Mistress Selina' in the cathouse, but Campbell ends up dead and Bruce narrowly escapes being blamed. Realising that he needs to operate with more methodology, he initially dons a cape and hockey mask — deliberately suggestive of the costume of Jason Voorhees in the *Friday the 13th* films. However, Bruce soon evolves a more stylised 'costume' with both form and function, acquires a variety of makeshift gadgets and weapons, and re-configures a black Lincoln Continental into a makeshift 'Bat-mobile' — complete with blacked-out windows, night vision driving goggles, armoured bumpers and a super-charged school bus engine. In his new guise as 'The Bat-

Man', Bruce Wayne wages war on criminals from street level to the highest echelons, working his way up the food chain to Police Commissioner Loeb and Mayor Noone, even as the executors of the Wayne estate search for their missing heir. In the end, Bruce accepts his dual destiny as heir to the Wayne fortune and the city's saviour, and Gordon comes to accept that, while he may not agree with The Bat-Man's methods, he cannot argue with his results. "In the comic book, the reinvention of Gordon was inspired," says Aronofsky, "because for the first time he wasn't a wimp, he was a bad-ass guy. Gordon's opening scene for us was [him] sitting on a toilet with the gun barrel in his mouth and six bullets in his hand, thinking about blowing his head off — and that to me is the character."

The comic and the script have many scenes in common — including Bruce Wayne's nihilistic narration (part Travis Bickle from *Taxi Driver*, part Rorschach from that other great late 80s graphic novel, *Watchmen*), a heroic Gordon saving a baby during a hostage crisis, Selina as proto-Catwoman, the beating Gordon receives from fellow cops as a warning to give up his war on corruption, his suspicion that Harvey Dent is The Bat-Man, and the climactic battle in the tenement building. But it acts as a jumping-off point for a much grander narrative. Although the script removes the subplot of Gordon's adultery, it goes further towards blurring the boundaries between accepted notions of good and evil: Gordon decries The Bat-Man's vigilantism as the work of a terrorist whose actions put him outside the law, not above it, unaware that it was as much his own televised declaration of war on crime and corruption which inspired Bruce to vigilantism as the senseless and random murder of Bruce's parents. The script contains numerous references for Bat-fans, including a brief scene with a giggling green-haired inmate of Arkham Asylum, and goes a long way towards setting up a sequel, as Selina/Catwoman discovers the true identity of The Bat-Man. Interestingly, neither the comic book nor the script provide an entirely convincing argument for Bruce Wayne's transformation into Batman: while *Year One* takes a more traditional approach — a bat smashes through the window of Bruce's study — the script has Bruce take inspiration from the Bat-shaped mark produced by his signet ring (shades of Lee Falk's superhero The Phantom) which leads the tabloids to dub him 'The Bat-Man'.

In a rare interview, Miller told *The Onion* about working with Aronofsky. "He's a ball," he said. "Ideas just pour out of his ears. We tend to have a lot of fun together. It's funny, because in many ways I think I'm the lighter one of the team, and I'm not used to that." Although he would not talk about the content of the film "because I think Warner Brothers would have somebody beat me up," he observed that asking a screenwriter what the movie would be like "is like asking a doorman whether a building is going to be condemned." Nevertheless, Aronofsky believes that his and Miller's approach would have made Tim Burton's *Batman* look like a cartoon. "I think Tim did it very well," he says, "especially on his second film, which I think is the masterpiece of the series. But it's not reality. It's totally Tim Burton's world; a brilliant, well-polished Gothic perfection concoction. The first one did have a certain amount of reality, but there were still over-the-top fight sequences, and I wanted to have real fights, [explore] what happens when two men actually fight, which you just don't see. Because once you start romanticising it and fantasising it into super-heroics, in the sense of good guys versus bad guys, and you're not playing with the ambiguity of what is good and what is bad... I just could not find a way in for myself to tell that story.

Of his own approach, Aronofsky admits, "I think Warners always knew it would never be something they could make. I think rightfully so, because four year-olds buy Batman stuff, so if you release a film like that, every four year-old's going to be screaming at their mother to take them to see it, so they really need a PG property. But there was a hope at one point that, in the same way that DC Comics puts out different types of Batman titles for different ages, there might be a way of doing [the movies] at different levels. So I was pitching to make an R-rated adult fan-based *Batman* — a hardcore version that we'd do for not that much money. You wouldn't get any breaks from anyone because it's Warner Bros and it's Batman, but you could do it for a smart price, raw and edgy, and make it more for fans and adults. Maybe shoot it on Super-16 [mm film format], and maybe release it after you release the PG one, and say 'That's for kids, and this one's for adults.'" Nevertheless, he adds, "Warner Bros was very brave in allowing us to develop it, and Frank and I were both really happy with the script."

In Burbank, Warner Bros was simultaneously pursuing an equally radical approach to its biggest franchise, as Aronofsky reveals. "They had a vision of a *Matrix* version that could have been really cool, but it just wasn't something I was really interested in doing." Aronofsky may be referring to the possibility of *The Matrix* writer-directors Larry and Andy Wachowski helming a *Batman* film — which Lorenzo di Bonaventura admitted "had crossed his mind" — perhaps even with Keanu Reeves in the role, a rumour which Reeves himself appeared to encourage when he told listings magazine *TV Times* how he would approach the role. "It'll have to be dark, very sombre," he said. "Something that'll make people think twice about whether they're actually watching a Batman film or not... I want to see more about what makes [him] tick — Bruce is far more than just your average wacko." As for The Joker, he went on, "He's the archetypal bad guy, the 'Bat-nemesis'. He's the dude with whom the Bat must battle — he's in the film, or I'm not! And Jack Nicholson has to do it again, definitely." Within days, Warner Bros sensibly dismissed talk of Keanu Reeves star-ring as Batman, causing rumour-mongers to turn their attention to an equally bogus suggestion: Ben Affleck. Speaking via his official web-site's message board, the future star of *Daredevil* hastily dismissed the claim as "pure fiction. There is no Batman script, no movie being planned, [and] they have not called me or my agent."

While the future of the live-action *Batman* remained up in the air, the Caped Crusader was flying high in a highly stylised and hugely suc-cessful TV show, *Batman: The Animated Series*, which amassed eighty-five half-hour episodes between 1992 and 1995, and spawned numerous feature-length spin-offs — beginning with the theatrically-released *Batman: Mask of the Phantasm* — and no fewer than four sister series. One of these, Paul Dini and Alan Burnett's futuristic *Batman Beyond* (aka *Batman of the Future*) — in which an ageing Bruce Wayne hands over the Batman mantle to teenage protégé Terry McGinnis — caught the eye of the studio, which was soon considering the possibility of a live-action version. "I know that it's one of the possible options that they have discussed on the lot," Dini told *Cinescape* in November 1999, adding that no script had been written. "I don't know what their plans are for it beyond just investigating several alternative ways to keep Batman going, as opposed to the way they've been doing the last two or three movies," he added. "It's a real idea that they're considering, but no one has asked us to be involved with it." Warner Bros registered several domain names related to *Batman Beyond: The Movie*, which were unconnected to the direct-to-video animated feature *Batman Beyond: Return of The Joker*, and in August 2000 *Variety* named Boaz Yakin (who had written a script for Marvel Comics' *The Punisher* and directed the surprise hit *Remember the Titans*) as director of the live-action *Batman Beyond*. As co-creator Paul Dini told website Comics Continuum, "Boaz is co-writing the script with [Alan Burnett and myself] as well as directing." Although such a script was almost certainly completed, soon after Dini's announcement the studio let it be known that it was no longer pursuing the *Batman Beyond* approach.

In the meantime, several former Batman interpreters threw their hats into the Bat-ring, with Val Kilmer expressing interest in returning to the role, comics writer Grant Morrison (*Batman: Arkham Asylum*) revealing that he had given the studio a "great pitch which got Batman out of Gay Gotham for a while and brought in some brilliant villains nobody's used yet", and even George Clooney offering his own take on the next film: "You do the movie cheap, in a *film noir* style," he told the Internet Movie Database. "Make Batman the Dark Knight, something Tim Burton didn't even do. You start at Alfred's burial, with a Sam Spade *film noir* narrator, talking to this Death figure standing there that only he sees. Go into the first big action set [piece] with Robin and he gets killed." Clooney's continuing contractual connection to the franchise did nothing to quell various rumours linking Brad Pitt, Nicolas Cage, Aaron Eckhart (*Erin Brockovich*), Brendan Fehr (TV's *Roswell*) and Christian Bale (*American Psycho*) to the role, despite the fact that neither Boaz Yakin nor Darren Aronofsky had ever discussed the potential casting of their respective projects, neither of which were being pursued.

With *Year One* and *Batman Beyond* both on the shelf, a more likely prospect seemed to be the big-screen team-up of DC Comics' two biggest heroes, a cinematic equivalent of the popular *World's Finest* title and the animated Batman/Superman adventures. The idea was first mooted in October 1998, when Jon Peters told *Cinescape*'s Beth Laski that a fifth Batman film was unlikely, "unless we put Batman and Superman together later." Warner Bros evidently saw a team-up movie as more than just a tantalising possibility, but a viable way of bringing the Superman and Batman franchises out of the development mire. It was soon confirmed that the studio was excited about a script entitled *Batman vs Superman*, written by *Se7en* and *Sleepy Hollow* scribe Andrew Kevin Walker and subsequently 'polished' by Akiva Goldsman (*Batman Forever*, *Batman & Robin*, *A Beautiful Mind*), in which the characters would begin as allies — albeit with radically different worldviews — but then face each other in a showdown concerning Bruce Wayne's desire for vengeance on a super-villain who murders his new bride.

The story begins five years into Bruce Wayne's life post-Batman, having put his costume back into the closet following the death of Robin. He has settled down, married a woman named Elizabeth, and is happier than ever. Over in Metropolis, however, Superman has not been so lucky in love, having been dumped by Lois Lane due to the myriad difficulties of being Clark Kent's girlfriend. When The Joker, previously thought dead, kills Elizabeth with a poison dart, Bruce takes it hard. First, he blames Superman, because the Man of Steel saved The Joker from a fatal beating just before the murder; second, he resumes the mantle of Batman — not, this time, under any pretence of metering out justice, but for the sheer cathartic pleasure of beating up bad guys. Superman, who has been busy wooing his first love, Lana Lang, in Smallville, tries to talk Bruce out of his vengeful ways, an act which ultimately pits the two heroes against each other. Eventually, it transpires that Superman's nemesis Lex Luthor was behind The Joker's return, hoping that Batman and Superman would kill each other. Instead, the two heroes unite to defeat first The Joker, and finally Luthor, the man fundamentally behind Elizabeth's death.

Opinions from Internet script reviewers were divided, either over the details of the Walker and Goldsman drafts, or the very idea of having Batman and Superman go *mano a mano*. Responding to an unfavourable review of Goldsman's rewrite by Coming Attractions' Darwin Mayflower, Batman on Film reporter 'Jett' said that, while he had not read the Goldsman draft, "I very much liked Walker's original... I thought it was a very dark and powerful script and had a very clever way of pitting Batman against Superman. Mayflower flatly does not like the squaring off of Bats and Supes... [whereas] I found it quite exciting — plus you know that they are going to end up as allies in the end. Mayflower also has a problem with Goldsman's (who many credit for the killing of the Bat-franchise with his p.o.s. *Batman & Robin* script) rewrites," Jett added. "The only reason I can come up with why WB let Goldsman do rewrites was to lighten the script up a bit. Walker's original — in my opinion — was dark. Perhaps WB thought too much so."

Nevertheless, the studio was sufficiently excited about the script to postpone its plan for a new stand-alone Superman film *and* a fifth Batman in order to fast-track *Batman vs Superman* for a 2004 release, with Wolfgang Petersen (*Das Boot, The Perfect Storm*) at the helm. "It is the clash of the titans," the German-born director told *Variety* in July 2002. "They play off of each other so perfectly. [Superman] is clear, bright, all that is noble and good, and Batman represents the dark, obsessive and vengeful side. They are two sides of the same coin and that is material for great drama." Petersen subsequently spoke to MTV.com about his love for the *Batman* and *Superman* films, "especially in both cases the first two. I saw them over and over again." *Batman vs Superman*, he added, would be part of the lore of the films and the comics, "but it's also different. First of all, the dynamics are different because if they are in one movie together it changes a lot of things and it gives you a new perspective on superheroes... You also have the look and feel of Metropolis, the bright golden city, and the feel of Gotham, which is a shadowy, sinister city, in the same movie. This is Superman/Batman of the time after September 11th, also. It takes place in today or tomorrow's world."

Unsurprisingly, the announcement of a fast-tracked *Batman vs Superman* movie led to a surge of speculation as to which actors might don the respective capes. "We have a script that really very, very much concentrates on the characters," Petersen told MTV.com. "It's really material for two great actors." Although he had previously cited Matt Damon as a possible star, Petersen later clarified that he was merely an example of the kind of actor he was looking for. "Someone [who] we so far did not really think of as a big action hero, [who] turned out to be a great actor who can also do great action... He's one of these guys, but there's a lot of these guys out there." As far as the rumour-mills were concerned, Jude Law and Josh Hartnett were apparently front-runners to play Superman/Clark Kent, while Colin Farrell and Christian Bale — the latter previously connected with the *Year One* role — were widely mentioned for dual duties as Bruce Wayne and Batman. ("No, that's

*Bateman*, not Batman," quipped Bale, referring to Patrick Bateman, his character in *American Psycho*.) Barely a month after the *Variety* announcement, however, *Batman vs Superman* seemed suddenly to have fallen out of favour with the studio, leading director Wolfgang Petersen to quit the project in favour of *Troy*, an epic retelling of Homer's *The Iliad* starring Brad Pitt.

The studio's swift about-face was based on a number of factors. Firstly, on 5 July, *Alias* creator J. J. Abrams had turned in the first eighty-eight pages of a new stand-alone Superman script, designed to be the first of a trilogy. Bob Brassel, a senior vice president for production at the studio, called producer Jon Peters, urging him to read the work-in-progress. "I did," Peters told *The New York Times*, "and it was amazing. In a world of chaos, it's about hope and light." Abrams delivered the remaining fifty pages of the script in mid-July, just as *Spider-Man* began its amazing assault on box office records, suggesting that light and airy, not dark and powerful, was the way to go with superhero flicks. At that point, Peters, Abrams and Brassel met in the offices of executive vice president for worldwide motion pictures Lorenzo di Bonaventura — the man behind the Harry Potter and *Matrix* movies, and a long time champion of *Batman vs Superman* — who said that he liked the script ("It had more epic ambition than earlier *Superman* scripts," he said later), but that he planned to release *Batman vs Superman* first. According to Peters, Abrams said, "You can't do that," suggesting that it was akin to releasing *When Harry Divorced Sally* before *When Harry Met Sally*.

Both sides had their points: with two iconic heroes for the price of one, *Batman vs Superman* arguably stood the better chance in a market-place soon to be crowded with superhero films, ranging from *Hulk* to *Daredevil*, and more sequels featuring Spider-Man and The X-Men; however, if the darker sensibility of *Batman vs Superman* did not connect with audiences, it could effectively kill both franchises before they had had a chance to be revived. Besides, if either *Batman* or *Superman* failed, the studio would still have the team-up movie to fall back on. As studio president Alan Horn told *The New York Times*, "In reintroducing these characters we wanted to do what was in the best interest of the company." Thus, in early August, Horn asked ten senior studio executives — representing international and domestic theatrical marketing, consumer products and home video — to read both scripts, and decide which of them stood the better chance in the post-*Spider-Man* market-place. "I wanted some objectivity," Horn explained. "Why not get an opinion or two?" At the meeting, di Bonaventura argued in favour of *Batman vs Superman*; others, however, felt that Abrams' three-part Superman story had better long-term prospects for toy, DVD and ancil-liary sales. Besides, even if the majority had not favoured the *Superman* script, Horn had the casting vote. "I said I wanted to do *Superman*," he told *The New York Times*. "At the end of the day it's my job to decide what movies we make."

The plan, Horn later told *The Hollywood Reporter*, was that *Superman*, the long-mooted *Catwoman* spin-off, and "a Batman origins movie" (presumably *Year One*) would revive both franchises, paving the way for a team-up movie. "I'd like to think that each character will evolve so that when we have *Batman vs Superman*, the meeting of the two will feel more organic," he said. Peters, the former hairdresser and *Batman* producer who had toiled through the development of a Superman film for eight years, was moved to tears when Alan Horn phoned to tell him the news. "I swear I heard the flapping of angel wings when Alan was talking," he said. Peters, in turn, called Christopher Reeve, who had played Superman in four films between 1978 and 1987, and had recently guest-starred on the small-screen Superman show *Smallville*, despite a crippling spinal injury he suffered in a fall from a horse. "He told me that his original idea was to do a film of *Superman vs Batman*," Reeve later recalled. "They were pretty far into it, and then Jon saw that documentary that my son made about me and how five years after the injury I started to move." According to Reeve, Peters began to rethink the idea: "'Why should [they] have two super-heroes fighting?' The movie that Warner Bros is making now will be a much more uplifting and spiritual story." In August, Warner Bros offi-cially switched off *Batman vs Superman*'s green light. Days later, on 4 September, its greatest champion, Lorenzo di Bonaventura, quit after twelve years at the studio, giving credence to the widespread specula-tion that Horn vs di Bonaventura — an epic battle of wills between two of the studios biggest guns over two of its biggest assets — had con-tributed to his departure.

Where all this left the Batman franchise was unclear until early

2003, when *Variety* revealed that Christopher Nolan, director of the tricksy *Memento* and a remake of Scandinavian thriller *Insomnia*, had been signed to direct a stand-alone *Batman* movie. "All I can say is that I grew up with Batman, I've been fascinated by him and I'm excited to contribute to the lore surrounding the character," Nolan said. "He is the most credible and realistic of the superheroes, and has the most complex human psychology. His superhero qualities come from within. He's not a magical character. I had a fantastic experience with the studio on *Insomnia*," he added, "and I'm keen to repeat that experience." Although *Variety* also reported that both *Year One* and *Catwoman* — scripted by John Rogers (*The Core*), starring Ashley Judd (later to be replaced by Halle Berry) and directed by visual effects veteran Pitof — were also on the cards, Nolan's untitled *Batman* seemed the most likely to move forward, although it was unclear which script would form the basis of the film. In March, *Variety* reported that David Goyer — who scripted *Dark City*, *The Crow: City of Angels*, the comic book adaptation *Blade* and its sequels, and unused drafts of *Freddy vs Jason* — was writing a brand new *Batman* script, apparently from a concept put forward by director Christopher Nolan. "You can make mistakes being too slavish to the source," Goyer told Boston's *Weekly Dig*. "You have to change things, collapse certain characters. We got a free pass with *Blade*. There's less of a burden to adhere to the mythology, since he didn't even have his own comic at the time. But then with Batman there's been TV shows and movies, so in terms of public consciousness the canon was already set. Chris Nolan and I had to meet with [DC Comics president] Paul Levitz and other high-ups, to make sure we didn't break the core rules of the character."

One persistent and intriguing rumour was that the Nolan/Goyer *Batman* may be based, at least in part, on a script entitled *Batman: The Frightening*, which appeared on the Internet in January 2003 — a fortnight before the Christopher Nolan announcement — and was promptly withdrawn at the request of Warner Bros. Apparently set after the events of *Batman & Robin*, the script opens with a dramatic escape from Arkham Asylum, reveals that Batman is wanted for the murder of Commissioner Gordon, and then tells — in flashback — of how The Scarecrow unleashed a fear drug on the citizens of Gotham, before releasing the inmates of Arkham Asylum onto the terrified populace.

Credited authors Terry Hayes and Rafael Yglesias (who shared credit, but did not physically collaborate on *From Hell*) issued strenuous denials distancing themselves from the project, and it was widely believed to be a work of fan fiction — until Warner Bros registered several Internet domain names related to the title. Rumours persisted that the script might form the basis of Goyer's rewrite.

In July, Batman news of a different kind caused a stir, as writer-director Sandy Collora unveiled arguably the most ambitious work of fan fiction in history: an eight-minute (six not counting the credits) 35mm film entitled *Batman: Dead End*, in which a comic book-costumed Batman (Clark Bartram) encounters The Joker (Andrew Koenig, son of Walter, *Star Trek*'s Chekov) in an alleyway, only to be set upon by an Alien and no fewer than four Predators (with the costumes superbly capturing the appearance of the creatures in Fox's *Alien* and *Predator* film series). Despite the extraordinary production values, cinematography, sound, make-up, costumes and special effects, Collora had no problem classifying the $30,000 *Dead End* as a fan film. "I'm a fan, and I made a film," he told Ain't It Cool. Describing *Dead End* as "my take on the Dark Knight", he explained that he had made it as a showcase for his abilities as a director, and had no wish to infringe on DC, Warner Bros and Fox copyrights. ("The legal department, I'm sure, will be sending me something soon, asking me to 'cease and desist'. Cease and desist *what* I don't know — I'm not selling the film, or even showing it for that matter. If people want to see it, it's all over the net and I have nothing to do with that.")

With no official Batman film having been seen for six years, it was to be expected that *Dead End* be greeted with fervour as millions of fans clamoured to get their hands (via their computer mouses) on the short, which premièred at the San Diego Comic Con. It was equally unsurprising that the film could not possibly live up to the hype. "The sheer amount of press and attention that this film has been getting is truly unfathomable, and quite unexpected," Collora admitted. "I don't think any film can live up to *that much* hype." Nevertheless, many — including legendary comic strip artist Alex Ross and writer/director Kevin Smith — felt that it represented the best Caped Crusader ever seen on screen. As pre-production on Nolan's film crawled forward, with Christian Bale donning the cowl, Bat-fans were given to wonder: if an unknown film-maker could manage to make a more than competent Batman short film for about the price of a new Volvo — what was taking Warner Bros so long?

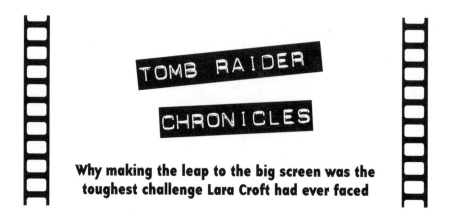

# TOMB RAIDER

## CHRONICLES

**Why making the leap to the big screen was the
toughest challenge Lara Croft had ever faced**

"We should have made a better movie. But we learned from
our mistakes and [the sequel] is a better movie.
For starters, it's got a plot."

— Tomb Raider *producer Lloyd Levin*

Computer and video games have never made the best basis for movies — whether commercially successful or not, they are almost without exception stultifyingly awful. Of course, since Hollywood is a business rather than an artistic endeavour, this has not prevented producers from going big game hunting, trying to turn the simplistic sequential narratives and one-dimensional characters of video games into big screen blockbusters. Although the computer revolution inspired such films as *Tron*, *The Last Starfighter* and *War Games*, the first brand name computer game conversion did not appear until 1993's *Super Mario Bros*, but it was another couple of years before British director Paul Anderson turned the smash hit 'beat-em-up' game *Mortal Kombat* into a phenomenal opening weekend, despite the universal derision the film received from critics. Studios had been quick to jump on the latest bandwagon, but films like *Street Fighter* and *Double Dragon* did not fare so well.

The thinking behind these ill-starred enterprises was simple: not only did brands like these have a ready-made international fan base, they tended to fall within Hollywood's most highly prized demographic: young males, aged twelve to thirty-four. If you play computer games, the logic goes, you probably go to the cinema, and vice versa — a theory borne out by the vast number of hit movies (*Die Hard*, *Men in Black*, *The Matrix*) converted into equally successful console games. One persistent problem has been that console gamers are a notoriously fickle bunch, and by the time many hit titles have reached the screen, a new game — or even a new console — has reached the shelves, and suddenly *Sonic the Hedgehog* looks about as cutting edge as *Pong*. Eventually, the studios wised up and decided to wait for a gargantuan global gaming success before swooping in for the movie rights. Finally, in November 1996, the largely male gaming population got its first female hero. Lara Croft was her name. And *Tomb Raider* was her game.

The brainchild of Simon Channing-Williams, Lara Croft was born at the offices of Eidos Interactive in early 1995. Part James Bond, part Indiana Jones, part glamour model, the luscious Lara was a twenty-something British aristocrat-cum-adventurer who eschewed the life of a debutante in favour of self-financed expeditions in which she braved lethal traps, dangerous creatures and treacherous rivals in order to steal relics from ancient burial sites. Lara made her début in November 1996, in what was essentially a platform game, and the platform in question was PlayStation, Sony's first entry into the risky but potentially lucrative console market, then dominated by Nintendo and Sega. *Tomb Raider* became an overnight success, propelling the pistol-packing virtual sex symbol Lara Croft to international stardom. Four sequels — *Tomb Raider II*, *Tomb Raider III: Adventures of Lara Croft*, *Tomb Raider: The Last Revelation* and *Tomb Raider Chronicles* — appeared year-on-year from 1997 to 2000, by which time Lara had become the biggest icon in the history of console games, selling more than twenty million games worldwide, appearing on more than 200 magazine covers, advertising products around the world, and appearing as the sole virtual entity on a Time Digital list of the fifty most important people in the cyber industry *and* a *Details* magazine list of the world's sexiest women. In the adventures themselves, she had travelled the globe from the frozen ruins embedded in an Arctic glacier to a forgotten valley filled with supposedly extinct creatures in a South American rainforest. It was only a matter of time before she found her way to Hollywood.

Such was the success of the first *Tomb Raider* game that rumours of a movie began as early as March 1997, less than six months after Lara

Croft's début appearance. By September of that year, model turned actress Elizabeth Hurley became the first in a long line of actresses to be linked to the role — by no less an authority than British tabloid *The Sun* — swiftly followed by such diverse names as Diane Lane, Sandra Bullock, Denise Richards, Catherine Zeta-Jones, Famke Janssen, Anna Nicole Smith, Demi Moore, Jennifer Lopez and Rhona Mitra — an unknown model who dressed up as Lara at trade shows (and later co-starred with Christopher Lambert in *Beowulf* and Ali G in *Da Ali G Movie*). Yet it was not until March 1998 that fan site The Croft Times broke the news: after one of the fiercest bidding wars in recent history — during which bidders were required to come up with not just the money, but also ideas and approaches — the film rights had finally been sold to Paramount Pictures. *Tomb Raider: The Movie* looked set to become more than virtual reality.

Making its official announcement a few days later, Eidos confirmed that it had entered into an agreement to license the worldwide film rights to Paramount, with plans to produce a live-action feature film — thus laying rest to rumours that the film might be fully-CG, *à la Toy Story*. "Mr Lawrence Gordon and Mr Lloyd Levin will produce the action adventure," the press release stated, referring to the prolific producers behind two *48 HRS* films, two *Die Hards*, two *Predators* and *Boogie Nights*. John Goldwyn, president of Paramount Motion Pictures, said, "We are thrilled by the possibilities of this film project. We are confident that the pairing of Eidos, a leading company in the cutting-edge world of video game, and producers Larry Gordon and Lloyd Levin, will result in a ground-breaking live-action adventure movie with worldwide appeal." Paramount had good reason to put the movie on the development 'fast track', since its deal with Eidos stipulated that if the project did not move swiftly through development, the rights would automatically expire. Thus, by March, the studio had already hired a screenwriter: Brent V. Friedman, co-writer of the console-game inspired sequel *Mortal Kombat: Annihilation*.

Friedman's first draft opens at a London boarding school in 1986 as sixteen year-old Lara — an expert gymnast and A-student — regails her fellow pupils with stories of her parents' daring exploits, soon revealed to be products of her over-active imagination, since her parents (Lord Desmond and Lady Vivian Croft) are not globe-trotting relic hunters but vacationing souvenir collectors, who attempt to make up for years of neglect by offering Lara a holiday anywhere in the world. Her choice — Tibet — turns out to be an unfortunate one, as their plane crashes in the Himalayas, killing her mother and injuring her father, whom she attempts to pull to safety on a makeshift sled-cum-stretcher. An attack by snow leopards shows Lara's precocious resourcefulness, as she uses one of her trademark flares to chase away the predators, only for Lord Croft to expire in front of the gates of a monastery, where a Tibetan monk named Karak takes in the newly-orphaned girl. From here the script leaps forward thirteen years to the Croft Estate in Hampshire, where an older, wiser Karak now serves as twenty-nine year-old Lara's trainer, guardian and companion.

Meanwhile, in the Caribbean, a grey-haired seventy year-old Scot named Darby Erikson — seemingly tailor-made for a Sean Connery cameo — sends Lara a videotaped message, alerting her to his discovery of a map which he believes might lead to El Dorado, the fabled South American city of gold. Unfortunately, an unscrupulous Australian named Larsen (the name of the evil Texan from the first *Tomb Raider* game) is on his trail, and Darby offers Lara a fifty-fifty split on the lost Incan gold, hoping to appeal to her charitable nature. Against Karak's advice, Lara takes the job, but before she goes, she pays a visit to Stuart, Liam and Wesley, three engineering eggheads — dead ringers for *The X-Files*' Lone Gunmen — who build gadgets and gizmos from designs drawn up by Lara, with whom they are besotted. Before she can leave for Curacao, where she must meet up with Darby, she returns home to find assassins prowling her estate, now inexplicably rigged with deadly traps. Of course, it's soon revealed to be the work of Karak and the gardening staff — presumably all part of her training.

Arriving in Curacao, Lara finds Darby dead, and narrowly avoids meeting the same fate. Although Darby's map has been stolen, she digitally enhances the one on his videotape, and follows it to Ecuador, where she purchases the services of Dodge, a rugged American guide as dodgy as his name suggests, and sets off up the Napo river in pursuit of the murderous Larsen and his fellow Aussies. After an eventful boat ride, during which the pair fend off deadly alligators and narrowly escape being sucked into a whirlpool, Lara ends up one step ahead of Larsen and his malevolent boss, Malvern, who have not figured out that magnetic north has shifted four degrees since 1523, when the map was made, nor that a lake featured on the map was drained by a volcanic earthquake in 1814. Entering through a volcanic fissure, Lara and Dodge discover Incan stone formations dating from the early 16th century, and make their way through a series of increasingly elaborate and ingenious traps. Finally breaching the tomb of Manco, an Incan king, Lara discovers that El Dorado does not mean 'Golden City,' but 'Golden Man' — a reference to Manco himself, who discovered the secret of alchemy, turning base metals into gold. She offers Dodge the same fifty-fifty split Darby offered her, if he will accompany her on the next stage of her journey: a trip even further into darkest Peru to search for Manco's alchemical device, a magical bowl known as 'The Black Veil'.

Of course, there are further revelations to come. No sooner have Lara and Dodge found the magical device than Malvern and Larsen turn up to claim their prize, revealing Dodge to be a traitor in their employ. Dodge regrets his betrayal, however, having grown fond of Lara during their shared exploits, and engineers her escape, getting himself shot in the process. With echoes of her struggle to save her father, she refuses to leave him behind, dragging him to safety and sneaking aboard Malvern's ship, where a last revelation awaits her: that Malvern is using the Black Veil not to turn non-precious metals into gold, but into an altogether more lucrative, dangerous and distinctly twentieth century treasure: weapons grade plutonium! Several daring escapes and one nuclear explosion later, Lara returns home, where she swaps her trademark togs — shorts, a form-fitting Lycra top, boots and mirror shades — for an evening dress to attend a society cocktail party thrown by her paternal aunt. After giving her bemused aunt the Black Veil for safe keeping, Lara makes her final escape — to a pub, where she fulfills an earlier promise to share a pint with 'The Gadget Boys' — further endearing herself to them by downing hers in one.

Friedman delivered his 108-page first draft on 17 July 1998. By 1 October, Internet movie-rumour site Ain't It Cool had posted a withering script review, courtesy of the anonymous 'Agent 4125'. "I'm sorry to report that the content is every bit as old and dusty as the ancient artefacts that Lara pursues in her gaming adventures," the reviewer claimed. "My first impression, upon reading the script, is that die-hard *Tomb Raider* fans will be shocked and dismayed at how much the game background and the character of Lara has been changed. For instance in the opening scenes, which depict the plane crash in the Himalayas, both of Lara's parents are killed — this is not the way *Tomb Raider* fans know it to be! On its own, this would only be a small matter," the report went on, "but there are plenty of other deviations and a general disregard for the *Tomb Raider* mythos throughout the script." The reviewer dismissed the Lara/Karak relationship as "an awkward contrivance" and "a lame take-off of the whole David Carradine/Grasshoper (sic) schtick from *Kung-Fu*," and likened Karak's surprise attack on Lara at Croft Mansion to Kato ambushing Inspector Clouseau in the *Pink Panther* films.

By the time the story gets to South America, Agent 4125 went on, "it seems like a mix of *Predator*-style chase set-pieces in the jungle, and an obligatory series of tricks and traps as Lara navigates her way through a subterranean temple." The reviewer grudgingly acknowledged the fact that Friedman's greatest challenge arguably lay in the fact that, with the exception of the gender of its hero, *Tomb Raider* was a thinly-disguised knock-off of the Indiana Jones movies, "but Friedman doesn't even seem to be trying — [Lara] even has a colourful peasant guide to follow her around and be amazed by her ingenuity in defeating the various traps (just like Satipo at the start of *Raiders of the Lost Ark*)." Although the reviewer conceded that Lara's level of flirtatious banter with Dodge was "about the one part of her character that they got right," the rest of her characterisation was "wrong, wrong, wrong... she relies way too much on contrived James Bond-style high-tech gadgets than her own ingenuity and her motivation is... well, a mystery. It's never really explained why she does these things that she does, or who it is she's trying to help. She just kinda... does them." Summing up, the reviewer described the script as a "shoddy... a cross between Allan Quatermain (remember that?) and *Anaconda*, with lots of steamy jungle, perilous situations and a whole ton of characters you really couldn't care less about."

Clearly, Agent 4125 did not appreciate the obstacles in Friedman's path, nor the structural gymnastics and character revisionism which would be necessary to convert a one- (or, at best two-) dimensional computer game character into a three-dimensional live-action figure. One obvious challenge was that, in the games, Lara's is a largely solitary pursuit (much like gaming itself), making it difficult to create effective scenarios for dialogue, a movie mainstay. Friedman solves the problem by having Lara *re*active rather than *pro*-active in verbal situations, preferring to let actions speak louder than words. And action *is* the operative word, as Lara tackles tricks and traps, each highly reminiscent of her console-based adventures, with an equally typical combination of problem-solving skills and gymnastic expertise. Scenes most typical of Lara's games heritage include a two-gun shoot-out with subterranean rats, a scuba diving sequence complete with harpoon gun and modified oxygen tank, and a sliding wall trap which snags her trademark pony-tail; these, along with quips like "Next time don't send boys to do a girl's work" and Lara's flirtatious dialogue with Dodge, seemed to prove that Friedman had done his homework, capturing the elusive spirit of Lara Croft in word and deed. Nevertheless, on 11 December 1998, a little over two months after Ain't It Cool published Agent 4125's negative review, the same site reported that Friedman had left the project, with another pseudonymous scooper ('ArchChancellor Ridcully') implying a causal link between one fan's assessment of a first draft script and Friedman's subsequent departure. Not so, says Friedman.

"I'd love to give you the whole story, but I'll spare myself the agony," he told *Premiere* magazine, before explaining that, twenty minutes after Paramount approved his script, he received a call from producer Lawrence Gordon, who asked him to "forget what Paramount says" and come up with more economically viable ideas. The studio, meanwhile, insisted that he continue working on the original concept. "The last thing you want to do is get caught in these tug-of-wars," Friedman added, "because you're a writer, nobody, just a casualty of war." Friedman did, however, try to reach a compromise with a second take on the film, but a week after Paramount approved the new draft, Eidos — which retained approval over script, director and star — rejected the script, for unspecified reasons. "My sense is, of all the people I met with, only one of the core group of producers and executives had played the game," Friedman explained. "But everybody has a different interpretation of what will make a lot of money."

In the meantime, Paramount had hired a female screenwriter, *X-Files* scriptwriter Sara Charno, to work on an alternative take. When she struck out, the studio knew that if the next writer did not hit a home run, it was game over. Thus, they went straight to the A-list, hiring Steven de Souza, who had worked with Gordon on such blockbusters as *Die Hard* and *The Running Man*, and had previously tackled another computer games conversion, *Street Fighter*. "I was hired in September 1998 to do a story, treatment, draft, rewrite and polish," says de Souza. "All that took six months, and I turned in my revised, polished script the first week of March 1999. At that point, I was contractually done," he points out. "The reaction to the script was universally positive, and it was the document that Stephen Herek read and which he signed on to film." In other words, he adds, "My script was the one that broke the dam of all the Development Hell."

De Souza says that by this time, acclaimed actress Angelina Jolie (who had co-starred in *Pushing Tin*, *The Bone Collector* and *Girl, Interrupted*) was everyone's first choice for Lara. But no mention was made of her in a *Variety* story, dated 11 April 1999 and headlined "Herek digs Par's *Tomb*", which reported that Herek, director of *Bill & Ted's Excellent Adventure* and *Mr Holland's Opus*, was close to a deal, with summer 2000 the new target release date. "Several scribes took a shot at adapting the vidgame," the report stated, adding: "it wasn't until de Souza submitted his draft that Paramount deemed the project ready for a director to come on board, according to Paramount Motion Picture Group president John Goldwyn."

'Necros', a script reviewer for Internet movie site Coming Attractions, shared Goldwyn's enthusiasm. "Thankfully," the review began, "de Souza's *Tomb Raider* does not begin with a silly and unnecessary backstory on Lara Croft. After a short 'hook' to set up the bad guys, we plunge right into a near-perfect cinematic realization of the best parts of the original *TR* computer game as Lara makes her way through the cavernous tomb of King Philip and retrieves the King's funeral mask. When she returns home she learns that her life may be in danger, and during the subsequent exhibition at the British Museum, a foreign minister from Kafiristan (the small third world country that Lara took the mask from) explains to Lara the mask's significance — that it may lead the way to the long-lost library of Alexander the Great. Lara's old nemesis Larson (the arrogant Texan featured in the original game) steals the mask from the museum that night, and it is now up to Lara to find the lost library before Larson can.

She gathers a small expedition team and sets out to find it, running into many difficult obstacles — some expected and some quite unexpected — along the way.

"Overall, this is an excellent script," the review concluded. "De Souza does a nice job of characterising Lara, and while the plot has touches of both Indiana Jones and James Bond films, it never feels like a rip-off of either series. Nor does the script suffer from an overdose of humour (although Lara has some great one-liners). It's a good, solid action-adventure story with a refreshing emphasis on adventure. With steady-handed direction and some good stunt choreography, TR could turn out to be one of summer 2000's real gems." Producer Lloyd Levin, however, remained unconvinced that de Souza's draft was ready for a green light. "The problem was that we kept falling back on stories and types of movies that were familiar," he told *Premiere*. "We hadn't gotten to the place where we were embracing what was special about the game, which was the character and how contemporary she was."

Herek also wanted changes, and the fact that de Souza had fulfilled his contract gave him licence to bring in new screenwriters, who would be cheaper and more accessible than de Souza. "Another motivation may have been — and of course I'm guessing here — Herek secretly wanted a writer less firmly in the producer's camp than me," de Souza explains. "My having done half a dozen pictures with Larry Gordon made Herek start to think that perhaps he should have a writer on board who would report to him, Herek, and not Gordon." It didn't help matters that, during this period, Gordon's comic book adaptation *Mystery Men* belly-flopped at the box office, which weakened Gordon's standing with Paramount. De Souza says that Gordon wanted to re-hire him — "maybe because I'm a genius, but also just possibly because I would be *his* guy in the shifting sand of studio politics post-*Mystery Men*" — but that his hands were tied. In any case, de Souza was no longer available, being buried in pre-production on his own film, *Possessed*, which he was also directing.

Whatever the reason, Gordon and Levin gave the next draft to two complete unknowns: Patrick Massett and John Zinman, who had adapted the pioneering wireframe arcade game *Battle Zone* into a screenplay for Lloyd Levin. At the pitch for *Battle Zone*, Massett and Zinman were drawn to a lifesize cutout of Lara Croft behind Lloyd Levin's desk, and

— even though they were unfamiliar with the game — decided to pitch for *Tomb Raider: The Movie*. As Zinman told *Creative Screenwriting*, "[The producers] said, 'The situation is this: we're running out of rope; we're looking to make a deal with someone who can give us some security.' They were very up front in saying, 'No one is going to roll the dice on you at this point.' Massett and Zinman chose not to take 'no' for an answer, writing a forty-page 'scriptment' — roughly half way between a treatment and a script — while their agent set up a pitch meeting with the producers. "Scene for scene, beat for beat, we told [them] the movie... from the opening to the final sequence," Massett said of the meeting. "We were riffing off each other the whole time. It was tight, like a forty-minute Jimi Hendrix show." According to Massett, neither producer spoke during the pitch, or after it; yet before the writers had left the lot, their agent called to say they had the go-ahead to turn their pitch into a script.

Only when they had the assignment did Massett and Zinman actually sit down to play the games, which Massett summarised as "a lot of puzzle solving; a bad guy tries to stop her, or beat her to the prize." The film, they felt, should be equally simple: "It was a franchise. It was cool. It was a chick as an action star." As Zinman explained, "The challenge is to create a story that's not going to alienate the fan base. But by the same token we wanted to expand the audience to people who weren't familiar with the game... Something we did incorporate was Lara's intelligence," he added. "Her success as an action hero is that she isn't just brawn. She figures things out; she's the smartest one in the room. I think that's the challenge of the game, that's why people get addicted to it." Seventeen days after getting the job, Massett and Zinman turned in their first draft, at which point, according to Zinman, they were "hailed as heroes." Not so, says de Souza. "Massett and Zinman's first attempt was not well received," he says, adding that it followed his draft in general, keeping the Alexander the Great idea but changing the 'MacGuffin' — Hitchcock's term for the motivating factor of most sto- ries — from Archimedes' Mirror to Achilles' Shield, an artefact they learned about in a PBS video on the Macedonian conqueror. "Of course the whole point of the MacGuffin isn't what it is, but how it is used and where it takes you," says de Souza. "So my original idea — that Alexander the Great stumbled on something very dangerous and hid it to protect civilization, and hid the only clue under the sea — led to a series of scenes and adventures that hardly changed in draft after draft."

Massett and Zinman were subsequently replaced by *Face/Off* scribes Mike Werb and Michael Colleary, who worked with Herek developing a new draft, subsequently reviewed by Darwin Mayflower on the website Screenwriters Utopia. "The script opens in Macedonia, 632 BC," he wrote. "Alexander the Great is mad with power: he has an ancient, supernatural breastplate, the Shield of Achilles, that makes him invulnerable. Alexander has begun to kill his own people, to feed the demon-dog Cerberus, and two of his men, Priam and Sophius, decide enough is enough and plot to take him down. They eventually do, with the help of one of Alexander's consorts, and break the breastplate into three pieces and bury them at the furthest reaches of the earth." Cut to the present day, in which Lara Croft is re-imagined as a Robin Hood-style figure who returns stolen artefacts to their rightful owners, the Shield of Achilles being her latest quarry. "Her frail Uncle Charles Powell hooks her up with Dr Alexis Toulin, who works for the Greek Ministry of Antiquities. Alexander's tomb has been found and Alexis fears that the three sections of breastplate, one of which Lara unknowingly found, might end up in the wrong hands (anyone who possesses it is invulnerable, remember)." Lara sets off with the bookish Dr Toulin. They arrive in Morocco, and gatecrash a party which is taking place above a cave which contains the second piece of the breastplate. Ultimately, Mayflower added, "Alexis winds up being a criminal. Her Uncle is in on it, too (he's dying and wants the breastplate so he can go on living). Lara gets together with the good-guy-she-thought-to-be-bad, [Theo] Rooker. And together... they track down the Shield of Achilles and try to stop Alexis and his dangerous wife."

Mayflower went on to describe Werb and Colleary's take on Lara as "a wonderful contradiction — she's beautiful but alone; she can speak six languages and knows her mythology like an average person knows his days of the week... she's ready to take on any challenge, but won't accept a man in her life. Lara's parents died in a plane crash," he explained. "Their bodies were never discovered and their empty mausoleum is like a self-torturing device to remind Lara her life with her parents never had a conclusion. Her butler dramatically tells her she helps find things for people because she's really looking for her parents." Unfortunately, he added, "Lara's problems aren't dealt with, and she just becomes another piece in the plot-puzzle. The lost-parents rap is also a little stupid: sure, it sucks to never find your parents' bodies, but she has accepted they are dead, and grieving over finding the mangled corpses of your loved ones isn't the best activity for a buxom heroine. Lara later runs into — wow! totally by accident! — those dead parents. And it's once again not a stroke of paint in Lara's personality, but another plot point.

"You're not asking much with a *Tomb Raider* movie. You want to sit down and see [Lara] kill bad guys, just make it under a gate as it's closing, and spout some cool one-liners. That the authors couldn't give us at least that much is both disappointing and baffling," he added, describing their draft as "dry and stagnant." Although impressed by an early scene which places Lara in an ancient-ruins-themed casino — and another in which Lara is tortured by being tied to a post while centipedes crawl up her body, only to crush one of them with her ample cleavage — Mayflower's overall disappointment was clear. "There's just not much going on," he lamented. "And when it does, it's Lara in some hackneyed action scene we've watched twenty years ago and were just as bored then as we are now."

This draft, according to de Souza, "spent a huge amount of time — like twenty-eight pages! — in ancient times with Alexander and company, sort of like *The Mummy* did before Brendan Fraser even showed up. This drove the studio *crazy*, because they were negotiating to pay [what was for] Angelina a record price to be in a ninety-minute movie, and now at the eleventh hour Herek wanted to take away a third of her time on screen, and replace it with millions of dollars of actors, sets and costumes that were all — essentially — a prologue!" This, along with the resulting time delays, may have contributed to Herek leaving the project, to direct Mark Wahlberg in the heavy metal drama *Rock Star*. "When Stephen Herek dropped out, they were in pre-production with a hard release date — the worst situation," de Souza recalls. "The movie was coming out next summer, so it had to start in September or October [of that year]. That's so far into the process, you can't even shop for directors. If you say, 'Who's available?' and start interviewing people, that takes six weeks."

It was at this point that someone at the studio remembered that British director Simon West — who had made the smash hit *Con Air* and, for Paramount, *The General's Daughter* — was entombed in a Paramount movie which had become bogged down in pre-production. West owed the studio a movie, so he would come relatively cheap, since the price for that film had already been set. Thus, says de Souza, "Paramount threw Simon West off a postponed film also on the lot and rolled his deal over to *Tomb Raider*. This seemed both wise and efficient at the time." West, however, did not like the direction the script was taking. "The old drafts had a lot of Mary Poppins representations of England," he told *Premiere*. "It was fairly horrendous, and I said, 'Look, I want to change everything but the title and the character.' I had to come up with it very quickly." As de Souza puts it, "As soon as he was locked into it, he took off his nice guy mask and completely hi-jacked the movie. He says all the right things to get the job, and once he's in he says, 'It's a piece of shit. I could write the script myself.'" Whether West was aggrieved that he had been manoeuvred into directing a potential blockbuster under the terms of an existing deal, meaning that he would not get the kind of payday he expected from a film like *Tomb Raider*, or whether he genuinely did not like the script, "he demanded he be given an additional paycheck to write his own script," says de Souza, "in lieu of the one already in 'prep' — mine."

West, who had spent more than a year developing a film based on 1960s TV series *The Prisoner*, made no secret of his initial scepticism at the prospect of taking on *Tomb Raider*. "Every time it came up I thought that we must really be desperate if we're looking to video games for film ideas," he commented. "I was a real prejudiced snob about it." Arguably tempting fate, he added: "No film based on a video game has ever worked." Neither did reading the script currently in favour endear the project to him. "The original script had scenes with people visiting the Queen and drinking tea," West told *Dreamwatch* magazine. "It was a tragedy waiting to happen." Describing his own vision of *Tomb Raider: The Movie* as "James Bond on acid" and "James Bond as it should be — slightly sadistic, supercool, with a surreal element," he said he had read all of the previous drafts, and decided that Massett and Zinman's was the one he liked best. As a result, West holed up in a London hotel room and bashed out yet another draft, which — according to a synopsis posted on Coming Attractions — combined elements of several earlier drafts. "The plot, briefly, involves adventuress/magazine editor Lara Croft's pursuit of the death mask of Alexander the Great," the report stated. "The mask was split into three pieces when Alex's hidden tomb was sealed to protect it from raiders (the closing of the tomb opens the film). The pieces of the mask were spread around the world. Lara unwittingly has one piece of the mask in a relic she takes in her introductory action sequence. The piece comes to her attention when a Greek man named Darius offers to buy the piece and, when she refuses to sell, he steals it. Lara then has to figure out what the piece is and find the other pieces before Darius.

"Darius wants to find the tomb because Alexander is said to have possessed the Shield of Achilles, which makes its holder invulnerable. Lara makes good use of her family butler, Jeeves, and a reluctant archaeologist friend she once had an affair with, Justin, to hunt down the mask pieces. The movie is full of action sequences with Lara finding her way through the tombs with Darius' men in pursuit... The final showdown is a bit hokey, as a plunge off a cliff ends with Lara saving herself with the shield. The plot is really an excuse for the action scenes, which range from the Middle East to the Khyber Pass to some nifty underwater work. The biggest problem with the movie is that Lara herself does not act particularly sexy and there is no real heat between her and Justin or even her and Darius. It's very PG in that respect. Fans may like to know that the script does show Lara grieving for her dead, rich parents and has her work as editor of an adventure magazine where she publishes accounts of her exploits. All in all," the report concluded, "this project needs some more work to make it stand out. Otherwise, it'll turn out to be just another action flick."

Few were surprised when the release date slipped again, this time to the summer of 2001, by which time many less powerful producers might have been fired by the studio; thus, it was perhaps for their own security that Gordon and Levin called in a series of 'closers' — *Mission: Impossible II* scribe Brannon Braga, Laeta Kalogridis, and Academy Award nominee Paul Attanasio (*Quiz Show*) — who continued to massage the script. According to de Souza, Mike Werb and Michael Colleary worked briefly with West, an experience they reportedly described as "horrible". Says de Souza, "Mike Werb said, 'The movie's called *Tomb Raider*, and there's no tombs and there's no raiding,' and Simon West said, 'That's my plan — I don't want to be obvious.' Other writers had told me that they would sit in a room with Simon West where they would say, 'You can't do that, it ruins the surprise,' and he said, 'I don't want any surprises in this movie — that's twentieth century. This is a twenty-first century movie. We're not here to surprise or play games with the audience or shock them or talk about characters and motivation — this is just pure kinetic energy and momentum.'" Basically, de Souza adds, "West went back to the scripts that were abandoned, and did a cut and paste and put them all together, and did his own rewriting across the top of it. He invented the storyline about the antediluvian Conan-esque Hyborean Age prehistory 'triangle of light' that was made from a meteor, and (with Angelina) added all the father/daughter scenes. Nobody wanted him to do that, but nobody could stop him. The studio was happy [with the script], but he kept saying, 'I want another rewrite.' He was driving them crazy." According to Lloyd Levin, however, "From a creative point of view, Simon totally turned it around."

West continued to work with Massett and Zinman, who wrote yet another draft — dated March 2000 — keeping the theme of immortality from the 'Shield of Achilles' drafts, but replacing it with West's idea: a search for an artefact called 'The Triangle of Light' by the 'Illuminati' — a secret order described in the *Illuminatus* trilogy by Robert Anton Wilson (for whom a newly-introduced character, Wilson, is presumably named). Said Zinman, "When we met with Simon his idea was the sacred shape, and there's only one sacred shape and that's the triangle. The trinity, the number three, the pyramids, the Masons, Christianity, the 'all-seeing eye' — it's just naturally there... We wrote in prose form what the mythology was, who the 'people of the light' were, what the pieces [of the triangle] were. I've got to tip my hat to Simon West," he added. "He said, 'Let's take it out of the known. Let's make it more mystical and unknown.' I think it was a wise choice."

Despite all these revisions, de Souza says that the script's basic shape and flavour remained close to his original: "We were still chasing after something Alexander had hidden, and Lara had a love/hate trust/don't trust relationship with a guy she was travelling with in partnership." West renamed all the supporting characters, including two held over from the de Souza draft — the cybernetic trainer, JEEVES, and the male lead, Kincaid — which he changed to 'SIMON' and 'West'. "I thought it revealing that he put the name 'Simon' on the robot, which is a mindless drone, and 'West' on the character who vacillates," says de Souza, "because — if you think about it — the film demonstrated completely mechanical storytelling, combined with a lot of indecision about which way to go."

As rewriting continued, so did the search for someone to fill Lara's boots. Despite earlier negotiations with Angelina Jolie, an edition of *Entertainment Weekly* dated 2 March 2000 quoted Simon West as saying that he was looking for an unknown actress to play what he described as the "James Bond of archaeology", for a June start date. "To some, she's the perfect woman, though others would say she's a total male fabrication of what a woman should be," he added. "We don't want to ram a Hollywood star into this thing, because Lara is visually [known]." The following day, however, *Variety* reported that Jolie — who was just two weeks away from winning an Academy Award for *Girl, Interrupted* — was in "final negotations" to play Lara Croft. *Tomb Raider* fans were divided on Jolie's casting: some celebrated the idea of an actress as intrinsically sexy and cool as Jolie playing Lara; others were not sure if her off-screen activities — she sported numerous tattoos (including a large one bearing her then-husband Billy Bob Thornton's name, ineffectually covered up during filming), and had admitted a proclivity for self-harm and knife wounds inflicted during sex — sat well with a game enjoyed by millions of pre-adolescent boys. (Fans may have been even more doubtful if they knew that Jolie wanted Lara to have a Mohawk hairstyle instead of Lara's plaited pony-tail, and that it took two weeks for the film-makers to convince her to get into a pair of Lara's trademark shorts.) "It was always Angelina," West later admitted to *Empire*. "I mean, Lara sleeps with knives and doesn't take shit from anybody. That's A. J. down to a tee." Nevertheless, it took some time for West to convince Jolie that the role fit her like a tank top and a pair of hot pants. "At first I thought *Tomb Raider* was a really bad idea," she told *Empire*. "Like most people I thought, 'Well, this is going to be silly and campy, and only based on that little outfit and the body.' But then Simon and I talked about her, about her relationship with her father, and she became kind of beautiful to me."

Certainly, one element of the *Tomb Raider* deal which may have helped swing the newly-minted Academy Award-winner into the film was the opportunity to work with her father, fellow Oscar-winner Jon Voight, from whom she had been estranged for many years. "It's taken us a long time to figure out if we could do a project together, for many different reasons," she said, "and it's very special. It's also very scary, because our relationship is very, very similar to these two people, [because] through my whole life, I've followed in his footsteps. And he's somebody who searches the world for information, different religions, different places, different myths..." West went a step further than casting Voight as Lara's explorer father, as de Souza explains: "One of the things that gave him leverage was she wanted to work with her father, so he said, 'I'll put your father in the movie, and I'll let you write your own scenes with your father.' So she and her father wrote those scenes they were in together. It shows how stupid everybody is because nowhere in the source material does it say the father's dead," he adds. "So if they want the father in the movie, let him be alive in the movie. They could have had a scene like in *The Mask of Zorro*, where the father dies in the daughter's arms. Instead, they get the father in the movie the hardest way possible, with all these dream sequences and flashbacks."

Despite de Souza's reservations, regular Ain't It Cool script reviewer 'Moriarty' was impressed by the shooting draft, not least the thematic resonance Massett and Zinman had been aiming for. ("It was always our intention for Lara to have a connection to the past, to the present, and to how those worlds collided and what that meant," Massett explained. "The Triangle of Light held the theme to understand God, or man's duty to understand the nature of Nature itself. That was the theme that came through.") "This script is first and foremost about Lara coming to some sense of peace with the loss of her father," wrote Moriarty. "This entire adventure serves only to take Lara to the next step, to get her over this particular pain. Loss informs her every choice in the movie, and it's one of the things that elevates the material, that gives it some heft and resonance."

Moriarty also approved of the script's "nimble wit", which included a sight gag where Lara, considering the options for her next mission, opens a file containing pictures of Egypt: "Right away, she tosses it aside, a welcome sight for anyone who's seen the Indy films and the new *Mummy*." As for the supporting characters, he thought the Q-like Bryce was an interesting foil for the heroine, noted the effective "sexual energy" between Lara and Alex Marrs, and highlighted her "antagonistic sparring" with the Illuminati villain Manfred Powell.

"I was surprised by how much I invested in Lara and her father by the end of the film," he added. "There's difficult choices that she makes that mark her as a hero of real conscience and strength, rather than just a babe in shorts who's good at killing thugs. Don't get me wrong, this isn't some talky chick flick by any stretch of the imagination. There's several great action set pieces... [and] each of them defines Lara or her relationships with Bryce, Powell, Marrs, and even her father. None of them are just action for the sake of it, and that's what intrigues me most about this film... These set pieces are all built on clever ideas, smart in both text and subtext. Lara's got a touch of angst in the film, as befits a story driven by the memory of her dead father, but she also loves what she does. She's not Batman... She seems to attack situations with two hands, digging in, drunk on raw experience. Jolie's got the exact right edge to play the role as written. There's something in Lara that seems almost out of control, and that makes her dangerous, and that makes her even more interesting."

Finally, Moriarty turned to the finale, as the characters vie for The Power of God in The Tomb of Ten Thousand Shadows. "The choices faced in this scene make the whole film pay off... I was unexpectedly moved by the big finish. There's a reason they didn't just pour a pair of tits into the lead role of this film. Jolie's got to go through some pretty harrowing beats to get to her final destination... The Lara Croft that comes out the other side is both tougher than she's ever been, and finally able to embrace some sort of life away from danger and death."

This shooting draft — credited to Massett, Zinman, Laeta Kalogridis and West himself — was dated 28 July 2000, just three days before production officially commenced at Britain's Pinewood Studios, before setting off for such diverse locations as Cambodia and Iceland. "Originally, I wrote the idea to be in China — the Great Wall — and I was going to use the Terracotta Army as an opposing force," West commented later. "But it was not possible to organise getting to China in time. And also, when I thought about it, I realised that the Great Wall would only give me one big element, and I needed so much more for that sequence. So I started looking around to other places, because the alternative was to build the Great Wall in Scotland, and the prospect of shooting in Scotland in winter didn't appeal to me that much — and I didn't think it was going to look that warm and 'Chinese-y!' So I looked around the world for other great settings and I happened to come across Cambodia."

As filming continued, numerous cuts made to the budget and schedule meant that there were fewer pieces to the plot puzzle. As Zinman explained, "We wrote a script that was just huge, and it needed to be scaled back. They had to omit a few costly scenes." Thus, he added, "In the shooting draft it's only two pieces of the triangle, [which is] symbolically less satisfying, because it's only two, not three. But of course, we only have 120 minutes and only have however many millions of dollars." Further cuts were made for budgetary reasons, including what would appear to be a crucial flashback in which Lord Croft (Jon Voight) explains the mythology, mysticism and might of the 'Triangle of Light' to seven year-old Lara, illustrated by cutaways of the action he narrates. "Long, long ago, a meteor crashed to Earth," he explains. "An ancient people excavated the meteor, and found, buried at its core, a mysterious, crystallised metal. They worshipped the metal for its magical powers, forging it into a sacred shape — a perfect triangle. They engraved upon it an emblem of its great power," he goes on, referring to the 'all-seeing eye'. "The mysterious Triangle induced great insights in its guardians, great knowledge in mathematics and science. They called themselves 'The People of the Light'. But others heard of the power of the Triangle and wanted it for themselves. A great war raged, and finally their beautiful Spiral City suffered under a terrible siege. As fire engulfed their homes, the sun appeared to go out. It was a total eclipse. Believing the end of the world to be upon them, their High Priest prayed desperately to the heavens — 'Let my enemies be vanquished.' And with the words still on his lips, his prayers were answered in a horrific instant!

"The High Priest knew that this power should not be held by any man," he continues. "A power that could explode the human mind.

The power of God. He ordered the Triangle cut into two smaller, right-angled triangles. One half was to stay at the Temple, while the other half was to be hidden at the end of the earth to prevent the Triangle's strange power from being used to change the fate of Humankind. In defiance of the High Priest, the craftsmen who had cut the Triangle in half secretly made a highly advanced clock to serve as a guide to find the hidden piece, and preserve the Triangle's awesome powers for future generations of their kind. They called themselves 'The Illuminati'. They all realised that the exact alignment of the planets necessary to activate the Triangle would not be due for another 5,000 years. But eventually, after many centuries, the People of the Light, the craftsmen, and their incredible Spiral City, and of course, their secret clock, disappeared, evaporating from the pages of history."

With this sequence cut, says de Souza, the search for the Triangle becomes meaningless, since "it was never clear what it could do. It just said [it had] 'the power of a God', or 'power over time and space', but Stephen Hawking has that, and he doesn't even get out of his wheelchair. What does that mean, really?" Besides, he says, "The villains were all just so campy and arch, like *The Avengers*. When I was on the picture they were saying, 'We want to get out of England by the end of the first act; we've got to be out of England by page thirty.' So I said 'OK.' And this one here it's barely ninety minutes long, but I think it really is like forty minutes before she leaves her house." Only three elements of de Souza's script remained in the shooting script: "Her fight against her household cybernetic opponent; her acrobatic gun battle with the invaders of Croft Hall; and the Harryhausen homage with the statues coming to life." This was not deemed sufficient for the WGA (which often arbitrates screen credits) to award de Souza a screen credit; instead, Werb, Colleary and Sara B. Cooper share story credit, with Massett, Zinman and West himself receiving credit for the screenplay. Screenwriters commonly fight for credit on a film, often claiming the best ideas as their own; in the case of *Tomb Raider*, de Souza says, "*all* the writers, who maybe under normal circumstances would say, 'That son of a bitch rewrote me and changed me,' were united in their dismay of this script, that had not been *written* so much as *un*written."

As if the development had not been hellish enough, problems plagued the production, with the *Sunday Express* breaking the news on 8 October 2000 that raw footage from the film had been stolen during a daring raid worthy of Lara herself. "Burglars escaped with a rucksack containing sensitive video tapes and a wallet during a burglary at the home of director Simon West," the tabloid reported, quoting West as saying he was woken by an intruder breaking the front door of his £1.1 million three-bedroomed home in Notting Hill, London. "I was in bed at home when I heard a huge crash downstairs at about 2am," he said. "I got up and went down but they just ran out. I didn't see them — just the front door swinging. I must have missed them by a split second. They snatched my bag which had two or three tapes including all the film so far, literally about half the film. It was everything we've done in the last two months." Two months later, the film made headlines again when Angelina Jolie injured her ankle, causing a week's delay, and adding $1 million to the already bloated budget, now edging towards $100 million.

Worse was to come, as one of West's assistants filed a lawsuit against Paramount, the director, and Bobby Klein, reportedly a former "psychologist specialising in stress management" who acts as West's manager (and received a screen credit as co-producer of the *Tomb Raider* film). Klein had hired Dana Robinson, a twenty-five year-old agent's assistant for Creative Artists Agency, but after quitting her job and relocating to London to work on the production, she became uncomfortable with Klein's sexual advances and other inappropriate behaviour. In a twenty-three-page complaint filed by her lawyers against Klein, West and Paramount, Robinson claimed emotional distress, sexual harassment and wrongful dismissal, since — she alleged — her complaints led to her being given the sack. Attorneys representing Paramount and West counter-claim that she was dismissed after three months for poor work performance, while West has said that claims of this kind come with the territory. "I've learned that when you get into this position in the entertainment industry, you get targeted," he told *Premiere*. "It's just one of those unfortunate things that when people don't work out, they look for someone to blame." Nevertheless, says de Souza, "I do not think there is parking space on the Paramount lot for Simon West."

In addition to such problems, de Souza alleges that West went "many, many millions over budget and two months over schedule, so the minute he turned in his interminable 130-minute cut, Paramount showed him the door. They didn't even let him in the editing room." Whether or not this is true — West was later invited back to direct minor reshoots in London, and provides director's commentary for the DVD — Paramount brought in Stuart Baird, a veteran trouble-shooting editor with credits as diverse as *Superman*, *Robin Hood: Prince of Thieves* and *Mission: Impossible II*, to re-cut the entire movie. "Stuart Baird has an executive producer credit on the movie," notes de Souza, "but all he did was re-cut the movie down to eighty-eight minutes (plus generous head and tail credits)." The studio also rejected the original score by Michael Kamen (*The X-Men*), commissioning *Pitch Black* composer Graeme Revell to produce a new soundtrack — sixty minutes of music — in the space of ten days. "The only way I could write so much music in ten days was to weight the approach in favour of electronics rather than orchestra," he told *Dreamwatch* magazine. "But this was as much a creative decision as anything because the style of the film does not support a big bombastic orchestral score." So rushed were the final stages of post-production, that several major effects shots appeared incomplete by the time the film hit theatres. Finally, says de Souza, "They released it and crossed their fingers."

Despite problems which stretched from development to post-production and a widespread critical drubbing, the film — now entitled *Lara Croft Tomb Raider* — opened on 15 June 2001 with a colossal $47.7 million, going on to gross over $130 million in the US alone, and a total of $275 million worldwide. By the time the weekend's box office figures were in, a sequel was already on the fast-track, but although Angelina Jolie was asked to fulfill her contract for a sequel — with a $5 million pay increase — director Simon West was not invited back. "I guess at some point somebody said, 'We're not going to go through that shit again,'" suggests de Souza. "'The director this time is not going to be someone who thinks he's a writer.'" Instead, producers Gordon and Levin hired Jan de Bont, whose directing career had derailed after early successes like *Speed* and *Twister* — his most recent credits had been as producer on *Minority Report* and

*Equlibrum*. James V. Hart (*Bram Stoker's Dracula*, *Hook*) and hot new-comer Dean Georgaris (*Paycheck*, *Mission: Impossible 3*) were among those hired to work on the script, which concerned a desperate search for Pandora's Box, the mythical source of all the pain in the world. "The first one did not have a strong story, I'll be the first to admit it," Levin later told *Entertainment Weekly*. "We should have made a better movie. But we learned from our mistakes and this new one is a better movie. For starters, it's got a plot."

Like West, de Souza did not expect to have anything to do with the *Tomb Raider* sequel — until he happened to see publicity stills featuring Angelina Jolie in the underwater temple of Alexander the Great. "I'm looking at her wardrobe, particularly in these underwater scenes, and it says, 'She's with a guy who's a British agent,' — and that was my leading man: I said, 'Put her with James Bond — it's perfect, who else would she date?' So that's when I called the Writers Guild and said, 'Listen, this may sound wacky, but when the *Tomb Raider II* script comes in for credit determination, could you check it against my "officially discarded" March 1999 script of *Tomb Raider I*?'" Sure enough, he says, "the Guild reader said, 'Hold on a second — the source of this script is obviously the de Souza script, resurrected.' At that point, the studio said, 'That's impossible, this script was a cold start — a totally brilliant fresh new approach of sheer genius-ity that just happens to have been written by our producer.'" This was a shock, de Souza says, "because I've known Lloyd [Levin] for a dozen years, and he's never written anything except a memo." (Even if Levin did contribute to the screenplay, as he claims, the WGA makes it even more difficult for producers to achieve writing credits than directors, for obvious reasons.)

De Souza can only guess what happened. "After the movie opened, on the following Monday, they probably said, 'We want to have a sequel out in two years.' 'That's impossible.' Then somebody went to the filing cabinet, found the script I wrote, which had been in pre-production with sets designed, and said, 'No it's not — we've got a schedule, boards, budgets, breakdowns and production design for the de Souza draft.' So they resurrected my script, which gave them a head start. It shows how crazy it can get." Nevertheless, he adds, "It actually showed some kind of efficiency for a change, that somebody had the sense to remember they already had a script they liked from before... returning to the script (and budget, board, location work, prop purchases, etc) all still lying around from only ten months earlier. (This is how fast this all happened.) So they already had the comp'd Scuba gear and underwater sleds, [the] design for Alexander the Great's library set, Hogan's alley, etc." What was more surprising for de Souza was that he had to find out by accident. "You'd think Larry Gordon would have called me to tell me this," he says. "I'd worked with him many times. But no — I had to find it out from the Internet."

Although Levin and Hart privately both state that de Souza had nothing to do with the script for the sequel, the WGA awarded him a shared story credit with Hart, with Dean Georgaris receiving sole screenplay credit. "The [sequel], with every line of dialogue changed, does essentially follow my script for about twenty minutes," says de Souza. "Then when the [MI6] men come to her house, she wasn't a bitch on wheels for no discernable reason, but she was thrown by the presence of the younger government guy. He was the male lead of the picture, and his moment where he betrayed Lara and Queen and Country was *in the movie*, mind-fucking the audience, instead of in the movie's back-story. Also, they didn't know what Alexander had hidden, but they knew the other heavies were killing their way towards it." Says de Souza, "The Guild said... *Tomb Raider II*'s genesis from my 1999 script was 'irrefutable' — the actual word used in the Guild paperwork — at which point the studio was bound by the sixty-five year-old contract that says, 'Guild determines credit, period.' And that's how I worked on *Tomb Raider* for six months, but got a screen credit for no months on *Tomb Raider II*!"

*Lara Croft Tomb Raider — The Cradle of Life* finally opened on 24 July 2003, with a disappointing first-weekend gross of $21.8 million — less than half that of the original. The reviewers had been slightly kinder than the first time around, but it was obvious that the paying public weren't impressed. Paramount was swift to try and place the blame for the film's failure elsewhere. "The only thing that we can attribute it to is that gamers were not happy with the latest version of the videogame," ventured the studio's Wayne Lewellen, referring to the recently released *Lara Croft Tomb Raider: Angel of Darkness*.

*Entertainment Weekly* had a different opinion: "If Paramount had spent a few bucks on polling, it might have discovered that despite its $131 million gross, nobody who went to the first *Tomb Raider* walked out saying, 'Can't wait for part two!'" Adds de Souza, "At least this [one] is a movie. The other one was not a movie. In my humble opinion, Paramount managed to make one lousy and one mediocre movie out of a very good script." Nevertheless, he adds, "I get a free poster and a free DVD, and they can't take that away from me!"

# INDEX OF QUOTATIONS

**Note:** Quotes taken from author interviews are marked AI. All available information on sources is given. Any omissions will be corrected in future editions where possible.

## INTRODUCTION

**Page 10:** "Trying to make a movie..." Douglas Adams, quoted in 'Douglas Adams' by Nicholas Wroe, *The Guardian*, 15 May 2001. "The writer turns in a script..." is from *Killer Instinct: How Two Young Producers Took on Hollywood and Made the Most Controversial Film of the Decade* by Jane Hamsher, New York: Broadway Books, 1997. **p11** "Everybody gives writers notes..." Richard Friedenberg, AI. "In Hollywood, ideas are anathema..." Gary Goldman, AI. "tweaking a draft..." William Farmer, AI.

## DISILLUSIONED

**Page 14:** "They wanted Indiana Jones..." and all other Ted Henning quotes, AI. "a small amount of TV..." and all other quotes from Lee and Janet Scott Batchler, AI. **p15** "Manipulating the laws of physics..."; "Whatever days I have left" are from the unproduced screenplay *Smoke and Mirrors* by Lee and Janet Scott Batchler. **p16** "Sounds great..." Jay Stern, quoted in *The Big Deal* by Thom Taylor, New York: William Morrow, 1999. "I'm looking for a million" Alan Gasmer, ibid. **p18** "I don't know if they got an answer..."; "I was concerned..." Stern, ibid. **p22** "Houdin travels to Algeria..." and all other 'Stax' quotes from 'The Stax Report: Script Review of *Smoke & Mirrors*' at IGN FilmForce (filmforce.ign.com), 19 December 2000. **p24** "The fact-based story..." quoted in 'Douglas, Zeta-Jones stoked for Smoke & Mirrors', uncredited, *Variety*, 22 May 2001.

## MONKEY BUSINESS

**Page 30:** "I thought it was gonna be fantastic..." and all other Don Murphy quotes, AI. "He told me the story..." and other Arthur P. Jacobs quotes, from 'Dialogues on Apes, Apes and More Apes' by Dale Winogura, *Cinefantastique*, Summer 1972. **p31** "I never thought it could be made..." Pierre Boulle, ibid. "The novel was singularly uncinematic," and other Charlton Heston quotes from *In the Arena* by Charlton Heston, London: HarperCollins, 1995. **p32** "The make-up was crude..." John Chambers, quoted in original 20th Century Fox production notes for *Planet of the Apes*. **p33** "I disliked, somewhat, the ending..." Boulle, quoted in 'Dialogues on Apes, Apes and More Apes' by Dale Winogura, *Cinefantastique*, Summer 1972. **p34** "Whether by design or accident..." Maurice Evans, quoted in original

20th Century Fox production notes for *Planet of the Apes*. "I had never thought of this picture..." Franklin J Schaffner, ibid. "I had always been a huge *Planet Of The Apes* fan..."; "but not a sequel to the 5th film..."; "*Spartacus* with Apes..." Adam Rifkin, AI. **p35** "The legend throughout the humans..." Rifkin, quoted in 'Evolution' by Daniel Argent, *Creative Screenwriting*, July/August 2001. **p36** "Fox was dead set on making this movie..."; "As soon as I was to turn in the cut down script..."; "quite unexpectedly and unceremoniously replaced..." Rifkin, AI. "[Fox wanted] a happy, harmonious ending..." Rifkin, quoted in 'Evolution' by Daniel Argent, *Creative Screenwriting*, July/August 2001. **p37** "Eventually the script evolved to a place..." and all remaining Adam Rifkin quotes, AI. "I imagine the conversation going something like this..."; "I watched the original movies again..." are from *Killer Instinct: How Two Young Producers Took on Hollywood and Made the Most Controversial Film of the Decade* by Jane Hamsher, New York: Broadway Books, 1997. **p38** "What if there were discovered cryogenically frozen Vedic Apes..." Oliver Stone, ibid. "Oliver Stone got Fox to take exactly..." ibid. **p39** "Oliver's notion is kind of in the Joseph..." Hamsher, quoted in 'Fox Goes Ape for Stone' by Leonard Klady, *Variety*, 14 December 1993. "I never worked out how to get back..." is from the unproduced script *Return of the Apes* by Terry Hayes. **p40** "one of the best scripts he ever read"; "What if our main guy finds himself in Ape land..."; "incredibly stupid" are from *Killer Instinct: How Two Young Producers Took on Hollywood and Made the Most Controversial Film of the Decade* by Jane Hamsher, New York: Broadway Books, 1997. **p41** "What we tried to do was a story..." Sam Hamm, quoted in 'Evolution' by Daniel Argent, *Creative Screenwriting*, July/August 2001. "once-proud porcelain features..." is from the unproduced *Planet of the Apes* screenplay by Sam Hamm. **p42** "Schwarzenegger ... is talking with Jim Cameron..." quoted in 'Arnold Wants Forman to take *Wings*' by Army Archerd, *Variety*, 28 January 1997. "I'm fourty-four..." James Cameron, quoted in *Premiere*, November 1998. "I would have gone in a very different direction" Cameron, quoted in 'Ape Crusaders' by Benjamin Svetkey, *Entertainment Weekly*, 27 April 2001. "The original movie is about race in America..." Albert Hughes, quoted in 'New Jack City' by Ian Freer, *Empire*, February 2002. **p43** "We wanted to take the premise..." Allen Hughes, ibid. "[Fox president] Tom Rothman called..." and other William Broyles, Jr. quotes are from 'Evolution' by Daniel Argent, *Creative Screenwriting*, July/August 2001. **p44** "I wasn't interested in doing a remake or a sequel..."; "introduce new characters and other story elements..." Tim Burton, quoted in 20th Century Fox production notes for *Planet of the Apes*. "When you say '*Planet of the Apes*' and 'Tim Burton' in the same breath..."; "[Broyles] came up with the characters...", Richard D. Zanuck, ibid. **p45** "Can I explain the *Planet of the Apes* ending..." Tim Roth, quoted in 'Empire Awards 2002', *Empire*, April 2002. "I thought it made sense..." Helena Bonham Carter, quoted in 'Helena Bonham Carter' by Mark Salisbury, *Total Film*, December 2001. "Tim had three months to edit the film..."

Estella Warren, quoted in 'Estella' by Justin Quirk, *Arena*, May 2003. "would have cost $300 million"; "I'm fascinated by the studio technique..." Burton, quoted in *The Independent*, reported by JAM! Showbiz, www.canoe.ca.

## CAST INTO MOUNT DOOM

**Page 48:** "When Gandalf is vanquished..." John Boorman, quoted on *The South Bank Show* edited and presented by Melvyn Bragg, LWT Productions, 2001. "In a hole in the ground there lived a hobbit" is from *The Hobbit* by J.R.R. Tolkien, London: Allen & Unwin, 1937. "My work has escaped from my control..." J.R.R. Tolkien, quoted in *The Letters of JRR Tolkien*, edited by Humphrey Carpenter with the assistance of Christopher Tolkien, New York: HarperCollins, 1985. **p49** "I had no sooner landed in London..." and all other Forrest J Ackerman quotes, AI. "I should welcome the idea..."; "entirely ignorant of the process of producing an 'animated picture'..."; "very unhappy about the extreme silliness..." Tolkien, quoted in *The Letters of JRR Tolkien*, edited by Humphrey Carpenter with the assistance of Christopher Tolkien, New York: HarperCollins 1985. **p51** "The problem was that, because Tolkien was not a regular moviegoer..." Brian Sibley, quoted in .Middle-Earth Man', uncredited, *Starlog*, January 2002. "We talked about it for a while..." Paul McCartney, quoted in *Beatles at the Movies* by Roy Carr, London: UFOMusic, 1996. **p52** "as a kind of opera, or a sort of..." and all other Heinz Edelmann quotes are from 'Tolkien: The Road Not Taken' by Ross Pleset, *Outré*, circa 2001. **p53** "like a Fellini movie in a never-land..." and all other Rospo Pallenberg quotes, ibid. **p54** "When you're faced with adapting..." Peter Jackson, quoted on *The South Bank Show* edited and presented by Melvyn Bragg, LWT Productions, 2001. "[We] used to get the giggles..." Boorman, ibid. **p55** "Look – only seven colours..." is from the unproduced *Lord of the Rings* screenplay by Rospo Pallenberg. **p56** "I was a Tolkien fan..." and all other Ralph Bakshi quotes, AI. **p58** "that was the key to it", Jackson, quoted in 'The Once and Future King' by Jenny Cooney Carillo, *Dreamwatch*, October 2003. "presents the characters that people love, and..." Jackson, quoted on *The South Bank Show* edited and presented by Melvyn Bragg, LWT Productions, 2001. "It's a huge uphill struggle..." Boorman, ibid.

## WE CAN REWRITE IT FOR YOU WHOLESALE

**Page 60:** "Ron [Shusett] said, 'You've done the Philip K. Dick version..." David Cronenberg, AI. **p61** "I think it was probably 1974..."; "This was the first story..." Ronald D. Shusett, quoted in the Artisan documentary *Imagining Total Recall*, circa 2001. "Ronny Shusett walked into my apartment..."; "Dick's story is short..."; "Quaid, Earth's top secret agent..." Dan O'Bannon, quoted in 'Dan O'Bannon On Why It Doesn't Work' by Carl Brandon, *Cinefantastique*, April 1991. **p62** "At the that time I was not a Philip Dick fan..." Cronenberg, quoted in *David Cronenberg* by Serge Grünberg, Paris: Cahiers Du Cinema, 2000. "It's a good thing I had a computer..." Cronenberg, AI. **p63** "I didn't want to do it as serious..." Shusett, AI. "I went to Dino..." Cronenberg, quoted in *David Cronenberg* by Serge Grünberg, Paris: Cahiers Du Cinema, 2000. "Cronenberg quit for a number of reasons..." Shusett, quoted in 'The Bizarre Mars of David Cronenberg' by Bill Florence, *Cinefantastique*, April 1991. "It's dead for me now..." Cronenberg, quoted in *David Cronenberg* by Serge Grünberg, Paris: Cahiers Du Cinema, 2000. **p64** "First of all, I really wanted to cast William Hurt..." Cronenberg, AI. "Quaid takes a cab driven by Benny..." is from 'The Bizarre Mars of David Cronenberg' by Bill Florence, *Cinefantastique*, April 1991. **p65** "They were creatures that lived in the sewers..." and other Ron Miller quotes are from 'The Bizarre Mars of David Cronenberg' by Bill Florence, *Cinefantastique*, April 1991. "I thought it was a bad movie..." Cronenberg, quoted in *David Cronenberg* by Serge Grünberg, Paris: Cahiers Du Cinema, 2000. **p66** "With Arnold Schwarzenegger in the main part..." Paul Verhoeven, quoted in commentary for *Total Recall* DVD. "Also I thought it was very tacky..." Cronenberg, quoted in *David Cronenberg* by Serge Grünberg, Paris: Cahiers Du Cinema, 2000. "As I recall it was seven directors..." Shusett, quoted in the Artisan documentary *Imagining Total Recall*, circa 2001. "I was asked to do a polish" and all other Gary Goldman quotes, AI. "Within a few hours..." Arnold Schwarzenegger, quoted in commentary for *Total Recall* DVD. "In 1981, eight years before I got the movie financed..." and all remaining Shusett quotes, AI. "about thirty" Verhoeven, AI. **p68** "Everything we have seen before..." Verhoeven, quoted in commentary for *Total Recall* DVD. "What's bullshit? That you're having a paranoid episode..." is dialogue from *Total Recall*. "That's the great thing about the movie..." Schwarzenegger, quoted in commentary for *Total Recall* DVD. "As much as possible..." Verhoeven, AI. "You are a top operative under deep cover..." is dialogue from *Total Recall*. **p69** "McClane tells him everything..."; "That part of the narrative..." Verhoeven, quoted in commentary for *Total Recall* DVD. **p70** "I think we were a very writer-friendly group..."; "There was an introduction..." Verhoeven, quoted in commentary for *Total Recall* DVD. **p74** "Somebody whose name I won't name..." Verhoeven, AI. **p77** "This is the perfect franchise opportunity..." Bob Weinstein, quoted in '*Recall* in New Dimension' by Rex Weiner and Anita M. Busch, *Daily Variety*, 15 January 1997. **p78** "Immediately after turning in that script..." and all other Matthew Cirulnick quotes, AI. **p79** "actively involved" is from 'Dimension eyes *Recall 2*' by Benedict Carver and Chris Petrikin, *Daily Variety*, 12 May 1998. **p80** "I'm very jazzed..." Jonathan Frakes, quoted in 'Inside Trek' by Ian Spelling, www.geocities.com/Hollywood/6952/st9.htm, March 1998. "Arnold is serious..." Frakes, quoted in interview with Louis B. Hobson, *Calgary Sun*, circa December 1998. "waiting for Mr Schwarzenegger's hands to free up..." Frakes, quoted in uncredited interview on Tripod (www.tripod.com), circa 1998. "*Totall Recall* is an old movie..." Frakes, quoted in *Starburst*,

February 2000. **p83** "That way, should we want to betray the agency..."; "Scientists say the Mars explosion..." are from unproduced script for *Total Recall 2* by Matthew Cirulnick. **p88** "After all, the real one..." is from 'We Can Remember It For You Wholesale' by Philip K. Dick.

**KEEPING UP WITH THE JONESES**

**Page 90:** "I was done with the..." Steven Spielberg, quoted in *Dreamwatch*, January 2003. "reading scripts" Harrison Ford, quoted at Venice Film Festival press conference, circa 1994. **p92** "When Jones gets wind..." is from 'From *Speed* to Ford Escort' by Baz Bamigboye, *Daily Mail*, 11 November 1994. "Baz Bamigboye was hungry for stories..." anonymous, AI. "While Nazis and various cultists..." is from 'Indy IV Delayed' by Michael Fleming, *Variety*, 21 March 1995. "About a year later..." and other Robert Smith quotes are from interview with Charles Deemer of the Internet Screenwriters Network, circa 1996. **p94** "In a New York minute..." Ford, quoted in interview with Barbara Walters, 24 March 1997. "We're working on a screenplay..." George Lucas, quoted at press conference for *Star Wars Episode I: The Phantom Menace*, circa 1997. **p95** "The script had to do with the lost city..." is from 'Indy IV Draft That Will Never Be!!' by Harry Knowles, Ain't It Cool News (www.aintitcool.com), 24 October 1997. "a fake or at the very least..." is from *Cinescape*, 11 April 1998. "We finished the script..." is from *Cinescape Online* (www.cinescape.com), 17 May 1998. **p96** "they would probably stick with..." is from Ain't It Cool News (www.aintitcool.com), 27 May 1998. "We just haven't really settled..." Ford, quoted in interview with Earvin Johnson on *Magic Hour*, 9 June 1998. "The Indiana Jones 4 hat..." Spielberg, quoted in interview with Cindy Pearlman, *Chicago Herald-Tribune*, circa July 1998. "Yes, there will be..." Spielberg, quoted on Ain't It Cool News (www.aintitcool.com), 25 July 1998. "there is no official..." Paramount spokesperson, quoted in AI for *Empire*, November 1998. **p97** "The script, labelled as the final draft..." is from Indyfan.com, 2 December 1998. "Indy, working in Egypt..." is from Ain't It Cool News (www.aintitcool.com), 13 December 1998. **p99** "The two of us wrote..." Michael Prentice, quoted in interview with Micah Johnson, Indyfan.com, circa January 1999. "We've got a fantastic script..." McCallum, quoted at press conference for Lucasfilm/LucasArts, 14 July 1999. **p100** "It takes place..." Makman, quoted on Ain't It Cool News (www.aintitcool.com), 17 July 1999. "I'm still quite fit..." Ford, quoted on *Entertainment Tonight*, 15 September 1999. "All I'm waiting for..." Lucas, quoted on *Entertainment Tonight*, circa October 1999. "ready when they're ready" Ford, quoted on *E! Online*, circa October 1999. "We don't want the fourth..." Spielberg, quoted on *Cinescape Insider* and elsewhere, circa October 1999. **p101** "If there was a script..." Patricia McQueeney, quoted in interview with Jeannie Williams, *USA Today*, 24 January 2000. "everybody having commitments..." McCallum, quoted in *The Sunday Express*, circa 2000. "Steven and George will not..." Ford, quoted on *The Big Breakfast*, 22 November 1999. "Harrison isn't too old..." Spielberg, quoted in interview with Larry King on *Larry King Live*, 10 December 1999. "I want it to happen..." Ford, quoted on *Inside the Actor's Studio*, 15 February 2000. "Dad, when are you going to..." Spielberg, quoted at Director's Guild of America, circa March 2000. "completely unconfirmed and graded as an 8..." is from Cinescape Online (www.cinescape.com), 15 February 2000. **p102** "in the process..." is from 'Arnold & Indy: They'll Be Back', uncredited, *Variety*, 22 June 2000. "There are a lot of things..." M. Night Shyamalan, quoted on MovieHeadlines.com, 29 November 2000. "I was never contacted..." Shyamalan, quoted on Ain't It Cool News (www.aintitcool.com), 31 July 2001. **p103** "looking forward..." Ford, quoted on the Internet Movie Database, circa October 2000. "but to be honest..." Kathleen Kennedy, quoted in interview with the *Calgary Sun*, February 2001. **p104** "We have a title..." Spielberg, quoted in interview with Roger Friedman for Fox News, 21 January 2002. "Right now, Steven's been described..." Marvin Levy, quoted in interview with *E! Online*, 22 January 2002. "We're in the process of hiring..." Lucas, quoted in interview with Master P for *MTV Movie House*, 24 May 2002. **p105** "George called about a month..." Frank Darabont, quoted in *Cinescape*, June 2002. "It's official that we have an ambition..." Ford, ibid. "wonderful" Spielberg, quoted in 'Indy Scriptwriter Signed', uncredited, *Dreamwatch*, June 2002. "Steven, Harrison and I..." Lucas, quoted on www.starwars.com, 25 June 2002. "Indy's pop will be back..." Spielberg, quoted in 'Indy Doesn't Get the Willies', uncredited, *Dreamwatch*, January 2003. "I absolutely don't want to do things..." Darabont, quoted in *Alameda Times-Star Online*, circa 2003. **p106** "I'm taking some time off..." Ford, quoted in *US Magazine*, circa 2003. "Harrison's the one..." Spielberg, quoted in 'Indy Doesn't Get the Willies', uncredited, *Dreamwatch*, January 2003.

### THE LOST CRUSADE

**Page 108:** "The story of the Crusades..." Verhoeven, quoted in interview with Neil Young posted on www.jigsawlounge.co.uk, 18 April 2002. **p109** "We were sitting outside Arnold's trailer..."; "Walon wrote a script..."; "We wanted to be honest..." Verhoeven, AI. **p111** "to wed and bed the true love..." is from the unproduced script *Crusades* by Walon Green. **p112** "It was always supposed to be a movie for Arnold..."; "There are touches of lightness..." Verhoeven, AI. **p114** "They came up with a draft or two..." and all other Gary Goldman quotes, AI. "We presented it in the way of *Total Recall*..."; "If you see other movies about the Crusades..." Verhoeven, AI. **p116** "the greatest unproduced script..." Damien Thorn, quoted on Ain't It Cool News (aintitcool.com). **p117** "*Crusade* doesn't want to take a religious stand..." anonymous, ibid. "I tested a lot of women..."; "I was too honest..."; "Carolco went through a terrible..." Verhoeven, AI. **p119** "serious talks"; "Long considered one of the best unproduced scripts..." is from 'Schwarzenegger Wooing Milchan to Join *Crusade*' by Michael Fleming, *Daily Variety*, 5 February 1999. **p120** "Even the *word* Crusade..." Verhoeven, quoted in *DVD Monthly*, circa 2001. "Of course, Bush not knowing what..." Verhoeven, AI. "We have to bring it up to date..." Schwarzenegger, quoted on *Cinescape Online* (www.cinescape.com), 9 November 2001. **p121** "At its core, it harkens to what's going on today..." is from 'Now Showing: The Flag' by Mike Medavoy, *Washington Post*, 6 February 2002. "In the end, you see the stupidity..." Walon Green, ibid. "The story of the Crusades..." Verhoeven, quoted in interview with Neil Young posted on Jigsaw Lounge (www.jigsawlounge.co.uk), 18 April 2002. "*The Crusades*, which began in the 11th century..." is from 'Fox, Scott Plot Crusade' by Michael Fleming, *Variety*, 3 Mar 2002. **p122** "It's a movie I've been thinking about for twenty years..." Scott, quoted in *The San Bernadino County Sun*, circa September 2003. "The subject has to be dealt with..." Scott, from a press conference for *Matchstick Men*, circa September 2003. "The answer is yes..." and all remaining Verhoeven quotes, AI.

### DE-RAILED

**Page 124:** "We were..." and all other Steven de Souza quotes, AI. "It was a sci-fi action thriller..." and all other Jim Uhls quotes, AI. **p125** "Sometime in 1988..." is from *H. R. Giger's Film Design* by H. R. Giger, London: Titan Books, 1999. "I have come close..." Ridley Scott, ibid. "he told me to just..." ibid. "If somebody is telling me something..." H. R. Giger, AI. **p126** "Shortly thereafter he telephoned..." is from *H. R. Giger's Film Design* by H. R. Giger, London: Titan Books, 1999. "I never got engaged and I never got paid..." and all remaining Giger quotes, AI. "a mutant professional fighter..." and all other Jere Cunningham quotes, AI.

### WHO WANTS TO BE A BILLIONAIRE?

**Page 136:** "I had lots of people calling me up..." and all other David Koepp quotes, AI. "Who else could have taken on the censors..." is from 'Howard Hughes: Tales of a Priapic Producer' by Peter Bart, *Variety*, 23 September 2001. **p137** "the greatest night in show business..." Charles Chaplin, ibid. **p138** "He had seen me in *Return to October*..." and all other Terry Moore quotes, AI. **p139** "I was caught up in a rushing stream..." Clifford Irving, quoted in interview with Mr Showbiz, April 1999. **p140** "That's a vast project..." Brian De Palma, quoted in 'Brian De Palma', uncredited, *ET Online* (etonline.com), 30 July 1998. **p142** "Leo's been phenomenal to work with..." John Logan, quoted on BBCi Films, uncredited, circa 1999. "Hughes was childlike in many ways..." Charles Higham, quoted in 'Imagine: Leo as Howard Hughes', uncredited, *New York Post*, 30 June 1999. "Leonardo has all of those qualities..." Michael Mann, quoted in 'Who's Hughes in H'wood' by 'Mr Showbiz,' mr.showbiz.go.com, 24 October 1999. "Hughes' formative years..." Michael De Luca, quoted in 'New Line Spruced Up' by Michael Fleming, *Variety*, 25 February 2000. **p143** "Much of what has been written about him..." Alan Ladd, Jr., quoted in 'Howard Hughes Biopic', uncredited, *Variety*, 23 March 2000. **p144** "Ten years ago, we would have said..." Scott Alexander, quoted in 'Hughes Intrigue Continues' by Michael Fleming, *Variety*, 13 January 2000. "As writers, the problem is..." Larry Karaszewski, ibid. "No one has worked harder to bring the story..." Pat Broeske, quoted in interview with Inside.com, February 2001. **p145** "As a result of these discussions..." and other details of the Evans lawsuit, ibid. "feature film or telefilm..." is from 'Helmer Friedkin to take on Hack's Hughes' by Army Archerd, *Variety*, 6 September 2001. "I've been fascinated by Hughes..." William Friedkin, ibid. **p146** "It was the extreme nature of his story..." Christopher Nolan, quoted in interview with *S.F. Chronicle*, reported on www.christophernolan.net, 17 May 2002. "It's about the extremes to which one man can live..." Nolan, quoted in 'Nolan on Hughes Project' by 'Lenny,' www.christophernolan.net, 2 June 2002. "It is the sort of great unmade Hollywood movie..." Nolan, quoted in 'Wide Awake & Living in a Dream' by Rob Blackwelder, Spliced Wire (www.splicedwire.com), circa 2002. "Jim was born to play Hughes...." Nolan, quoted in 'Chris and Carrey Tackle Legendary Howard Hughes', uncredited, *The Calgary Sun*, 24 April 2002. "Hughes is like everyone else..." Jim Carrey, quoted in 'Hughes Grant' by Liana Bonin, *Entertainment Weekly*, circa 2002. "Mann apparently agreed to step aside..." is from 'Helmers Ganging up on Hughes' by Michael Fleming, *Variety*, 24 January 2002. "I was never, like so many others..." Martin Scorsese, quoted in *Variety* report by Marilyn Beck and Stacy Jenel Smith, circa February 2003. **p147** "There's no sense of any kind of race..." Nolan, quoted in 'Howard Hughes Biopic Update', uncredited, The Z Review (www.thezreview.co.uk), 29 August 2002.

**PERCHANCE TO DREAM**

**Page 148:** "The *Sandman* movie has nothing to do with me..." Neil Gaiman, quoted in *Cinescape*, 16 August 1999. **p149** "Looking back, the process of coming up..." Gaiman, from the afterword to *The Sandman: Preuludes & Nocturnes* by Neil Gaiman *et al.*, New York: DC Comics, 1991. "to read *The Sandman* is to read something more..." Mikal Gilmore, quoted on dustjacket for *The Sandman: The Doll's House* by Neil Gaiman *et al.*, New York: DC Comics, 1995. "To make it film-shaped..." Gaiman, quoted in *The Sandman Companion* by Hy Bender, New York: Vertigo Books, 1999. **p150** "After turning in a draft that we felt..." Ted Elliott, quoted on Coming Attractions (corona.bc.ca), circa May 1998. "Since its inception, Terry and I..." and all other Elliott quotes are from Word Play (www.wordplayer.com). **p152** "[Elliott and Rossio] had been paid a king's ransom..." and all other Roger Avary quotes are from Avary.com (www.avary.com) **p153** "one of the best I've read in quite some time..." 'Widget', quoted on Coming Attractions (corona.bc.ca). "It's very hard to dislike them..." Gaiman, quoted in interview with Cold Print (www.cold-print.com). **p155** "I read the graphic novel..."; "Basically, it was clear from the start..."; "The reply was basically..."

William Farmer, AI. **p156** "Where *The Sandman* movie is concerned..." Gaiman, quoted on Ain't It Cool News (www.aintitcool.com) circa 1998. "When all was said and done..." Farmer, AI. **p157** "Mistake number one..."; "Rose Kendall is the daughter..." 'Moriarty', quoted on Ain't It Cool News (www.aintitcool.com) **p158** "The horrible line..." Farmer, quoted on Comics 2 Film (www.comics2film.com). "Well, of course the hospital..."; "Gaiman never, ever cheated us..."; 'Moriarty', quoted on Ain't It Cool News (www.aintitcool.com). "the worst one yet..." Gaiman, quoted in interview with the *Philadelphia City Paper* (www.citypaper.net). **p159** "not only the worst *Sandman* script..." Gaiman, quoted in interview with Andy Mangels, reported on Ain't It Cool News (www.aintitcool.com). "If any of you are waiting for Mr Gaiman's..." Farmer, quoted on Coming Attractions (corona.bc.ca). "mixed feelings" and all other Farmer quotes, AI. **p160** "I think right now they're licking..." Gaiman, quoted in interview with Andy Mangels, reported on Ain't It Cool News (www.aintitcool.com). **p161** "They always have ideas for casting..." Gaiman, quoted in interview with Cold Print (www.cold-print.com). "been in contact with Neil Gaiman..." Fairuza Balk, quoted on www.fairuzasfansite.com, circa July 1999. **p162** "I was approached by Brian Manis..." and all other David J. Schow quotes, AI. **p164** "I couldn't quite see why they got him..." Gaiman, AI. "for another [version of the] movie..." Gaiman, quoted on Universo HQ (www.universohq.com) "the strange, sad, development hell..." Gaiman, AI. **p165** "I just desperately hope that it's a good movie..." Gaiman, quoted in interview with Cold Print (www.cold-print.com). "My own hope is that some time in my lifetime..." Gaiman, AI.

## CRISIS ON THE HOT ZONE

**Page 166:** "We had Redford, Ridley Scott..." and all other Richard Friedenberg quotes, AI. "He mentioned Ebola..." Richard Preston, quoted in 'Crisis in the Plot Zone' by Rebecca Ascher-Walsh, *Entertainment Weekly*, 24 March 1995. **p167** "I want people to know..." and all other Arnold Kopelson quotes are ibid. **p168** "Fox and I had won..." and all other Lynda Obst quotes are from *Hello, He Lied* by Lynda Obst, New York: Little Brown, 1996. **p169** "I had just finished *Contact*..." and all other James V. Hart quotes, AI. **p174** "I got the scripts the same day..." Wolfgang Petersen, quoted in 'Crisis in the Plot Zone' by Rebecca Ascher-Walsh, *Entertainment Weekly*, 24 March 1995. **p175** "an eleventh-hour, page-one..." and all other Tom Topor quotes, AI. **p183** "It was like a train wreck..."; "When the Fox project exploded..." Preston, quoted in 'Film Clipped' by Richard Corliss, TIME, 5 September 1994. **p184** "an old poker buddy"; "every draft by every writer"; "Ted Tally contributed..." Robert Roy Pool, quoted in 'Crisis in the Plot Zone' by Rebecca Ascher-Walsh, *Entertainment Weekly*, 24 March 1995. **p186** "I'm just sitting there laughing..." Preston, ibid. "ripped off" and all other Pool quotes are from a letter printed as part of 'Inside *Outbreak* Fever', uncredited, *Entertainment Weekly*, 21 April 1995. **p188** "It's a great script..." Scott McGehee, quoted in

*Variety*, 2 July 2002. **p189** "watching people break and enter..." Preston, quoted in "Crisis in the Plot Zone" by Rebecca Ascher-Walsh, *Entertainment Weekly*, 24 March 1995. "I would have loved to work with Jodie..." Ridley Scott, quoted in *Ridley Scott: The Making of his Movies* by Paul M. Sammon, London: Orion, 1999. **p190** "It's not like *Alien*..." Preston, quoted in 'Film Clipped' by Richard Corliss, TIME, 5 September 1994.

### THE DARK KNIGHT STRIKES OUT

**Page 192:** "I told them I'd cast..." and all other Darren Aronofsky quotes, AI. "I remember when I was..."; "Batman and Robin were always punning..." Bob Kane, quoted in 'Bob Kane, 83, Cartoonist Who Created Batman', *The New York Times*, 7 November 1998. **p193** "a definitive Batman movie..." Michael E. Uslan, quoted in 'Batman' by Alan Jones, *Cinefantastique*, November 1989. "The first treatment..." Tim Burton, quoted in *Burton on Burton* edited by Mark Salisbury, revised edition, London: Faber and Faber, 2000. **p194** "The success of the graphic novel..." Burton, quoted in 'Batman' by Alan Jones, *Cinefantastique*, November 1989. "I tried to take the premise..." Sam Hamm, quoted in 'Batman' by Taylor H. White, *Cinefantastique*, June 1989. "In my mind I kept..." Burton, quoted in *Burton on Burton* edited by Mark Salisbury, revised edition, London: Faber and Faber, 2000. **p195** "I see what they're doing..." Hamm, quoted in 'Batman' by Taylor H. White, *Cinefantastique*, June 1989. **p196** "When I was hired..." and all other Wesley Strick quotes, AI. **p197** "The Joker is coming..." Jack Nicholson, quoted in various sources from *As Good As It Gets* press conference, circa 1997. **p198** "He's not Batman..." Jon Peters, quoted in interview with Beth Laski, *Cinescape Online*, 9 October 1998. "If there is another, I'd do it..." George Clooney, quoted in interview with *E! News Daily*, 19 September 1997. "I felt I had disappointed..." Joel Schumacher, quoted in *Variety*, 9 January 1998. "If your only memory..." is from the introduction to *Batman: Year One* by Frank Miller, New York: DC Comics, 1990. **p203** "It'll have to be dark..." Keanu Reeves, quoted in interview with *TV Times* and reported on *Empire Online*, 1 October 1999. "pure fiction..." Ben Affleck, quoted in Comics 2 Film (www.comics2film.com), 29 December 1999. "I know that it's one of the possible options..." Paul Dini, quoted in interview with Cinescape Online (www.cinescape.com) by Patrick Sauriol, 5 November 1999. **p204** "Boaz is co-writing the script..." Dini, quoted in interview with Comics Continuum (www.comicscontinuum.com), circa 2000. "great pitch which got Batman out of Gay Gotham..." Grant Morrison in interview with Comics Newsarama reported on Comics 2 Film (www.comics2film.com), circa August 2000. "You do the movie cheap..." Clooney, quoted on the Internet Movie Database, 8 September 2000. "unless we put Batman and Superman..." Peters, quoted in interview with Beth Laski, *Cinescape Online*, 9 October 1998. **p205** "I very much liked Walker's original..." 'Jett', quoted on Batman on Film (www.batman-on-film.com), reported on Coming Attractions (www.corona.bc.ca), 26 January 2003. **p206** "It is the clash of the titans..." Wolfgang Petersen, quoted in 'WB Finds Helmer for *Batman vs Superman*' by Dana Harris, *Daily Variety*, 8 July 2002. "especially in both cases..."; "We have a script..." Petersen, quoted on MTV.com circa 2002. "No, that's *Bateman*..." Christian Bale, quoted in an interview with Movie Hole (www.moviehole.net), 15 August 2002. **p207** "I did, and it was amazing..." Peters, quoted in 'In This *Superman* Story, the Executives Do the Fighting' by Laura M. Holson, *The New York Times*, 15 September 2002. "In reintroducing..."; "I wanted some objectivity..." Alan Horn, ibid. **p 208** "a Batman origins movie..." Horn, quoted in *The Hollywood Reporter*, circa December 2002. "I swear I heard the flapping..." Peters, quoted in 'In This *Superman* Story, the Executives Do the Fighting' by Laura M Holson, *New York Times*, 15 September 2002. "He told me that his original idea..." Christopher Reeve, quoted on Comicon.com, 20 January 2003. **p209** "All I can say is that..." Christopher Nolan, quoted in '*Batman* Captures Director Nolan' by Michael Fleming, *Variety*, 27 January 2003. "You can make mistakes being..." David Goyer, quoted in interview with *Weekly Dig*, circa 2003. **p210** "I'm a fan, and I made a film..."; "The sheer amount..." Sandy Collora, quoted in interview with Ain't It Cool News (www.aintitcool.com), circa July 2003.

## TOMB RAIDER CHRONICLES

**Page 212:** "We should have made a better movie..." Lloyd Levin, quoted in 'Angelina Jolie is One Tough Mother' by Benjamin Svetkey, *Entertainment Weekly*, 18 July 2003. **p214** "Mr Lawrence Gordon and Mr Lloyd Levin..." is from a press release announcing the *Tomb Raider* film, circa 1998. "We are thrilled by the possibilities..." John Goldwyn, ibid. **p216** "I'm sorry to report that the content..."; "it seems like a mix of Predator-style chase set-pieces..." are from 'Tomb Raider Script Review' by 'Agent 4125', Ain't It Cool News (www.aintitcool.com), 1 October 1998. **p218** "I'd love to give you the whole story..." Brent V. Friedman, quoted in 'Tomb with a View' by Christine Spines, *Premiere*, July 2001. **p219** "I was hired in September 1998..." and all other Steven de Souza quotes, AI. "Several scribes took a shot..." is from 'Herek Digs Par's *Tomb*', uncredited, *Variety*, 11 April 1999. "Thankfully, de Souza's *Tomb Raider*..."; "Overall, this is an excellent script..." 'Necros,' quoted on Coming Attractions (www.corona.bc.ca). **p220** "The problem was that we kept falling back..." Levin, quoted in 'Tomb with a View' by Christine Spines, *Premiere*, July 2001. **p221** "[The producers] said, 'The situation is this..." John Zinman, quoted in 'Tomb Raider' by David Goldsmith, *Creative Screenwriting*, July/August 2001. "Scene for scene, beat for beat..."; "a lot of puzzle solving..." Patrick Massett, ibid. "The challenge is to create a story..." Zinman, ibid. "hailed as heroes" Zinman, quoted in "Tomb with a View" by Christine Spines, *Premiere*, July 2001. **p222** "The script opens in Macedonia..."; "a wonderful contradiction..."; "You're not asking much..." Darwin Mayflower, quoted on Screenwriters Utopia (www.screenwritersutopia.com). **p224** "The old drafts had a lot of Mary Poppins..."; "Every time it came up I thought..." Simon West, quoted in 'Tomb with a View' by Christine Spines, *Premiere*, July 2001. "The original script had scenes with people visiting the Queen..." West, quoted in *Dreamwatch*, circa 2001. **p225** "The plot, briefly, involves adventuress/magazine editor..." is from a report on Coming Attractions (www.corona.bc.ca) **p226** "From a creative point of view..." Levin, quoted in 'Tomb with a View' by Christine Spines, *Premiere*, July 2001. "When we met with Simon his idea was..." Zinman, quoted in 'Tomb Raider' by David Goldsmith, *Creative Screenwriting,* July/August 2001. **p227** "James Bond of archaeology..." West, quoted in *Entertainment Weekly*, 2 March 2000. "It was always Angelina..." West, quoted in 'Not Just a Pretty Face... Balls of Brass Too' by Mark Dinning *Empire*, August 2001. "At first I thought *Tomb Raider* was a really bad idea..."; "It's taken us a long time to figure out..." Angelina Jolie, ibid. **p228** "It was always our intention for Lara..." Massett, quoted in 'Tomb Raider' by David Goldsmith, *Creative Screenwriting,* July/August 2001. "This script is first and foremost about Lara..."; "nimble wit..."; "I was surprised by how much..."; "The choices faced..." 'Moriarty', quoted on Ain't It Cool News (www.aintitcool.com). **p229** "Originally, I wrote the idea to be in China..." West, quoted in interview for Paramount press materials for *Lara Croft Tomb Raider*. **p230** "We wrote a script that was just huge..." Zinman, quoted in 'Tomb Raider' by David Goldsmith, *Creative Screenwriting,* July/August 2001. "Long, long ago, a meteor crashed to Earth..."; "The High Priest knew that this power..." is dialogue cut from *Lara Croft Tomb Raider*. **p232** "Burglars escaped with a rucksack..." is from a report in *The Sunday Express*, 8 October 2000. "I was in bed at home..." West, quoted ibid. "psychologist specialising in stress management" reported in 'Tomb with a View' by Christine Spines, *Premiere*, July 2001. "I've learned that" West, quoted in ibid. **p233** "The only way I could write so much music..." Graeme Revell, quoted in *Dreamwatch*, June 2001. **p234** "The first one did not have a strong story..." Levin, quoted in 'Angelina Jolie is One Tough Mother' by Benjamin Svetkey, *Entertainment Weekly*, 18 July 2003. **p235** "The only thing that we can attribute it to..." Wayne Lewellen, quoted in 'Lara Plays the Blame Game', uncredited, *Dreamwatch*. October 2003. **p236** "If Paramount had spent a few bucks..." is from 'Summer Winners and Losers' by various, *Entertainment Weekly*, circa September 2003.

# SELECTED BIBLIOGRAPHY

Bartlett, Doland L. and James L. Steele, *Howard Hughes: His Life and Madness*. London: Andre Deutsch, 2003.

Bender, Hy, *The Sandman Companion*. New York: Vertigo Books, 1999.

Brown, Peter Harry and Pat H. Broeske, *Howard Hughes: The Untold Story*. New York: Diane, 1996.

Carpenter, Humphrey (ed.), *The Letters of J.R.R. Tolkien*. New York: HarperCollins, 1985.

Carr, Roy, *Beatles at the Movies*. London: UFOMusic, 1996.

Dick, Philip K., *Minority Report: Volume Four of the Collected Stories*. London: Gollancz, 2001.

Dick, Philip K., *We Can Remember It For You Wholesale: Volume Five of the Collected Stories*. London: Gollancz, 2001.

Gaiman, Neil, *The Sandman: Preuludes & Nocturnes*. New York: DC Comics, 1991.

Giger, H. R., *H. R. Giger's Film Design*. London: Titan Books, 1996.

Grünberg, Serge, *David Cronenberg*. Paris: Cahiers Du Cinema, 2000.

Hamsher, Jane, *Killer Instinct: How Two Young Producers Took on Hollywood and Made the Most Controversial Film of the Decade*. New York: Broadway Books, 1997.

Heston, Charlton, *In The Arena*. London: HarperCollins, 1995.

Miller, Frank, *Batman: Year One*. New York: DC Comics, 1990.

Obst, Lynda, *Hello, He Lied and Other Truths from the Hollywood Trenches*. New York: Little Brown, 1996.

Salisbury, Mark (ed.), *Burton on Burton*, revised edition. London: Faber and Faber, 2000.

Sammon, Paul M., *Ridley Scott: The Making of his Movies*. London: Orion Books, 1999.

Taylor, Thom, *The Big Deal: Hollywood's Million Dollar Spec Script Market*. New York: William Morrow, 1999.

Tolkien, J.R.R., *The Lord of the Rings*. London: Allen & Unwin, 1937.

# INDEX OF NAMES, FILMS AND TV TITLES